THE
WOMAN
DETECTIVE
GENDER & GENRE

THE WOMAN DETECTIVE

GENDER & GENRE

Second Edition

Kathleen Gregory Klein

University of Illinois Press
Urbana and Chicago

Illini Books edition, 1995
©1988, 1995 by Kathleen Gregory Klein
Manufactured in the United States of America
P 5 4 3 2 1

This book is printed on acid-free paper.

Library of Congress Cataloging-in-Publication Data

Klein, Kathleen Gregory, 1946–
    The woman detective : gender and genre / Kathleen Gregory Klein.—
    2nd ed., Illini Books ed.
        p.   cm.
    Includes bibliographical references (p.   ) and indexes.
    ISBN 0-252-06463-1 (pbk. : acid-free paper)
    1. Detective and mystery stories, English—History and criticism.
    2. Detective and mystery stories, American—History and criticism.
    3. Women detectives in literature.   4. Women in literature.
    I. Title
PR830.D4K58   1995
823′.0872′09352042—dc20
                                                    94-24616
                                                    CIP

for
Rick Klein
and
Mary Cox Gregory

Contents

Acknowledgments

This book began as a brief response to a friend's comment, "I didn't know there were any professional women detectives." It was supposed to be an article. After a decade of reading and writing about this detective fiction, I owe many debts of gratitude. My first is to the feminist critics whose work has energized my life and enhanced my ability to read; I would not be who I am today without the women's movement.

My research would not have been possible without the major bibliographic compilation of detective fiction by Allen J. Hubin and the research on women detectives by Michele Slung. Friends and strangers sent me titles, lent me books, or provided secondary materials; I especially appreciate the timely help of Kathi Maio, Jim Leachman, Candida Lacey, Jane Bakerman, Neysa Choteau, Mary Jean DeMarr, and Carol Brenner of Murder, Ink. Librarians—particularly Mike Sutherland of Occidental College, Susan Glover Godleski from the Lilly Library (Bloomington, Indiana), and the Interlibrary Loan staff at the University Library of IUPUI—located little-known novels with reassuring ease and good nature.

I have been especially fortunate in finding many willing readers of the entire manuscript during its various incarnations. Throughout many revisions, I have been continually grateful for the careful reading and informed suggestions of my colleague Ray Keller. Other colleagues at my own institution—Barbara Cambridge, Alan Purves, and Ed Casebeer—offered good advice as did members of the Detective

Fiction Caucus of the Popular Culture Association, particularly Marty Knepper and Fred Isaacs. And, both Lillian Robinson and John Reilly helped shape the final version with their proposals for revision.

My own university has provided encouragement and resources from the outset: the School of Liberal Arts, English Department, Women's Studies Program, and Center for American Studies have funded my research. And, I could not have finished the manuscript without my student assistants, Deborah Mayor and Beth Miller. Similarly, two supportive women at the University of Illinois Press, Carole S. Appel and Carol Bolton Betts, made everything seem easier.

And my friends—you know who you are—always knew what to do.

My final debt is to my husband, Rick Klein; his encouragement never wavered. I have relied on that.

Introduction

A commonplace of mystery fiction is that the detective-hero solves crime. From Sherlock Holmes to Spenser, he unravels the tangled complications of murder and intrigue. When the detective is professional and paid for his work, his success is expected—by his clients and by the readers. However, when the paid detective is a woman, this anticipated pattern of successful crime solving suddenly collapses.

Since the 1864 appearance of the first professional woman detective, she and her professional competence have been consistently undercut despite overt claims for her abilities, successes, intelligence, and cunning. Although she is identified as the hero, her authors—whether female or male—seldom allow her to function like one; her failures can be found among all the major sub-genres.[1] Because detective fiction follows rather than parallels social reality, the genre's inherent conservatism upholds power and privilege in the name of law and justice as it validates readers' visions of a safe and ordered world.[2] In such a world view, criminals and women are put in their proper, secondary places. In consequence, despite enormous differences in the detectives themselves and the societies for which they were produced, the underlying plot in almost three hundred novels denies these characters either as detectives or as women.[3]

The unacknowledged sabotage of these purported heroes is the focus of this book. The principal methodology of this investigation is feminist analysis. Feminist critique, as Elaine Showalter defines it, dominates the analysis as I trace the contradictions between "woman" and "detective" appearing in novels written by women and men for female and male readers. I am primarily concerned with the moment of intersection between gender and genre, recognizing how both are socially constructed and validated. Consistently, I trace the ways conventional sex/gender bias predominates over the generic conventions or the mimetic possibilities in order to reinforce a nostalgic mythology of women's position. My analysis examines both textual strategies of authors and the materialist position of women to locate the subversive messages of these novels. Then, in the final chapter, "An Unsuitable Job for a Feminist?," which examines consciously feminist attempts to expand the genre, I consider women as producers of textual meaning and redefiners of generic conventions; how likely, I ask, are current writers to change the formulaic restrictions and break the dichotomy between "woman" and "detective" with their characters?

The secondary methodology, which determines the structure of each chapter and of the entire book, is historical—literary and social. I have organized the chapters chronologically from 1864 to 1987, dividing them into periods of significant generic development from which I draw the definitions and modifications of "detective." Each chapter also includes a description of the changes in women's lives, primarily in the public sphere. These sections provide information about the scripts available—however unattainable—to women. Thus, I mark the fictional limitations of the genre and the social promise from history as the narrowest and the broadest extensions of the term "woman detective" which might be used by the authors.[4]

Throughout this book, I compare the woman detective implicitly and explicitly with the preeminent male detectives whose portrayals describe and delimit the norms of the profession and the genre. She has three role models: Sherlock Holmes, the classically ratiocinative sleuth; Sam Spade, the ultimate hard-boiled private eye; and Spenser, a stand-in for the sons of Sam in the seventies and beyond.[5] The characteristics of these three establish the standard for the woman detective as well as the restrictions which her creators encountered. As the brief summaries of the changes in the genre, its formula, and its conventions in each chapter make clear, no single detective character or sleuthing style (not even as practiced by these three) completely dominated at any time.[6] Nonetheless, no other models have successfully challenged the preeminence of those established by Arthur Conan Doyle, Dashiell Hammett, and Robert B. Parker.

Although less easily and less succinctly established, the scripts for women since 1864 generally labeled her as "not-man," what Simone de Beauvoir called "other." Certainly, a woman's script did not include setting up professionally in a job which so clearly required acknowledged masculine virtues like physical strength, logical thinking, and worldly experience. Women might be successful amateur detectives so long as they employed the more stereotypically feminine talents of gossip and intuition, but they were barred from detective careers. There are two ways to examine the changing definitions of women and their place throughout the years covered by this study. The first, considering what the majority of women or the typical woman would do, is inappropriate for looking at the woman detective whose behavior throughout this century and a quarter is continually described as unusual for a woman. Therefore, just as each chapter examines developments in the genre, it also reviews the more radical changes in middle-class women's subordinate social position.[7] I use legal changes, employment opportunities, education, political participation, movie images, and other social changes for women with which detective fiction readers would be familiar as markers to contrast with the more slowly changing women detectives. How much does the detective resemble the most socially advanced women of her historical period? In examining this scenario I borrow Tzvetan Todorov's distinction between *fable* and *subject* (45) to compare the story of women's life histories with the narrative plot the authors make of women detectives.[8]

Because both the genre and women's history have changed markedly since 1864, the fictional portraits of the women detectives vary considerably. Thus I cannot provide the same kinds of information—even if it were desirable—for each of the seventy-one characters I consider here. Instead, I represent each character as she appears as both a woman and a detective, with emphasis on those features of the text significant to my thesis. Where a series character appears in several books—anywhere from two to fifty—I have used characterization and character development, personality, and explicit comparison of the various cases to chart her balancing act between the scripts of "woman" and "detective." I have been more restricted where a character appears only in a single novel. In both cases, however, the covert message of the author—the undercutting of the woman detective in one or both of her roles—is encoded in theme or structure as well as in characterization.[9]

What stands out most sharply is the problem these authors had in reconciling two divergent scripts. Readers of detective novels, whether of the police notebooks and dime adventure stories which preceded Sherlock Holmes or the hard-boiled adventures which followed him, not only recognized the formula on which the fictions were built, they also expected it. Opening a novel about a private investigator, readers anticipated finding—from one sub-genre to another—logic, action, ratiocination, violence, crime, scientific methods, and more. Authors from Waters to Robert B. Parker have not disappointed them. However, these readers were also members of societies whose sex-role definitions allocated all the detectives' usual talents to men.[10] The script labeled "detective" in readers' minds did not naturally overlap or even mesh with that labeled "woman." Attempts to raise the detective script to a paramount position by abjuring the conventional image of women and creating a woman detective who followed the male pattern failed as the inevitably conflicting script for women intervened; the unity of the novel's formula was then destroyed. Similarly, attempts to raise the "woman" script undercut the necessary elements of the detective formula. To succeed commercially, authors decided that their character was either not a proper detective or not a proper woman. Occasionally, they drew both conclusions.[11] Difficulties encountered by both experienced and novice writers of detective fiction attempting to replace the male detective with a woman detective emphasize the extraordinary power of the patriarchal script.

Why did the woman detective deliberately created by her author to fill a well-defined fictional role have to fail? The answer is encoded within the text and the reader. Popular fiction, like high culture, provides a form of catharsis for its readers. Detective fiction is designed to raise emotions of both fear and pity only to assuage them through the agency of the sleuth who solves the mystery, captures the criminal, and restores order.[12] When that detective is a woman, a similar, equally strong response is raised. Like the criminal, she is a member of society who does not conform to the status quo. Her presence pushes off-center the whole male/female, public/private, intellect/emotion, physical strength/weakness dichotomy. Therefore, her façade of normal respectability—like the criminal's—must be stripped away. If she can be shown as an incompetent detective or an inadequate woman, readers' reactionary preferences are satisfied; their second catharsis is achieved.[13] The detective novel is then doubly a moral tale. A slight extension of critic Robert Champigny's description of mystery stories as hermeneutic tales explains the undercutting of the female/detective; clues to the understanding of "truth" and the subsequent resumption of social order trap both the criminal and the captor in the end.

Recognizing that detective fiction as popular literature is more a commodity produced for mass consumption than a valid social history makes it easier to understand that whether written by women or men, the product is usually responsive to society's demands. Not until the 1970s is there a consciously articulated response to social change by women writers who challenge the sexist assumptions of hero formation apparently required by the formulaic demands of this fiction. That they are only partially successful in challenging the sexist boundaries of popular fiction—as previous women detectives were also limited in adopting masculine professions—testifies again to the strength of society's given scripts. Additionally, revisionist feminist attempts to redefine the genre and to reclaim it for women's uses pose serious ideological problems: can or should a feminist detective operate professionally to bolster the patriarchal system? Should she remain part of Virginia Woolf's "society of outsiders" instead?

This study is unlike the other critiques of the field—Michele Slung's *Crime on Her Mind* or Patricia Craig and Mary Cadogan's *The Lady Investigates*—in which gender provides an overriding focus, linking the woman as amateur, police officer, private eye, spy, girl detective, and criminal. Instead, I deliberately limit this analysis to the paid, professional woman detective who is the protagonist of the novel. As a member of Western capitalistic society, the private investigator who offers herself as a professional for hire would be expected to provide competent service for her employer. Thus readers could anticipate that the woman detective would (or should) be successful in the terms defined by the formula: out-think the police and outsmart the criminal. I have excluded amateurs and policewomen like Miss Marple or Sgt. Nora Mulcahaney as neither is comparable to the paid professional. The amateur is allowed extraordinary scope for error, foolishness, and luck as she solves a mystery; she has no client, no responsibility, and no commitment to investigation as a profession. Her accepted lack of credentials means that readers have no standard against which to compare her. Police, on the other hand, are bound by bureaucracy, hierarchies, and politics. Historically, they are paid by a system which inhibits individual action and decisions; they are assigned to cases, bound to standard investigative behavior, and responsible to the state's vision of justice. Fictionally, police novels are widely divergent, borrowing from casebook, classical, and hard-boiled formulas; and, since the 1950s, they form a separate sub-genre. Both generalizations and comparisons are, therefore, difficult and of limited value. Conflating the professional with either her official or amateur counterparts reinforces the critical assumption that there are no significant variations within the field.

My sources are Anglo-American book-length works in which the woman detective is the protagonist;[14] I consider short story collections, but not individual short stories because of the difficulties in locating such examples and because the crime and its solution rather than the detective are the focus of shorter works. I also omit novels in which the woman detective appears as the wife, secretary, assistant, or underling of a male protagonist; but, in such cases where female and male detectives have established an actual or understood legal or contractual partnership, I have included the novels in the chapter on partnerships whether or not the woman functions as the protagonist.

In analyzing these novels, I have decided not to use contemporary reviews to gauge the novels' popularity or readers' responses to them for two reasons: first, detective fiction does not always receive serious treatment except in fan magazines, which skews assessments of the fiction's popularity; secondly, reviews are always flawed by the convention that the murderer and the novel's conclusion cannot be revealed.

Finally, although I do not claim this study is exhaustive (forestalling inevitable embarrassment as additional novels surface), I have not settled for a representative sample of characters which might produce charges of feminist bias.[15] Instead, I have provided both a bibliographic survey and a critical analysis of an area previously not isolated for study.

Neither readers, writers, nor reviewers immediately flocked to the new detective fiction upon Edgar Allan Poe's creation of C. Auguste Dupin in 1841. His few, finely crafted stories which introduced locked rooms, improbable criminals, misdirection, and the now-famous ratiocinative method were almost drowned in a sea of adventure, police, criminal, and action stories which did not privilege intellect or puzzles. Instead, it was Arthur Conan Doyle's "nemesis," Sherlock Holmes, who is best described as the model and the signifier of the great detective. Created forty-six years after Dupin, Holmes's persona continues to be recreated and redefined by contemporary authors. Only the American hard-boiled detective introduced in the 1920s could match his popularity and his dominance in the genre. The counterparts of Sam Spade and the novels in which they appear were deliberately created to challenge the imposing figure of Holmes and his Victorian London; that Raymond Chandler considered the body in the library and the improbable amateur sleuth their targets does not deflect serious attention from their primary rival.

Still, the overall popularity of the genre cannot be overstated.[16] Allen J. Hubin's massive bibliography lists approximately 60,000 crime fiction titles. As early as the 1830s, a printer called James Catnach provided millions of copies of murderers' confessions to large numbers of willing readers (Knight 9). Although no detective novels or short story collections appear on the British best-seller lists from 1800 to 1900, sales were still substantial (Altick 383–86). Conan Doyle's *The Hound of the Baskervilles* was first to reach the yearly lists in 1902 and was followed in 1909 by Mary Roberts Rinehart's *The Man in the Lower Ten* (Hackett, *Fifty Years* 96). Either Rinehart or E. Phillips Oppenheim, each with at least one new book per year, appeared on the list throughout the 1920s; Rinehart's average yearly sales reached 300,000 copies (Hart 245). The popularity of mysteries in the United States during the Depression is attributed to readers' need to relax without being forced to confront their own lowered expectations; in addition, mysteries had become more respectable because of the polished and sophisticated output of the twenties (Hart 257–58). The genre historian Howard Haycraft notes that during the 1930s in the U.S., 25 percent of new novels published were mystery-detective fiction (Hart 259). Statistics from *Publishers Weekly* indicate that this popularity continued into the 1960s (Escarpit 77); and, according to an unnamed survey quoted by Elliot Gilbert in 1978, one of every four U.S. sales in books (not merely fiction) is a detective story (xxx). For sheer individual numbers, Agatha Christie's sales figures are unmatched: nearly 500 million copies by 1979 (Knight 107).

The best-seller records of American publications including reprints of British books between 1895 and 1975 compiled by Alice Payne Hackett from *The Bookman* and *Publishers Weekly* chart the popularity of the genre numerically. The mystery and detection bestseller category for 1895–1955 lists 112 books which had sold over a half million copies; 56 are by Erle Stanley Gardner and 29 by Ellery Queen. The top seven novels on the list are all by Mickey Spillane (*Sixty Years* 53). By 1965, best-seller status required sales of at least one million in paperback or 7,500 in hardback; still the number of novels on the list increased to 151. Added to Queen and Gardner among the most popular authors was James Bond's creator, Ian Fleming. Again, Spillane led in sales of individual titles with over four and one-half million copies of each of the top seven titles (*Seventy Years* 61). When sales of two million were required by the 1975 edition of the list, fifty-five novels were included on the mystery and detection list (*Eighty Years* 49). On the overall best-seller list for this entire period (1895–1975), the following crime novels appeared: *The Godfather* at number 1; *I, the Jury* at number 39; other Spillane novels at numbers 48, 55, 56, 57, 58, and 61; *Thunderbolt* at number 86; and the first detective novel, Gardner's *The Case of the Sulky Girl*, appeared at number 117 (*Eighty Years* 10–13).

Unlike other examples of formula fiction, detective fiction is read by both women and men whereas romances typically draw female audiences and westerns attract male ones. Recent shifts in science fiction readership do not obscure the fact that it had a primarily male audience until the 1970s. However, crossover by readers among the sub-genres of detective fiction (classical, hard-boiled, police procedural, etc.) makes suspect most statements about reading preferences by gender.

Despite enormous and varied readership for all versions of the genre, women detectives—even the amateurs—do not appear frequently on readers' polls of all-time favorites. Haycraft's 1941 "Cornerstones" includes only sixty-seven male detectives (*Murder* 302–6). A 1946 survey of readers of *The Pleasures of Publishing* approved ten authors with only Christie having a female detective (Hackett, *Sixty Years* 54). And *Newsweek's* 1985 "Sleuth's Hall of Fame" includes ten favorite novels and five runners-up; one woman writer and no women detectives rate approval. A more extensive survey of readers of *The Armchair Detective* (*TAD*), a popular American fan and critical magazine first published in 1968, reveals similar preferences for male characters.[17] These aficionados ranked detectives as disparate as Sherlock Holmes (first, with fifty-two votes) and Dr. Thorndyke (eighteenth, with four votes) but included only one woman detective, the amateur Miss Marple, in the first eighteen. Two authors listed in the top twenty—Stout and James—have secondary series detectives who are women but none of the novels in which they appear is among the twenty favorites (Seidman and Penzler 128–30). The magazine's regular publications reflect the same preferences. In eighteen years, only Madame Rosika Storey has had an entire critical article devoted to her fictional development; brief bibliographical notes about Mrs. Gladden and Miss Silver complete the very short list of paid women detectives meriting separate attention in *TAD*.

General critics of the genre are equally sparing in their attention to any kind of women in detective novels much less the narrow category of professional women protagonists. After all, this fiction is primarily a man's story, Marjorie Hope Nicolson noted, with major female roles limited to villain or victim. She concludes, "One or two authors have experimented with the woman detective, but for the most part with little success" (123). Dorothy L. Sayers agreed. When Colin Watson devotes a chapter to women, they are not detectives but suspects or encumbrances; their parts are passive (151–52, 158). To explain these passive roles, Jerry Palmer turns to society's valuation of women: "If the succession of women who 'surrender' to the thriller hero can, within the thriller, serve to enhance his stature, and thus his competitiveness, it is because in everyday life such events are traditionally valued, and men like this are thought to be 'a helluva guy' " (143). He recognizes that attempts by both the church and the women's movement to challenge this concept have had little effect.

The male model which receives so much attention from authors, readers, and critics alike is widely varied. Private detectives can be blind, fat, homosexual, aristocratic, lazy, crooked, clever, violent, intuitive, sexist, logical, racist, and more. Yet, it usually goes without saying that they are male and thus privileged in society as a result. Although each of the three model detectives used in this study—Holmes, Spade, and Spenser—has distinguishing individual characteristics, he also displays the basic, general characteristics of the classical, hard-boiled, and modern detective which typify his competitors.

All three are professionals. Critics as disparate as Palmer and W. H. Auden recognize the importance of this distinction: "The professional detective has the advantage [over the amateur] that, since he is not an individual but a representative of the ethical, he does not need a motive for investigating the crime; but for the same reason he has the disadvantage of being unable to overlook the minor ethical violations of the suspects . . ." (Auden 21). Palmer makes a more precise distinction among characters, separating the professional from both the amateur and the bureaucrat. The amateur, by definition, is permanently incompetent; he cannot learn from experience because everything is always new. The bureaucrat cannot learn because he requires organizational predictability. Only the professional can learn because he is both knowledgeable and responsive (11–12).

Primary among these professionals is the master Holmes. Stephen Knight is unlikely to be challenged in his assertion that Sherlock Holmes's name is a synonym for "detective" (67). He is preeminent among early detectives who used reason to bring order out of chaos, gain some degree of control, find the criminal, and triumph over evil, all the while remaining supremely confident of his abilities (Carter 404). As a master scientific detective, he is "midway between Poe's extravagant celebrations of human reason and mid-Victorian fears about its limits" (Gilbert xv). Conan Doyle's Holmes is more active than Poe's Dupin, but still deductive in his methods. His ratiocination poses as straightforward, common sense observation and natural, if heightened, logic. This pose may be either cause or effect of his arrogant stance; similarly, the arrogance may be correlated with his isolating genius and eccentricity (Palmer 104). Virtually all critics recognize his position of detective-as-aesthete (Ruehlmann 5). Readers, however, are more likely to agree with Knight's conclusion comparing the detective with Lord Raglan's mythic hero: "Holmes with magnifying glass and London fog has attained the same status [as Robin Hood], epitomizing the rational hero who resolves urban disorder" (104).

Deliberately unlike Holmes in most respects, Sam Spade shares one characteristic—he is the prototype of the detective in his era (Wolfe 119). Several critics have noted the direct line between Dashiell Hammett's creation and James Fenimore Cooper's Leatherstocking (Geherin 1; Dove, "Criticism" 205): both are physically able, honest, and compassionate. Hammett himself says of Spade: "Your private eye does not . . . want to be an erudite solver of riddles in the Sherlock Holmes manner; he wants to be a hard and shifty fellow, able to take care of himself in any situation, able to get the best of anybody he comes in contact with, whether criminal, innocent bystander, or client" (Wolfe 119). Spade's action is very different from Holmes's; more than just physical movement or investigation, it involves violence—fights, beatings, chases. He is tough without being brutal, committed to those he cares about, and willing to take risks. Far less arrogant than Holmes, he faces temptation and moral tension. For generations of mystery fans, Sam Spade has the look of Humphrey Bogart (Marcus 198; Ruehlmann 73). David Geherin concludes, "in the character of Sam Spade in *The Maltese Falcon*, he gave shape to the image of the tough, cynical detective that was to serve as the model for all later private eyes" (1).[18]

With Chandler's Phillip Marlowe, the hard-boiled detective began to change; vulnerability and complexity were added to the original form. By the 1970s when Robert B. Parker introduced his Boston-based, tough but literate Spenser the image had shifted noticeably. Spenser's principal characteristic is his articulate understanding of the code which motivates his behavior. This self-awareness is honed in his encounters with Susan Silverman, the enforcer Hawk, and the teen-ager he chooses to parent. Nevertheless, other challenges to Spenser's code are less willingly received; he is firmly committed to his own vision of moral behavior against a corrupt or uncommitted society. And he is willing to use extraordinary amounts of violence to support his view.

In the minds of writers, readers, and critics, these are the images of the private detective. For well over a century, creators of women detectives have seemed to challenge that view.

Notes

1. Based on a limited sample of six characters (Silver, Cool, Bay, Bonner, Gray, and McCone), Barbara Lawrence concludes that the products of male writers are sexist whereas those of female writers are not. I find this generalization inadequate even for these characters and completely unwarranted for the field as a whole.

2. The same point is made by Carter (404) and Mason (39) but extended by Porter, who suggests that readers' tastes and values be considered (5), and Mann, who insists the form must "reflect the prejudices and aspirations of the reader" (93).

3. In a positive response to the recovery of previously unknown characters, Patricia Craig and Mary Cadogan conclude that "the general idea behind the use of a female detective is bound to appear progressive, irrespective of how it is worked out" (12). Because they discuss amateurs, policewomen, and spies as well as professional, paid detectives, their approving view—like Carolyn Heilbrun's assessment in *Hecate*—can accommodate a wide range of behavior by the detectives. Although also involved in recovery, I am concentrating on the sharp contradiction between apparent progressiveness and the actual working out for a single, narrowly defined group of female detectives.

4. I am sensitive to Lillian Robinson's suggestion that anachronism ought not be elevated into criticism "demanding that writers of the past meet present-day expectations of political awareness" (33). Because of this I have tried to judge each novel on the basis of its formulaic integrity and historical possibilities.

5. I have, obviously, borrowed this phrase from David Geherin.

6. Some readers of detective fiction will argue that reducing my models to these three characters oversimplifies the genre; for example, Archer is different from Spade although both are clearly hard-boiled detectives. My point is that Hammett, like Conan Doyle, set the standard which subsequent writers had either to follow or reject while being unable to disavow their predecessors' influence. Parker's Spenser represents exactly such a deliberate "misreading" of Hammett.

7. Throughout, white middle-class women are used as a point of reference because the female detectives (except Violet Strange and Baroness Linz) were or wished to be considered middle-class and, therefore, respectable. In this desire for respectability, they are similar to the "traveling heroines" described by Ellen Moers (179). The only black detective appears in a series which is both sexist and racist. However, none of these generalizations about race, class, or social mobility apply to Kat Guerrera.

8. I have used social history as a model for the female detective even though portraits of male detectives often did not match with reality. There is still mimetic fidelity in male characters being portrayed differently from social history because of the wide range of options available to men; for female characters, their authors' persistent rejection of available social roles denies mimetic truth and announces an ideological stance about sex/gender behavior.

9. Early in *Sexual Politics*, Kate Millett identified the power of such covert messages: "However muted its present appearance may be, sexual dominion obtains nonetheless as perhaps the most pervasive ideology of our culture and provides its most fundamental concept of power" (25).

10. Kathlyn Ann Fritz and Natalie Kaufman Hevener also consider the detective's attributes identical with exclusively male qualities: independence, assertiveness, decisiveness, problem-solving, and (when necessary) bravery (107).

11. Although Jane Austen might be surprised to find her characters compared with women detectives, Rachel Brownstein's work on heroines is applicable here. Like the classic, realistic English novel, the detective story with a female protagonist has the opportunity to explore connections between the inner self (the desire/decision for a professional, investigative career) and its outward manifestations (the social role demanded of women) (xix).

12. The fear and pity which readers feel is for themselves as members of a society in which such things can happen. For another view of catharsis for detective fiction readers, see Dorothy L. Sayers, "Aristotle on Detective Fiction," 180.

13. In their dialogue/conversation about feminist literary criticism, Carolyn Heilbrun and Catharine Stimpson explain literature's tendency to reinforce this attitude: "Literature has tended to masculinize most activity, particularly worldly activity, even as it has recorded it. The women in literature who try to act, or who exercise will, are by the books' denouements either prisoners or paralytics, literally or psychically. What tends to be aggressive and egocentric in a woman might easily be considered a quest for liberty and self in a man" (62).

14. Reliable informants and my own extensive investigation have found no professional women private detectives except in Canada, Britain, and the U.S. The most promising European character, Arlette van der Valk, is really a social worker and amateur detective despite her second husband's joking comparisons of her with California private-eye Phillip Marlowe.

15. For the chapter on American dime novels, I have been unable to obtain more than a handful of the novels whose titles appear in various secondary sources; therefore, my conclusions are limited. In several chapters I occasionally have drawn conclusions about characters based on a sample of the novels in which they appear and have noted this where done. Omitted entirely are the five books about Charlie's Angels by Max Franklin (1977–78); all are novelizations of the television series.

16. Dennis Porter insists on this popularity as a reason for paying attention to popular literature (2). Part of its appeal comes from the kind of re-

reading which formula fiction provides; like the fairy tale, it combines familiar form (a limited number of structural constants) with unfamiliar specifics (an infinite number of "decorative variables") (99).

17. The 198 results are based on 1800 questionnaires with a 47 percent response rate.

18. As the hero who knows his way around the dangerous world of the 1930s and 1940s, Bogart also appeared, fittingly enough, as Raymond Chandler's Phillip Marlowe (Jameson 140).

1

British Policewo/men: 1864

Most readers' familiarity with detective fiction usually begins with Conan Doyle's stories and novels about Sherlock Holmes, but the reputation of these works is not due to their premiere chronological or structural status. The three detective stories of Edgar Allan Poe featuring C. Auguste Dupin, "Murders in the Rue Morgue" (1841), "The Mystery of Marie Roget" (1842–43), and "The Purloined Letter" (1845), first introduced the ratiocinative mode which came to dominate the genre. Initially, however, the most popular sub-category of the new genre was formed by the ostensibly factual stories of the lives and exploits of members of the newly formed London police force. These accounts owed their genesis to the early story of a Bow Street Runner, *Richmond: or, Scenes in the Life of a Bow Street Officer*, published in 1827 (Bleiler, viii), and to the *Memoirs* of Vidoq, founder of the investigations unit of the Paris police, published in 1829. E. F. Bleiler describes them: "The stories concerned were narratives of detective work, usually told by a professional detective, reasonably factual in subject matter, but usually melodramatic and sensational in presentation" (viii). Following the successful sales of these real-life stories, would-be novelists seized upon the same subject matter; the first was Waters's "Recollections of a Police-officer" (1849) published in Chambers's *Edinburgh Review*. After Waters, authors vied for interesting variations on the casebook with minimal concern for the plausibility of their detectives. Joining London detectives were French and New York police detectives, amateur and professional detectives, customs officers, spies, lady detectives, and rustic or rural detectives (Bleiler, viii). Generally, these early casebooks were awkwardly narrated, lacked more than minimal plot or structure, and omitted character development. They offered few investigative techniques expected by readers today as detectives succeeded through unimaginative questioning and a good bit of luck.

Attached to the Bow Street magistrates office and paid a retainer, the Runners had much more in common with private detectives than police officers. They were free to accept cases from anyone who could afford to pay them the going rate of a guinea a day plus expenses and they could expect to receive a reward from their employer (Dilnot 16). They worked less for the general good of the population than for the recovery of private property or retribution of personal wrongs. The provisions of the 1829 Police Act led to the formation of a regular metropolitan London police force whose primary responsibility was to prevent crime; detecting crimes already committed and capturing those responsible was a secondary function (Critchley 52). Then in 1842, the need for a specific detective force to replace the extinct Bow Street Runners became a priority; still, anyone who chose to pay their expenses might employ one of these detectives. Not until 1884 was the system of rewards to detectives in special cases abolished since, by then, salaries had been regularized and improved. Women did not enter the police force officially until 1915 and despite great opposition during the postwar period, twenty were retained by a 1922 Act of Parliament (Dilnot 181).

Although the nineteenth-century British public might not envision women police officers, they were forced to acknowledge one woman in a role overwhelmingly perceived as male. No doubt, the strongest impact on the perception of women's place in the public or private sphere was generated by Queen Victoria—monarch and mother. The visible and inevitable contradictions between her roles influenced national attitudes about family and women from the time of her ascension to the throne in 1837. But she was the ruler—England in person—so her privilege to challenge expected behavior was not shared by her female subjects. On the other hand, queen or not, she often found her options limited because of her sex.

The general cause of women's rights was widely argued in the context of the French Revolution and beyond. However, although Mary Wollstonecraft's *A Vindication of the Rights of Women* (1792) was initially well received, by 1803 the book's reputation had declined (McGuinn 191). In 1825 William Thompson, a socialist, published the first book-length argument for the full emancipation of women and their admission to the legislature (Stenton 321). A number of specialized journals supported the cause of women's education and rights early in the nineteenth century. Nevertheless, parliamentary attempts in 1831 and 1848 to extend voting rights to all householders regardless of gender were soundly defeated (Strachey, cited in Stenton 333), accurately reflecting widespread public opinion about women's rights.

As threatening as the unlikely prospect of women voting were the proposed changes in laws regarding married women, their property, and the control of their children. Throughout the 1840s and 1850s, the Law Amendment Society and such determined women as Caroline Norton and Barbara Leigh Smith worked to increase married women's independent status. Although only limited rights were granted in these decades, the prospect of such changes affected many more households indirectly.

A different kind of independence had been available to women through the spread of birth control information since the 1820s. Richard Carlile's "What is Love" (1822) redirected concern from the Malthusian fear of surplus poor to the rights of women and men to control their family size (Rowbotham 37). These new attitudes were reinforced by Knowlton's *Fruits of Philosophy* (1832) which was about both birth control and sexuality; it sold thousands of copies and was republished as late as 1877 (Rowbotham 75).

There is no indication that the issues of women's public responsibilities and rights troubled the first two female police detectives appearing in ninteenth-century British fiction. They are devoted exclusively to their work, unconcerned with the political or social implications of their professions. Nor do the books themselves explicitly address sex-role stereotyping; the characters' gender is mentioned only when conventional attitudes would suggest women's traditional skills might be useful. As protagonists and narrators, these women detectives are used by their creators to gain variety and commercial attention for the sub-genre; this authorial strategy is shared, in particular, by writers of dime novels and hard-boiled pulp stories. All three are adventure- and action-based variations whose parameters seemed especially unsuited to female stereotypes. Like the dime novels, police-notebook novels are precursors to the actual genre of detective fiction; similarly, these women detectives are advance models whose undermining signals the strategies which subsequent authors adopted.

These tensions correlate with the "contradiction of genre and gender" which Sandra Gilbert and Susan Gubar identify: "Most Western literary genres are, after all, essentially male—devised by male authors to tell male stories about the world" (67). And, as Joanna Russ has convincingly demonstrated, replacing male heroes with female protagonists does not transform men's stories into women's ("What Can a Heroine Do?"). By using women detectives as though this sub-genre were gender neutral, Forrester and Hayward are revealed as products of their cultural education which assumed that male activity constitutes the norm for human behavior; the novels replicate culturally dominant myths. Dale Spender, recognizing that "male values are the basis of society," accurately notes that any alternative is both invisible and incomprehensible (9).

In May 1864, predating the official acceptance of women in Britain's police force by over fifty years, the first fictional woman detective to appear introduces herself as Mrs. Gladden, in the first-person narrative *The Female Detective*.[1] Although the title page indicates that the work was only edited by Andrew Forrester, Jun., it seems clear that this is not an actual police officer's casebook but his imaginative creation. From the outset, Forrester hides the details of his protagonist's female existence. Her name is a pseudonym chosen to protect her identity and her privacy. Also, she alternately uses "Miss" and "Mrs." with her assumed name, concealing or confusing her marital position. Finally, she declines to admit whether she is a widow working to support her children or an unmarried woman responsible only for herself, thus screening her parental status. These omissions and evasions deny the character's definition in societal terms. In refusing to clarify her identity as a woman, the author redirects attention to her position as a detective.

Six of the seven cases related in the book are typical of the period's factual and fictional output, but one, "The Unknown Weapon," is marked by a deliberately experimental fictional style. Here, characters besides the detective and criminal show definite personality characteristics, are developed although not fully rounded, and operate in more than a functional way. At the outset, the narrator describes

her decision to "give the particulars . . . in the form of a narrative"
and to "analyse" the mystery at Petleighcote (3).

Frequently, Mrs. Gladden uses the narrative as an opportunity
to comment on the capabilities and motivations of her colleagues
among the detective ranks: they are "simple, and accept a plain and
straightforward statement with extreme willingness" inasmuch as "the
general, the chief motive power in the detective is gain" (23–24). A
former police constable, she makes explicit both her reservations
about the kind of behavior required by the job and her acceptance of
the greater good to be achieved:

> And indeed it is the great gain and drawback of our profes-
> sion that we have to doubt so imperiously. To believe every
> man to be honest till he is found out to be a thief, is a
> motto most self-respecting men cling to; but we detectives
> on the contrary would not gain salt to our bread, much less
> the bread itself, if we adopted such a belief. We have to
> believe every man a rogue till, after turning all sorts of
> evidence inside out, we can only discover he is an honest
> man. And even then I am much afraid we are not quite
> sure of him.
>
> I am aware this is a very dismal way of looking upon
> society, but the more thinking amongst my profession con-
> sole themselves with the knowledge that our system is a
> necessary one (under the present condition of society), and
> that therefore in conforming to the melancholy rules of
> this system, however repulsive we may feel them, we are
> really doing good to our brother men. (43–44)

Beyond this, she justifies not only her colleagues' behavior but also
her own specific acts: "if the reader complains that there is much
falsity in what I state, I would urge that as evil-doing is a kind of lie
levelled at society, if it is to be conquered it must be met on the side
of society, through its employes [*sic*], by similar false action" (37).
Clearly, she is experienced, comfortable, and confident in a profession whose complexities she fully understands.

Still in London reading only the newspaper accounts of a case,
Mrs. Gladden decides to take on the Petleighcote investigation although the inquest strongly suggested accidental death and despite
the prospect of only the limited government reward of one hundred

pounds given in cases of death by foul play. Her curiosity is aroused by "several peculiar circumstances" (24). The body of a young man has been found outside the door of his parents' vacant country house with an arrow-like barb caught behind his ribs. Promptly, because "with us detectives action is as nearly simultaneous with determination to act as it can be," she travels to the site (25). There the inquest report and interviews with local inhabitants increase both her knowledge of events and her certainty that the case has been bungled.

During this investigation she reveals a whole spectrum of investigative approaches and talents despite her assertion that in "most of the great detected cases on record . . . you will find a little accident has generally been the clue to success" (54). Pure luck plays a fairly small part in Mrs. Gladden's success; instead she organizes the case logically. Her methods of solving the case are threefold: she interrogates witnesses, uses her previous experience in detecting, and takes advantage of what luck she has. A wide range of testimony is her best source of information. No one is immune from her persistent questioning, not even a stupid, unhappy young servant prone to convulsions. She bullies the local police constable for whom she has no respect; she labels him "a stupid, hopeless dolt, as I found to my cost, who was good at a rustic publichouse row, but who as a detective was not worth my dog Dart" (17). She disguises her official status as much as possible, rightly believing that she will have more success by offering bribes than by producing police papers. For the same reason, she is willing to lie as well as to mislead indirectly in order to keep the intention of her questions secret. Showing no reluctance to use whatever source she can, the detective initially collects information widely and freely which she can later reconsider for accuracy and relevance. She notes that "all these particulars I learnt readily after the catastrophe, for the townsfolk were only too eager to talk of the unfortunate young man" (6). Her assessment of the inquest proceedings serves as a model for her evaluation of all kinds of testimony; she looks for order, comprehensiveness, and common sense.

In addition to her astute questioning, which any interested person might have also done, Mrs. Gladden reveals her professional capabilities and her previous experience in the approaches she takes to solving the crime. Her earliest remarks on the case both criticize the inefficient local constable and reveal a certain pride in her own intelligence and her effectiveness:

... for I may tell the reader that boot-marks have sent more men to the gallows, as parts of circumstantial evidence, than any other proof whatever; indeed, the evidence of the boot-mark is terrible. . . . [I]f I were advising evil-doers on the best means of avoiding detection, I would say by all means take a second pair of boots . . . [however] I flatter myself I have a counter-mode of foiling such a felonious arrangement as this one of two pairs of boots. And as I have disseminated the mode amongst the police, any attempt to put the suggestions I have offered actually into action, would be attended with greater chances of detection than would be incurred by running the ordinary risk. (18)

In an early example of scientific detecting, she extracts a bit of lint from the coat pocket of the victim to send to a chemist for microscopic analysis. Because the almanac she regularly carries revealed rain the night of the murder, Mrs. Gladden questions the local police constable about the state of the victim's clothing. However, the constable's standards of observation and insight do not match hers; he notices nothing. Even while in the country, she keeps well informed by receiving the *Times* daily. In short, she loses no opportunity to provide herself with whatever evidence might help solve her case.

Cleverly, Mrs. Gladden manipulates the investigation to increase her access to the crime scene. Sending to London for a female police officer, she places her assistant at Petleighcote as a servant working secretly under the detective's orders. Hoping to find a way of safely searching the house herself, she places an advertisement in the *Times* to lure the housekeeper to London. Finally, when all the available evidence seems completely contradictory, she invokes an "ordinary detective law," drawn from her previous experience: "In all cases which are being followed up by the profession, a lie is a suspicious act, whether it has relation or no relation, apparent or beyond question, with the matter in hand. As a lie it must be followed to its source, its meaning cleared up, and its value or want of value decided upon. The probability stands good always that a lie is part of a plot" (51). When scientific information, police procedures, and experience are combined and focused on the investigation, the detective's ability to solve the crime is rewarded. Nonetheless, as the detective herself admits, luck plays some role in her eventual solution of the case.

Three specific instances provide Mrs. Gladden with opportunities which neither her questioning nor her skills and experience could have given. But none was entirely a gift; each was generated by her careful and astute preparation.

Throughout "The Unknown Weapon," Mrs. Gladden's detective methodology is clearly logical and rational; almost too frequently and obviously she marshalls the available information and sets herself a list of questions to be answered. These result in a range of responses which generate what she describes as "inferences—if I may use so pompous a word" (47). Unlike the later ratiocinative style of Holmes, Mrs. Gladden does not seize upon a single interpretation and follow it to the conclusion, but deliberates among many possibilities. Some lead her astray; most, however, form a part of the pattern of thought which leads her to question apparent improbabilities.

When the killer is finally revealed as Mrs. Quinion, the Petleighcote housekeeper, the novel's emphasis on clever, resourceful women is complete. In having kept her professional identity a secret, Mrs. Gladden was spared challenges to her abilities based on sex. Even the constable whose evidence she demands is curious but ignorant: "Under my corkscrew-like qualities as a detective he had no more chance than a tender young cork with a corkscrew proper. I believe that to the end of the chapter he never comprehended that I was a detective. His mind could not grasp the idea of a police officer in petticoats" (25). Throughout, the other men investigating the case are as unsuspicious as the unfortunate constable. Being a woman, the murderer is also overlooked; initially, even Mrs. Gladden does not suspect the housekeeper, describing some specific behavior in the case as "unwomanly." However, the woman detective and her female police assistant quickly discard such prejudice when the evidence warrants. In the story's final episode, the suspect recognizes the trap which has been set for her and returns to Petleighcote. There she entraps the two detectives and sets the house on fire, making her successful escape. Undaunted, Mrs. Gladden and her assistant "to our honour as detectives . . . did not lose our presence of mind," (64) even though they do not apprehend the criminal or make their evidence public. "I carried the case no further. I had no desire to do so— had I had, I doubt if I possessed any further evidence than would have sufficed to bring me into ridicule. I left the case where it stood" (66). Nonetheless, all three women have succeeded in some way: Mrs.

Quinion, who had accidentally killed her employer's son (who may also have been her nephew), escaped retribution although not detection; Mrs. Gladden and her subordinate followed a case abandoned by other detectives to unassailable knowledge of the truth. Although the criminal seemed to get away with murder, Mrs. Gladden's conclusion, "I acknowledge she conquered me," is incomplete (65). Mrs. Quinion's former life, her security and peace of mind were all taken from her by the knowledge of Mrs. Gladden's accurate deduction of the crime. But by contrast, in formulaic terms, Mrs. Gladden has failed: the murderer escapes and the detective receives no reward. The criminal has outwitted the detective; one woman has triumphed over another.

In "The Unknown Weapon," Forrester offers three escape routes for readers troubled by the unusual sight of a woman detective. Throughout, he makes it easy for them to forget that she is a woman, emphasizing her portrayal as a detective. For the less easily distracted, he structures the conclusion so that this unusual character fails both professionally and financially; readers are free to infer that a male detective might have succeeded. Finally, he creates a case where a woman's quarry is another woman; gender rather than professional ability is then identified as the investigator's important characteristic. As this is a quality Mrs. Gladden possesses by birth rather than by training or talent, she can claim no special skill in using it; she solves the case by *being* more than by *doing*.

Although this woman detective's tenacity and talent are not easily dismissed, the fiction acknowledges no positive correlation between her gender and her profession. Clearly recognizing the separateness of the scripts in contemporary societal terms, Forrester splits the character into two components, detective and woman. The former is fully acknowledged as Mrs. Gladden operates within the framework introduced by Waters; however, the latter is minimized as the author develops a character who seldom identifies herself as a woman. Even use of a gender-specific, third-person pronoun which would ordinarily remind readers of the protagonist's gender is limited here by the subgenre's convention of a first-person narrator. Therefore, casual readers aware of Mrs. Gladden's important difference from the usual detective would still be able to ignore this distinction when the action-filled pages of the story seldom noted it. This omission, or "gap" as Pierre Macherey names it, demonstrates how incidental the protagonist's gender is in *The Female Detective;* instead, Forrester has created an honorary male. He has thereby lessened the impact of his experimentation by submerging the protagonist's sex-role characteristics under her professional definition.

More articulate about his innovation in the sub-genre, W. Stephens Hayward identifies his creation, Mrs. Paschal, as "one of the much-dreaded, but little-known people called Female Detectives" (3). Following Mrs. Gladden by only six months, Mrs. Paschal is the only other known female police detective.[2] Nonetheless, she introduces herself in *The Experiences of a Lady Detective* not as a unique or singular person but as part of a British group modeled on an existing European force: "Fouché, the great Frenchman, was constantly in the habit of employing women to assist him in discovering the various political intrigues which disturbed the peace of the first empire. His petticoated police were as successful as the most sanguine innovator could wish; and Colonel Warner, having this fact before his eyes, determined to imitate the example of a man who united the courage of a lion with the cunning of a fox, culminating his acquisitions with the sagacity of a dog" (2). Later, when her uniqueness and authenticity are challenged by a criminal, Mrs. Paschal denies them matter-of-factly, " 'in this country it is not so uncommon a thing' " (44). Her gender is acknowledged intermittently throughout the book although it is conventionally treated; the ramifications of her untraditional behavior and employment are never specifically explored.

How she came to be employed by Colonel Warner, chief of the London Police Detectives, is almost as much a mystery as the ones she solves. Her husband died just before she was forty, leaving her without a sufficient income; she then was approached about joining the force although her self-defined qualities as well-educated, well-bred, and having some talent as an actress are never used to explain her hiring. Her superior adds little to the catalogue of her abilities; vaguely he claims: " 'I do not know a woman more fitted for the task than yourself. . . . I am aware that you possess an unusual amount of common sense . . .' " (4).

Mrs. Paschal solves ten cases in *The Experiences of a Lady Detective:* three have been assigned by Colonel Warner while seven are private investigations. The three police cases involve theft and murder as do the private cases which also include kidnapping, forgery, impersonation, and rescuing an impressionable young man from being fleeced by his attractive mistress. In all of the cases Mrs. Paschal sets her own schedule, requests and organizes police information or backup assistance, plans the pattern of the investigation, and receives expense payments as needed. In addition, she is eligible for a reward when the cases are successfully completed. Apparently she receives no salary from the police department, depending only on the success of her talent and ability for her financial support. When assigned to a police case, she is guaranteed to be the only detective working for that reward; however, in a private investigation she competes with others for information and the reward. In these latter cases she is often aided by Colonel Warner's willingness to provide special information and police assistance when she requests it. In offering her the case of "The Mysterious Countess," the colonel recognizes both her talent and her need; he offers " ' . . . to entrust a serious case to your care and judgment. I do not know a woman more fitted for the task than yourself. Your services, if successful, will be handsomely rewarded, and you shall have no reason to complain of parsimony in the matter of your daily expenses . . .' " (4). In order to assure her ability to compete successfully, she employs a former pickpocket whom she has taught to read and write, and in whom she has "inculcated high moral precepts" (101); his job is to "discover minute and petty details which it was inconvenient for me to investigate myself" (103). Of course, she is free to work without the expectation of a financial reward if she chooses; but the absence of any guaranteed salary makes this an infrequent luxury.

Mrs. Paschal's determination to succeed is especially evident through her first-person narrative descriptions of her behavior and her thoughts: ". . . I had not long been employed as a female detective, and now having given up my time and attention to what I may call a new profession, I was anxious to acquit myself as well and favourably as I could, and gain the goodwill and approbation of my superior" (3). Her preparation is deliberate and thoughtful. She trains herself for her profession thoroughly by learning how to use a Colt revolver and by coming to feel more comfortable having it with her than not. She practices tailing suspects and moving through a strange house, up and down stairs, silently and without arousing suspicions. Even her emotions are schooled to her profession; when a confidante is killed, Mrs. Paschal concludes: ". . . but I, too, was somewhat callous through experience and contact with a hard world, so I dashed away the tear which was the apotheosis of the deceased woman, and applied myself with renewed ardour to the task before me" (71). When a young client compliments her on being " 'prepared for everything' " her attitude about her responsibility is clear: " 'If I were not, I should be unfit for the position I hold and unworthy the confidence [*sic*] that Colonel Warner places in me' " (155). In fact, noting that she concentrates all her energies on fulfilling her duties, she even finds that work seems to be her pleasure: "I undertook it [case of stolen letters]; for it was a task of some difficulty which I fancied would occupy a week or so most agreeably. I was always happier in harness than out of it. I do not mean to say that I despised reasonable relaxation, but I depricated any great waste of time" (116).

Mrs. Paschal proceeds on each assignment with intelligence and care. She credits herself with making minute observations, deductions from evidence, and deliberate reflections, thus setting up her successes. She considers herself unusually hardened for a woman and therefore willing to accept dangerous cases. In all this, she recognizes the role of her quick mind: "I was usually fertile in expedients, and I thought I should be able to find my way out of the dilemma in some way. I was not a woman of one idea, and if one dart did not hit the mark I always had another feathered shaft ready for action in my well stocked quiver" (27). Mrs. Paschal's impressive self-confidence is typical of the detective casebooks of the period; almost off-handedly, she announces: "I had been in many perplexing and exciting situations before, and I had taken a prominent part in more than one extremely perilous adventure" (21). At the novel's opening, when she insists that her dramas of real life will require "nerve and strength, cunning and confidence, resources unlimited," she feels no uncertainty about claiming all these qualities (3).

Only occasionally does it seem that both Mrs. Paschal's assignments and her successes are directly correlated to her sex. Several times she and the Colonel agree that stereotyped expectations about women can provide her with an advantage: "I suppose that Colonel Warner imagined that a service of so deliberate a nature would stand more chance of success if confided to a woman than it would if put in the hands of the regular police. Men are less apt to suspect a woman if she plays her cards cleverly, and knows thoroughly well how to conduct the business she is instructed to bring to a successful termination" (43). However, she, her colleagues, and the moneylender involved are all willing to acknowledge her abilities as well as her sex when she successfully solves the famous Rustenburgh diamond case. She acknowledges that the competition is fierce: "I was aware that in engaging in this matter I was undertaking a contest with the keenest wills and most fertile brains in the force." But she also recognizes that solving this cause célèbre "would rebound to my credit and give me a higher position than the one I now occupied" (95, 96). In a backhanded compliment, one of the Colonel's policemen assures her that even though no one has solved the crime quickly, " ' I shall think more than ever of the Lady Detectives if you accomplish what you lead me to suppose you can' " (105). The moneylender she eventually tricks into revealing his role is more direct: " 'Another time when I essay a similar affair I shall be more on my guard against lady detectives' " (114).

Mrs. Paschal's style of detection is unmarked by the behavior readers have come to expect from later fictional crime solvers. She operates more by intuition (never described as a woman's special gift) and by perseverence and courage than through collecting and investigating clues or material evidence. The turning points in her cases come from imaginative insights leading her to be in the right place at the right time. Although she sometimes calls in police assistance with great success, she prefers to work alone. This solitary investigation is not so much a necessary style of operation as a sign of her need for recognition: "If I ever achieved a triumph, which I sometimes did, I did not like my laurels shared with anyone else. Such as they were I approved of wearing them myself without any partnership in the wreath" (98).

Despite the qualifying references to a "lady" detective and some characters' surprise and dismay that a lady might be sagacious, courageous, clever, and self-directed, on the whole, the first-person narrative makes little reference to Mrs. Paschal's sex inhibiting either her investigation or capture of criminals. Once, she even slips out of her petticoat when it proves too cumbersome to allow her to climb down a drain tunnel, completely overturning references to the "petticoat police." Traditional femininity overwhelms her on only one occasion. Having been discovered at the hideout of a criminal group by their fierce leader and threatened with torture and death, she is released by the police. She summons them with a whistle she invented, having thrust off the criminal who held her up to the moment when lightning struck him dead. Then she admits, "When I found myself amongst friends and freed from the great danger which lately menaced me, I showed that I was a woman and swooned away" (88). Ordinarily, however, Mrs. Paschal aligns herself with her profession rather than her sex, saying, "I believe the end justified the means, and detectives, whether male or female must not be too nice" (156).

Over half the stories in this collection refer specifically to the character's gender although few inferences are drawn. Ordinarily, the dual identity of the protagonist as both woman and detective is acknowledged; criminals she captures or her employer describe her operation as a "lady detective," usually recognizing that part of her success is due to others' stereotyped image of a detective as male. Despite her talent and skill, her success is often attributed to surprise which catches criminals off guard. She does not contradict praise which labels her as "courageous beyond the average run of women" although such distinctions between women foster a competitive atmosphere and guarantee that someone must always lose (155).

In two stories, however, Hayward addresses episodes which directly challenge social stereotyping. Hired to investigate thefts from the post office, Mrs. Paschal infiltrates the all-male work force in "Stolen Letters." To disguise her investigation, "two other women had been introduced at the same time, but we were not by any means regarded favorably. The men scowled, and looked upon us as if we intended to take the bread out of their mouths. I took no notice of their hostile glances" (117). Already employed, she can afford to ignore the workplace harassment which is introduced without any amplification. Later, "The Secret Band" pits Mrs. Paschal against a master Italian criminal whose masculine, heroic qualities impress her. She is "dispirited" by Zini's love for a mindless, frivolous wife (51), while admitting that the woman's prettiness and engaging manner "will in the eyes of some men cover a multitude of sins" (47); still, she had expected him to choose a commanding and dashing woman. In the contrast between Zini's wife and the woman—not unlike herself—Mrs. Paschal would have him marry, Hayward plays on readers' stereotyped expectations. Those disapproving of a woman detective would not only find a traditional wife but could also mock Mrs. Paschal's implied personal interest in Zini; their rejection of the woman detective would be reinforced by the criminal's choice of a dependent, unintelligent wife. However, at the same time, Hayward's narrative also allows objections to the passive, doll-like woman as a socially approved wife; readers willing to reject sex-role stereotyping found double reinforcement here.

Certainly, nothing of the historical realities for women in 1864 anticipates the portraits of these two characters. Even as the authors do not explicitly address their replacement of a male hero with a female one, they also do not deliberately show their protagonists as stereotyped women failing in a traditionally male profession. The authors' provocative decision to use female protagonists is qualified by treating them more as neuter than female; they are honorary men.[3] Thus, it is probably coincidental that these novels were published in the same decade as John Stuart Mill's *The Subjugation of Women,* for Mrs. Paschal and Mrs. Gladden were no harbingers of change for literary or real women. No doubt the newness of the genre and the type of protagonist encouraged these authors to experiment more freely than the constraints of established literary forms would have allowed. The use of first-person narrators in both volumes, as in most of these casebook novels, also redirects the attention of the readers from the detective to the actions of the case; this mode was quickly abandoned in favor of the now-familiar emphasis on the great detective. Written by men, these two novels narrated by women avoid overtly undercutting their protagonists based on society's sex-role expectations. However, among the numbers of casebook novels published, only two are known to be about woman detectives. These characters are anomalies; the novels apparently led to neither imitators nor followers. Even Forrester and Hayward abandoned their innovations after the first attempt. It is impossible to know whether subsequent authors were self-censuring, publishers uninterested, or the reading public rejecting; undoubtedly, all three groups affected the limited adoption of these models. Certainly, the lack of additional similar characters and the absence of further British female private detectives until the 1890s diminishes the status of these precursors through silence and omission.

Notes

1. Both Mrs. Gladden and Mrs. Paschal (see text, below) belong in a book on the women private detective in fiction although they are described as members of the police. During this part of the nineteenth century,

members of the police detective force were also allowed to operate in a private capacity (e.g., Wilkie Collins's Sgt. Cuff) and, like bounty hunters, did so for the rewards.

2. E. F. Bleiler demonstrates that *The Experiences of a Lady Detective* thought to be published in 1861 is a ghost issue; the actual first printing was released October 1864 as *The Revelations of a Lady Detective*. My own research contradicts Craig and Cadogan's claim that British Library book stamps prove that *The Revelations of a Lady Detective* did appear in 1861. In the British Library copies, *The Revelations of a Lady Detective* is stamped 23JA65 (23 January 1865) and *The Experiences of a Lady Detective*, 17NO84 (17 November 1884). Nevertheless, exact dating of Hayward's book is not crucial to my argument. [Douglas G. Greene, in a personal letter dated 26 October, 1988, states that *The Lady Detective, a Tale of Female Life and Adventure* (n.d., British Library date stamp, 30 Jan. 61), *Revelations of a Lady Detective* (1864), and *Experiences of a Lady Detective* (n.d., c. 1884) have the same text.]

3. Not seen by characters in the novels or by readers as sexual women, Gladden and Paschal are—in some respects—like the postmenopausal women in Pacific cultures whom Margaret Mead saw being accorded male privileges (*Male and Female* 139).

2

Women Detectives in the American Dime Novel: 1880–1904

The dime novel was an American phenomenon in the last forty years of the nineteenth century. From the first Beadle and Adams publication in June 1860 until the change in postal laws eliminated their second-class mailing privileges and signaled their fall in 1901, these ten-cent paperbacks were a major force in American publishing and reading history. It is impossible to know how many copies were published or how many readers each copy may have had. One large publisher alone issued over three thousand titles in thirty-eight years, and during the Civil War train car loads were sent from Washington to Union soldiers in the field (Pearson cited in Durham 33–34). The first novel to mention detecting in its title was *The Bowery Detective* released on 28 March 1870, but the publications two years later by and about "Old Sleuth," the pseudonym of Harlan P. Halsey, signaled the popularity of the new hero (Hoppenstand 1). So significant was this introduction that Old Sleuth's publisher later successfully sued the rival firm of Beadle and Adams for using the term "sleuth." After 1890 the latter firm was enjoined against using the word as a title, pseudonym of an author, name of an author, or name of a series. Although Howard Haycraft does not wish to grant dimes the "dignity of detective novels" (*Murder* 83), they clearly were big business (Johannsen 67).[1] A typical detective dime novel emphasized action over investigation, physical over mental power, and a superhuman ability to succeed (Hoppenstand 3). Most of the novels were set in the cities as the dimes turned from the "Garden of the West" to the "City as Protector," to use Hoppenstand's metaphors; the detectives were the protectors of capitalism and the status quo (6).

The first appearance of a woman detective in the dime novels cannot be determined, but Hoppenstand's survey of two major publishers' offerings gives some indication of how infrequently women detectives turn up. Of 801 detective novel titles listed by Tousey Publishing Company, only four indicate the presence of a woman detective (36–69). In Munro's Old Cap Collier series, eight of 822 detective novels feature women (100–135). The percentages improve slightly in the Old Sleuth series: in Old Sleuth Library, four of 101 titles indicate women (162–65); in Old Sleuth Weekly, four of 203 titles feature women detectives (167–74); in Young Sleuth Library, five of 143 titles indicate that the Young Sleuth has teamed up with a girl or woman detective (176–81). Of approximately 5,800 fiction titles published by Beadle and Adams, only fifteen of the almost 500 detective novel titles suggest the presence of a woman detective. With the percentage of women detectives for these series coming to 1.5, they are only one of the interesting variations on the main theme: there was also the New York detective, the baseball detective, the gamin detective, the road agent detective, etc.[2] Additionally, many of these titles are deceptive in that the woman identified may be a minor character, an assistant to the male detective, or even a man in disguise.

Readers and writers of the detective dime novels would have been influenced by three major developments in the nineteenth century: the decline of the family-centered economy, the rise of women's education, and the development of organized women's activities (Chafe, *Women and Equality* 9). Undoubtedly, women and men identified white, middle-class women's values as those appropriate for all women. Indeed, the 1830s elevation of the "lady" cult to a status symbol, as Gerda Lerner defines it, reinforces this notion (190). It was not that the nineteenth-century woman necessarily had fewer responsibilities than her eighteenth-century counterpart but that her leisure "whether hypothetical or actual was increasingly treated as the most interesting and significant thing about her. . . . [H]er function was obscured and intended to be so, and evaluations of her worth consequently tended to become exercises in indirection" (Douglas 63).

The decline in the family-centered economy directly affected all women. Those of the middle class found themselves receiving less approval for work outside the home than they had in colonial America (Lerner 184); meanwhile, the positive image of working-class girls in New England mills began to decline with the introduction of immigrant labor and mechanization (189). Professionalized out of medicine and law, limited as shopkeepers to those businesses serving women exclusively, and growing in numbers only in teaching, women inevitably regarded work as a temporary, premarriage activity. This attitude resulted in their continuing as untrained casual labor with the lowest paid, least skilled jobs (189–90). Nonetheless, during the Civil War, women proved their abilities in fundraising, business economy, and taxing work. The Civil War Sanitary Commission (although run by men) offered seven thousand local women's societies an opportunity to participate in the work force and the war work. They raised $50 million, recruited nurses, provided supplies and food, campaigned against unsanitary hospital ships and convalescent homes, searched for the missing, and escorted the wounded home (Flexner 107). Others either struggled to keep their families together and fed in the absence of male wage-earners, worked in cities to earn salaries, or nursed the wounded.

The impact of women's education on their attitudes about themselves and men's attitudes about the women with whom they came in contact cannot be underestimated. By 1860, even in farm communities girls were as likely as boys to be enrolled in primary school (Degler 309) and by 1870, some eleven thousand women were enrolled in 582 institutions of higher learning (O'Neill 13). In 1833, Oberlin College was the first "seminary/college" open to all; its first female graduate of a full course received her diploma in 1841. At Vassar, founded in 1865, the courses were the same as those demanded elsewhere of men. Nonetheless, physical education was the first department listed in the school's "General Scheme of Education" and was strongly promoted to counteract the supposedly negative effects of studying on women (Rothman 29). By 1870 women constituted 21 percent of the total undergraduate population, probably due to the shortage of male students caused by the Civil War (Graham 764). Still, a paradox persisted. Colleges may have offered women

the opportunity to leave home; but at the same time, they also perpetuated the idea of limiting women's activities to a socially acceptable sphere (Rothman 41).

Education was not the only area in which women became more
active. America in the 1830s began to see the rise of numerous female
reform societies designed to promote temperance and purify public
morality (Chafe, *Women and Equality* 8). In the name of holy causes,
nineteenth-century women could become aggressive and even angry,
thus exceeding limits laid down by sexual stereotyping (Douglas 10).
However, the closer their nondomestic activities were to their approved domestic and moral sphere, the more likely these were to be
condoned. Thus church work and a discreet antislavery stance were
acceptable; active feminism and public appearances were not (Degler
306). Nonetheless, the public lecture series, an important feature of
nineteenth-century American cultural life, also drew women speakers
who were both vilified and praised. As an institution which reached
enormous audiences, it consolidated attitudes toward cultural and social issues (Scott 800).

No matter how undesirable women's rights seemed to the population at large, they posed vital legal, political, and moral issues for
nineteenth-century America. An 1801 Connecticut publication, *The
Female Advocate,* proposed that the two sexes were equal in talent,
genius, morals, and intellectual worth, and that only male arrogance
rejected that equality (Cott 171). Founded in 1833, the Philadelphia
Female Anti-Slavery Society met in 1837 for a twelve-state convention with a woman as the presiding officer (Flexner 42). Of course,
abolitionist women were charged with being unwomanly by church
and society as they were busy learning to organize, hold public meetings, conduct petition campaigns, and speak in public.

Despite opposition, in 1848 the First Women's Rights Convention was held at Seneca Falls, and in 1850 the first National Women's
Rights Convention convened in Worcester, Massachusetts. The first
state suffrage referendum was held in Kansas in 1867, marking the
beginning of serious attempts to achieve women's suffrage (Flexner
294). However, the early women's rights movement did not focus
exclusively on the vote, but also concentrated on the control of property and income, guardianship, divorce, legal status, education, and
employment (Flexner 82). In 1863 Elizabeth Cady Stanton, Susan
B. Anthony, Lucy Stone, Angelina Grimke, and Ernestine Rosy founded

the National Woman's Loyal League, which obtained 400,000 signatures between May 1863 and August 1864 for the passage of the Thirteenth Amendment (Flexner 110). Women were not only learning how to organize but also were showing their potential political power. As might be expected, women's rights activity stopped during the Civil War, and women were subsequently excluded from the Fourteenth Amendment passed in 1868. But, the first federal women's suffrage bill was introduced in the Senate that same year and in both houses of Congress in 1869 (Flexner 149). The federal legislation moved more slowly than bills in the individual states, for by 1870 both Utah and Wyoming had passed a women's suffrage bill. Ellen DuBois characterizes the underlying fears of women's suffrage with recognizing its challenge to distinctions between public and private (63).

The existence of fictional women detectives also threatened the distinctions between public and private spheres of action. The examples of women detectives both on the frontier and in the cities parallel the experiences of male heroes of the dimes to a considerable degree.[3] However, like female sleuths who follow them, these women are split by their male authors into two categories: woman or detective. None of the seven characters discussed in this chapter is allowed to blend the two roles successfully to stand as a fully integrated, successful character.

Unlike Forrester and Hayward, who placed their women police detectives squarely within the models provided by the sub-genre, three dime novel authors—Harlan P. Halsey as Old Sleuth, Albert W. Aiken, and Edward L. Wheeler—chose to challenge and subvert the established conventions of their form. The early dimes with their stories of history, frontier adventure, and heroes served a myth-making function for a still young country. Even if the demographics of their readership—primarily young and male—are not known exactly, the texts themselves inscribe their consumers. Terry Eagleton's claim that "every literary text intimates by its very conventions the way it is to be consumed, encodes within itself its own ideology of how, by whom and for whom it was produced" clarifies the roles of authors, publishers, readers, and texts in this profitable and popular sub-genre (quoted in Barrett 77). Detection was not the principle function of these variations on the form; reinforcement of American capitalistic, individualistic, heroic achievement was. Explicit and implicit com-

plicity between authors and readers with a clear, if unspoken, awareness of the moral of these tales demanded that the scripts of woman
and detective which were temporarily conflated at the outset of the
novels be ultimately separated into their usual and stereotyped channels.

Because this confusion of scripts need never have arisen if the
authors had not introduced women detectives, modern readers and
critics might question the writers' motivation and suspect a thwarted
liberalizing attempt either to extend the genre or to redefine women's
roles. But, in view of the persistent sabotage of female protagonists,
Michele Barrett's concept of recuperation seems a more plausible
explanation. She defines recuperation as an "ideological effort that
goes into negating and defusing challenges to the historically dominant meaning of gender in particular periods" (82).[4] In the dozen
years preceding the first identifiable dime novel with a woman detective protagonist, fear of the radical demand for women's suffrage
which had begun before the Civil War intensified; a federal bill was
introduced, and two frontier states—sites of typical dime novel adventures—had ratified state suffrage. The fictional undercutting of an
independent woman provided a powerful dose of "wish fulfillment of
[the] patriarchy" to readers of the dimes (Barrett 80).

Thus, the novels are not what they seem to be. The author and
the narrator tell different stories, relate different plots. What M. M.
Bakhtin calls the "double voiced discourse" persists throughout the
texts (324). The seven novels discussed in this chapter resonate not
merely with two different points of view but with two contradictory
plots also. Always there is the foregrounded plot of detection. But, in
three novels, the apparently dominant plot is structurally matched by
the conventional marriage plot; in two others it is paralleled by a
competing, male-dominated detection plot. In these works, the back-
grounded plot gradually moves into the primary position, reducing its
story of the female-as-detective-as-protagonist to a contributing episode. Two other novels resolve the difficulty of imagining a woman
as a detective by redefining the character as unwomanly to account
for her ability as an investigator.

The marriage plot quickly comes to dominate *The Lady Detective,* the earliest and the longest of these dime novels featuring a
woman detective, written by the man who virtually copyrighted the
term "sleuth"—Harlan P. Halsey. Kate Goelet, the protagonist, is

apparently a sleuth worthy of the name, without parallel in New York, and a fitting first woman in the field a full decade after the introduction of male detectives in dimes. However, she is eventually consigned to romance; her status as a marriageable woman takes precedence over her unique career.

As though to establish her credentials to a potentially unbelieving audience, Halsey initially provides a more detailed and explicit description of Goelet's characteristics than is typical for her male counterparts. At the opening of the novel, she is reported to be a twenty-three-year-old rare beauty with the countenance of a lady, suited to "the glare of gas-jets, glittering in silks and jewels" (5). She combines a graceful figure with a sweet and pleasant voice. These qualities are then matched with those which would account for her perspicacity as a detective: she is intelligent and has "the courage, cunning, patience, endurance and sagacity of the most experienced officer on the whole detective force" (6). But, descriptions of her physical courage are lessened by references to her expected gender limitations; thus Halsey notes: "[S]he had resources for self-protection ingeniously arranged, and felt perfectly able to take care of herself, although but a young and delicate woman" (77). To assure the reader of the lady detective's proper feminine feelings, the narrator announces her sympathy for both unfortunate criminals and innocent victims early in the story. Finally, even more reassuring to readers is her stated desire to leave the profession altogether as soon as she can earn sufficient money to do so. Only necessity, the narrator implies, has driven her to such an unladylike trade in which a woman has "associated in all kinds of rough company and mixed in all kinds of horrid scenes while performing her duty as a professional detective" (135). Thus Halsey forestalls criticism by acknowledging the inappropriateness of his character's behavior and offering a plausible explanation for it.

The story itself revolves around two tasks for the woman detective. The first is to find a large sum of negotiable bonds and collect the ten percent reward on which she will retire. The second is to prove the innocence of Henry Wilbur, the supposed thief, whose honest and decent appearance initially appeals to her feminine intuition and later touches her heart. The detection plot makes way for the marriage plot as throughout the case she worries that the "refined, highly cultured, well born and bred" bank clerk (who still lives with and respects his mother) will find a woman detective socially and morally beneath him (135). That she succeeds in finding the bonds and saving Wilbur does not mean that she considers herself worthy of him. He must assure her that not only does he love her but also that he has seen through her many disguises and reservations to accept her. Wilbur becomes a stand-in for the readers who also recognize that Goelet's detecting persona masks her true status as potential wife.

There is no doubt that Kate Goelet is qualified to undertake this investigation. Like Halsey's male detectives in the dimes, she is a master of disguise. She defends herself against physical attack easily, relying sometimes on an undescribed instrument which she carries and other times on her own strength. Once, she demonstrates how she might have overcome Henry Wilbur had he been a criminal: with an unseen movement she causes two six-inch stilettoes to shoot out from her sleeves. In her perceptive, thorough, and imaginative observations she sometimes uses scientific devices which allow her to hear conversations through keyholes and easily unlock doors. She is quick to take advantage of coincidences which abound in the book—meeting Wilbur moments after she has been assigned to the case, getting hired by the villain's wife, and encountering another enemy of the villain when she breaks into his country home to recover the stolen bonds. Finally, she manages to ingratiate herself with even those who should be most suspicious of her, manipulating them to her own advantage while trying to reinforce their initial assumptions of her innocence. These talents are matched by a confidence which allows her to insist to Wilbur: " '[A]lthough I am but a woman, I do say, had I not come into the case, you would have been convicted as the thief' " (41). Her self-deprecating reference to the gender stereotype, by contrast, is unconscious and virtually automatic.

Halsey makes clear to recalcitrant readers that women as detectives, while more unusual than men, are a recognized extension of the profession. Henry Wilbur knows that "there was a corps of lady detectives on hand to pipe [investigate] and prepare the way for more able-bodied officers" in addition to men who can assume a woman's disguise (25). The villain recognizes that he is operating against a wily and cunning woman detective, a fact which the chief of the detective agency has already verified on the novel's opening page. Kate Goelet herself explains in a mundane and somewhat disillusioned way the value of women as detectives: " 'There are some things in our profession that a woman can better perform than a man; you know all the great thieves are not men?' " (40). With this statement, she reclarifies the legitimate reason why she has been employed in this case as in others: a fine, noble young man is presumed to have been manipulated by a scheming woman whom only another of her sex can ferret out successfully. This competition between two women for a desirable man transmutes a typical ploy of the romance novel into the middle of the investigation, structurally bridging the detective plot and the marriage plot.

Halfway through the novel, the author shifts the story's structural emphasis, explicitly introducing the theme of romance which reinforces Kate Goelet's primary identification in the plot as a woman in love rather than a woman detective:

> Kate Goelet had led a strange and romantic life; but within the few weeks that she had been acting as a detective to discover the stolen bonds, she had fallen upon the real romance of a woman's existence.
>
> It was not alone the hope of a reward that was inciting her to work up the mystery.
>
> Ever since the night she had first met Henry Wilbur, a new motive had agitated her.
>
> Like a sudden gleam of sunlight flashing into a dark corner, a radiant hope had blazed way down in her heart.
>
> She was but a woman, and women are strange beings where the affairs of the heart are concerned. (67)

Although she seems able to win Wilbur's affection in one of her disguises as a beautiful young woman, she is repeatedly uncertain about his reaction if he should discover the profession which has turned her from an unsophisticated girl to a woman fully acquainted with crime and vice; "she feared that, when the truth became known, he would despise her, and treat her with contempt and scorn—even worse—absolute hatred, for having deceived him" (96). Should this happen, she decides, she would prefer to die. Wilbur claims that as long as her purity is assured, he is unconcerned with her past, which he inaccurately assumes has to do with impoverished or socially unacceptable parents.[5]

With the marriage plot now dominant, the male character is granted control; both the fictional plot and the social reality guarantee his dominance. In the closing pages of the novel, Wilbur assumes superiority over the disguised Kate, first rejecting her masquerade cooly and claiming to love the absent Kate Goelet. When Kate admits having betrayed him through the disguises, Henry Wilbur insists that with the power of love he has seen through all her masquerades. The reader knows that this is merely a lover's claim, proven false in the text of the story. However, whether Kate believes or simply accepts this fiction, she falls "into the strong, brave arms outstretched to receive her in their warm embrace" (138). Although she has earned enough money to support her own family, herself and Wilbur, and, presumably, his dependent mother, all this goes unmentioned. That she has cleared him of one crime and helped him make financial restitution for another he committed is also allowed to fade into the background. The romance of a strong man and an apologetic but forgiven woman assumes center stage.

The narrator's final remarks concentrate on Wilbur's evaluation of his wife; she is not-so-strangely silent. Had she been born a man, Henry Wilbur insists, his wife would have rivaled Napoleon; having been born a woman, she cannot hope for that distinction. However, he is willing to acknowledge that she is the "best, handsomest, and smartest woman in the world" (138). One expects him at any point to refer to her as "the little woman."

Completely overshadowed by this conventionally happy ending is a cautionary tale against marriage introduced earlier. One of Kate's unexpected accomplices is the bigamous wife of the real thief, Henry Wilbur's employer, George Cameron. Their clandestine marriage thirteen years earlier had left Florence Clarke completely in her husband's power. Every husband's legal and financial control assumes a physical reality here when Cameron, tired of his supposed wife's company, imprisons her in an attic cell. Pretending to be insane for the privileges this disguise gains her, Florence joins Charlotte Brontë's and Charlotte Perkins Gilman's madwomen in the attic; all are paradigmatic representations of married women. Only some form of insanity, the model suggests, could lead women to abandon their limited independence and separate identity for the non-person status of a wife. Marriage, the symbol further implies, is a woman's prison complete with bars and guards. Even Clarke's bigamous alliance traps her as Cameron protects his public reputation. The implications of this exposure of marriage's institutionalized inequity are submerged in the detection plot. Cameron's behavior toward Florence Clarke is attributed to his criminal habits, not his masculine position in a patriarchal society. In fact, when Goelet reveals his banking crime, Cameron is neither prosecuted nor punished but allowed to relocate abroad; no mention is made of Clarke's fate.

The final chapter's romance parallels this earlier tale of marriage. Like his criminal employer, Henry Wilbur had declared himself in love with two women, Kate Goelet and Mary Clarkson (actually Goelet disguised). Hypocritically, Henry does not initially reveal that he has seen through her disguise as Kate desperately attempts to discover which of her personalities he really loves. He manipulates Kate's capitulation before he admits having always known the truth. Like Cameron, Wilbur has controlled all the facts and used them to his advantage without seriously considering how his deceptions might affect the woman he plans to marry.

Neither Halsey nor his narrator and characters recognize the limitations of marriage as a social institution in these paired episodes. Despite its legal and contractual ramifications, marriage is persistently treated as a personal agreement whose success or failure depends on the individuals involved. No inference that marriage serves ideological ends appears even subliminally in any of these dime novels. And yet the pattern of marriage followed by retirement for these women detectives reveals the values and beliefs of the work and the culture which has engendered it (see Kolodny 147). Through repetition plus supposed mimetic fidelity and naturalness, these conclusions achieve the force of fictional conventions, unelaborated by writers and taken for granted by readers.

Like Kate Goelet, the unnamed detective called "La Marmoset" abandons her detective activities for marriage; in Albert W. Aiken's *La Marmoset, the Detective Queen*,[6] however, the propriety of her professional behavior is at the root of the challenge to her competence. Although she is always in disguise and therefore unrecognizable, her work is well known, leading to her reputation as "the most expert agent that the police could command in all France—the queen of detectives" (4). She reveals only at the novel's conclusion, when guilt forces her into confession, that she has been masquerading as the heiress she was hired to find.

La Marmoset's guilty confession and flight from Paris and from her profession are extreme. She sails for America in the company of her client whom she has not only duped but also drugged and imprisoned. She explains: " '. . . at the last moment I discovered that the game was not worth the candle. I wanted the fifty millions of francs with which to purchase something, but when I went to buy I found that not ten times fifty millions would secure what I wanted; I had schemed and schemed for naught. Of what use was it, then, to lead a lying life longer? I grew sick of France and wished to bury myself here, in this new world, where in a new life I might forget the old one' " (27). The deluded client immediately proposes and the reader is assured that they are married within six months. Inasmuch as this is no punishment, perhaps her real penance was in knowing how her absence was explained in Paris where she had been considered invincible. The police chief, unaware of the truth, announced that she had been captured and murdered by a scoundrel whose imprisonment she had previously engineered.

The moral of the story is clear: liars are rewarded and lady detectives have no ethics, so it is better in the long run that they abandon their profession for marriage. The detective's moral flaw is integral to both her failure as an investigator and her success as a bride. In the unnecessarily confusing ending of the story, the five years of police-spy work done by La Marmoset are seen as a temporary meal ticket and a vocation to which she had no commitment or loyalty. The chief of police and his other male employees labor on while the woman spy is apparently redeemed through marriage.

Certainly, no character in the detective dimes seems less likely to develop into a romantic heroine than Nell Niblo. Unlike Kate Goelet or La Marmoset, she is young, boyish, and untraditional in style; nonetheless, Nell follows their lead—down the aisle. In 1886, the creator of Deadwood Dick, Edward L. Wheeler, introduces her: " '[A] new one they've got on the force—a gal, by the way, just over from N. Y. Nell Niblo, she calls herself, and they do say she's reg'lar smart' " (2). Dubbed "the boy-girl detective," Nell is perfectly disguised as a street Arab who is also clearly feminine and attractive under her rough appearance. Everyone involved seems to have some difficulty placing her: the characters are alternately confused and definite about her gender; the author wants to have her disguises impenetrable and yet keep her transparently a girl. Nell herself is certain about her gender yet unconvinced of what it might mean: " 'But I ain't a woman; I'm only a gal. They call me a little cuss over in York, 'cause I allus hoe out my own row, and keer fer No.1' " (4). Wheeler even introduces an interesting legal reference to the option police had to arrest Nell for wearing clothes "not natural with her sex," which they forego because of her contradictory abilities to behave modestly and still defend herself from insulting behavior (10). In this, the tension between her two, still-conflated scripts is evident.

New York Nell begins as a newsgirl who leaves New York rather than be imprisoned in the Tombs for poisoning a dog. At some point her career as a detective begins to take shape; she announces her credentials as a member of the New York Detective Force (an undefined entity) but seems to operate alone, independent of any affiliation. " 'If you want help and want to pay for it, I'm ready for biz— New York Nell, at your service, perfeshional detective, an' ef I can't win a case I take hold of, I don't charge a cent' " (12). Wheeler uses repeated announcements of Nell's status both to explain her presence and, especially, to allow reiteration of her commitment and her self-confidence: " 'Professionally, heretofore, I have been a detective and a newsgirl, the latter serving me in the former capacity. Professionally, henceforth, I am a detective. I tell *you* [the criminal] this because I would rather battle with an armed villain than an unarmed one. The victory is keener. the satisfaction keener. Look at me I am a mere chit of a girl—17 years of age only—and never had the advantage of a common school education. Still, there is a heap of sense and understanding in my curly head, and I have eyes like a hawk' " (11). This detective suffers from no doubt that she can achieve her goal and more as she stalks both cases and criminals. Local villains who are wiser than her enemies are content to avoid her or " 'she'll turn a trump on you' " (20).

Nonetheless, at the story's conclusion, having been financially rewarded for her professional skill, she apparently gives up her career to marry a "noble husband" who is said to be justly proud of the auspicious results brought about by his wife's detecting experience (31). There is no suggestion that she will continue in this vital work for which she is so well suited. And, as written, her material rewards and her noble husband are so neatly juxtaposed in the text as to make a reader wonder whether the spouse is not a part of the well-deserved reward. This superimposition of the marriage plot over the detection formula, coming in the novel's last page, emphasizes its importance by this placement in the ultimate position. But, the marriage plot is unanticipated and unjustified by earlier events in the novel; similarly, it is unexplained. Wheeler's structural undermining of what had seemed to be the only plot is so completely taken for granted as to insist it is inevitable in a novel with a female protagonist.

Undercutting the sleuthing qualities of his woman detective without resorting to a compensatory romance, Harlan P. Halsey as Old Sleuth twice creates a parallel and intersecting detection plot starring a male protagonist. As in the earlier stories, the apparently dominant plot of a woman detective recedes, allowing a more familiar story to assume center stage. Halsey includes the name of one of his male series characters in the title of a novel about a female protagonist: *Cad Metti, the Female Detective Strategist; or Dudie Dunne Again in the Field*. This reassures the reader of a familiar constant in the series character and counterbalances the less familiar idea of a woman detective with a recognized male hero. In this novel, the two work as a kind of team although Dunne claims that Cad Metti is his "detective aid" (11) and the government specialist who hires them describes her as Dunne's "lady pal . . . one of the bravest and brightest women that ever entered the profession" (6). This conflict between an announced partnership and an actual subordinate relationship continues throughout the novel as Dunne trails the criminals, overhears their plots, and focuses most of the reader's attention. Meanwhile, Halsey allows Cad Metti to shadow Dunne or other suspects but to come into the case only in conjunction with Dunne, while he is often centrally present in the story in her absence. On one occasion Dudie even orders her away from the criminals' location as a precautionary measure which she describes as "generous" (17).

Her partner's cautious behavior seems inappropriate to the reader when Cad Metti's talents are revealed. Like Dudie she is able to safeguard herself by remaining unrecognized; once she even fools the government security man who has hired them. When necessary she can shadow criminals without their being aware of her and, as a result, can warn the impressionable Dunne of a duplicitous woman. She demonstrates her strength on an unbelieving villain and, as the narrator clearly indicates, is a real hero: "The wonderful Cad was not much behind when it came to a shindy. She could have given the famous strong woman who a few years ago appeared on the stage points in many athletic fields" (98). A criminal she knocked down and out puts it more succinctly: she has "the force of a Goliath" (27). But Dunne vacillates between acknowledging her ability and trying to protect her. Even Halsey's descriptions of her admit these contradictions. ". . . [W]hen it comes to quickness, nerve, cunning, and courage she cannot be excelled" (11). Nonetheless, she titters girlishly and inappropriately to work off her excitement and defers unnecessarily to Dunne when they are planning, refusing even to make suggestions.

As seems true throughout the dime novels of detection, the primary talent and device of the investigators is disguise. Whereas Dunne is generally adept at disguises, Cad Metti is described as a scholar of them who has studied them scientifically. Most frequently Cad adopts the image of a young boy despite her natural appearance as a youthful beauty with a dazzling smile. This tendency to assume the appearance of a young man, much like Shakespeare's Rosalind or Viola, allows the detectives (Cad, New York Nell, and Kate) to gain some advantages of the male world without entirely giving up their respectable female status.

Structurally, the novel persistently acknowledges the male detective; coincidental good luck surrounds "our hero," as Dunne is regularly called. Criminals freely discuss every aspect of their plans when he is within hearing and, when faced with alternate suspects to tail, he invariably chooses to follow the right man. Cad, who claims to know his rashness, usually follows Dunne to rescue him from dangerous situations. But at the end, he and the secret police capture the dangerous Italian gang while Cad Metti is conspicuously absent. If Dunne and Cad's participation in the ultimate moment is inequal, so are their shares of the reward. Although both are given verbal credit by the narrator, Dudie Dunne is named "the detective of the age" by the head of the secret police and goes "up to the top as a great officer", his woman detective partner is never mentioned (106). At the story's conclusion, the reader is promised further narratives of the two wonderful people and "the romance of the life of the bright, beautiful Italian girl who from choice became a female detective strategist" (106). Of course, there are no further adventures of Cad Metti recorded.

The ease with which Halsey displaces his protagonist when she is female suggests that he does so *because* she is female. However he may have experimented with an unusual detective protagonist, he finally opts for the traditional male hero. His reluctance to deviate from the conventional expectations of "Old Sleuth's" readers inscribes their definition on the text. Halsey's two voices as author and narrator merge, like his two distinctive detectives, into a single nostalgic view reifying sex-role stereotyping; his commercial success implies that readers approved.

The same pattern is followed in Old Sleuth's third novel about a woman detective, *Mademoiselle Lucie: The French Lady Detective*, which is actually less about Mlle. Lucie and her exploits than about the machinations of the villains against the innocent characters; like *Cad Metti*, it quickly shifts its protagonist from female, to a female-male team, to a male. Eventually, the woman who describes herself as "a sort of female detective" joins forces with a male detective who knows the story of her past and promises to assist in her current case (8). As the narrator makes clear, the man becomes the primary investigator: "The detective was to investigate as to what had become of Agnes, and the mademoiselle also determined to do a little investigating on her own" (24). Although they are together in rescuing Agnes Tift from her in-laws, the use of the term "detective" for Jerry Mack and "mademoiselle" for Lucie grants him the professional status and her an identification by gender alone; further, the woman's contribution to the solution of the case is minimized by calling it "a little investigating." In the final lines of the story, Mlle. Lucie's personal case is solved and her inheritance restored. The proof has been uncovered not by the female detective but by Jerry Mack. So, he has taken over at least half of the Tift case from her and later appropriated all of the "Mlle. Lucie case," leaving her without a professional position from which to operate. This problem is effectively solved by the author in having Lucie abandon the profession which brought her notoriety, an income, and status. Clearly, she need never have become a detective at all; the novel's conclusion implies that she, like the victimized Agnes Tift, should have been the client not the investigator. By Halsey's definition, women either have or are the problems; men are or provide the solutions.

Displacing the detection plot is not the only technique used to undercut the dime novel's women detectives; in two novels, Albert W. Aiken redefines the protagonists' characteristics to achieve the same reassuring effect for his readers. The fictional development of both Hilda Serene and Mignon Lawrence emphasizes the unwomanly behavior or appearance which accords with their unfeminine choice of a profession.

As is true with a number of other dime novels of detection, Aiken's *The Actress Detective; or, The Invisible Hand: The Romance of an Implacable Mission* has a title which both tells and teases the reader. Is she actress or detective? Which is the disguise for the other? Is there to be romance of the usual sort or the heroic sort? For the reader of such a novel almost one hundred years after its publication, these are not unimportant questions. The readers' confusion over the title can be taken as a paradigm for the characters' confusion about the protagonist. Which is her disguise—woman or detective? They do not believe she can be both.

From the novel's opening it is clear that Hilda Serene is destined to be more than an actress or, more accurately, other than an actress, as her qualifications for success in her chosen profession are questionable. Her talents clearly lie elsewhere. Her physical fitness, record of having done gymnasium practice, and decidedly masculine appearance are described, apparently to prepare the reader for her active role in a physical scuffle: "[W]ith the cunning of a veteran boxer the actress threw up her left hand, warded off the blow without any trouble, then there was a momentary stiffening of the lithe, muscular figure—the 'gathering together'—as the pugilists term it—out shot the right arm, and the man, who got the blow on the neck under the ear on the jugular vein, received the impression that he had been struck by a fist of iron, not of flesh and bone" (4). This early introduction to the masculine talents of the ill-named Miss Serene becomes the focal point of the novel's description of the protagonist. Inaccurately, she calls herself a "knight of old on adventure" but later attributes her interest in solving the mystery of her new friend's inheritance to woman's curiosity (12).

Had Hilda Serene set out to be a detective, she could hardly have had better training. Raised in the West, she is experienced in handling weapons; she is not hesitant to use her double-acting revolver or her eight-inch Bowie knife. In less deadly circumstances, she is equally prepared to defend herself: " 'Well, you know it is a popular fad nowadays for ladies to take fencing and boxing lessons, and only the other day there was a regular prize-fight between two women . . . still it is not a bad idea for a woman who is possessed of sufficient muscular strength, to know how to take care of herself, in case she is attacked by ruffians' " (5). She is skilled at observation, not terrorized by the sight of blood, able to run despite being encumbered by skirts, well educated, and able to drink without getting drunk. The police chief compares her eyes with those of a cat which might see in the dark and turns to her in his bewilderment for "counsel from the shrewd, fresh young wits of the girl" (19); being unfettered by stereotype or expectation, she is able to press the supposedly respectable people whom the police ignore. She is, they conclude, "one woman picked out of a million" (25).

This praise is ironic in view of the one accusation repeatedly leveled at Hilda Serene: she is more like a man than a woman. The police and criminal she captured walk off chatting about her masculine strength. The latter's cohorts, convinced that no man in the New York police force could find them out, conclude that their discoverer must be more than mortal; later they revise this judgment by acknowledging that Hilda Serene is like a man compounded with the magnetism of Cleopatra. When challenged by a jealous actress who insists that she must be a man, Hilda Serene's response is a disappointed negative. She considers it unfortunate that she is a woman as she hates such traditional signs of femininity as clothes, shopping, and jewelry, has never been in love, and, at age twenty-five, is uninterested in marriage. With 140 pounds of muscle, she looks masculine but is female. Even her defender Louise Amherst compliments her as "a strange man-woman," "a great, big, horrid, dear, delightful, masculine fighting girl" (24). And she herself does not question this charge: " 'I ought to have been a man; there is not the least doubt about that. All my tastes are masculine and not feminine, and the best proof of my assertion is the liking I have for the life of a detective' " (26).

So, throughout the novel and particularly at the end, all the characters conspire to praise the detecting qualifications of this woman who is consistently portrayed as unfeminine. Her traditional feminine qualities are clearly nonexistent and therefore unrelated to her success as a detective. Her dominant characteristics and inclinations are emphatically attributed to a masculine tendancy which is both cause and effect of her ability as a detective. Aiken divides the character so clearly into feminine and masculine parts without allowing for the possibility of *human* characteristics which might be useful in solving crime that readers can draw only one conclusion: detection is a masculine pursuit whether done by an actual man or a woman-man.

Aiken again declares his protagonist unwomanly to account for her professional choice in *The Female Barber Detective: or, Joe Phoenix in Silver City*. Although its title—like *Cad Metti*— suggests the presence of a male colleague or even a male detective in female disguise, this novel is precisely what it represents itself to be. New York police spy Mignon Lawrence establishes a barber shop in the mining town of Bearopolis, New Mexico, as a cover for her detecting.[7] Her talents are established immediately; she is a detective of whom her mentor Joe Phoenix could be justifiably proud.

Nonetheless, Aiken is at some pains to make it clear to the reader that like Hilda Serene, Mignon Lawrence is no typical woman. Her physical strength, clever planning, determination, and courage are regularly noted. But the author goes further to clarify how untypical a woman this detective is; she explains to her landlady: " 'I will have to make a clean breast of it, I suppose, Mrs. Hauser. The fact is, I am unfortunate enough to have a horrid mustache, so that I have to shave just like a man. . . . It is an awful nuisance. But if I didn't shave I would have a regular mustache, and as a woman can't very well go to a barber I am compelled to shave myself. Just think now what an amount of talk it would create if I should walk into the barber's shop in town and announce that I had come to be shaved' " (5). This physical characteristic of the detective is not specifically mentioned again. But, needing to support herself, she opens a barber shop and handles razors, talks about razors, goes off to buy new razors, shaves and barbers a number of men in the town; her activities generate frequent talk about the "she-shaver."[8] All these references consistently remind the reader not only of this unfeminine attribute of Mignon Lawrence and the masculine occupation of the detective as barber but also suggest the masculine occupation of the detective as detective. The novel does not so much question a woman's suitability for a typically masculine profession as challenge her womanliness itself. Without ever being explicit about the character's unsuitability for at least one of the roles he establishes for her, Aiken manages to undercut the protagonist's heroic position. He suggests something faintly ludicrous about a mustached woman, clearly undermining her womanly attributes. The reader is then not likely to take her exploits— investigations, rescues, and arrests—seriously either. By rejecting what he has seemed to champion, Aiken undermines reader identification with or admiration for his detective-hero.

Aiken, Wheeler, and Halsey have shifted the emphasis and redefined the importance of the two plots their novels employ. Beginning with an apparently liberal approach to women's fictional (if not historical) options, they foreground an adventurous, exciting detection plot. Gradually, and more explicitly in some novels than others, they develop a conservative, gender-limited perspective through a background story which eventually replaces its competition. The detection plot, for as long as it holds its position, shows the female detective solving crimes, saving the innocent, and serving justice. The female script clearly demonstrates how pretty, feminine women inevitably accept marriage proposals while unwomanly women do not receive any and look for compensating activities. Both the sub-genres of adventure and romance are manipulated for traditional purposes: however good a detective the woman may be, marriage is her proper destiny; only the unwomanly evade it.

If, as John Farahger has demonstrated, the nineteenth-century American frontier offered fewer opportunities for breaking sex-role stereotypes than other historians have suggested, it is apparent from these novels that urban settings were no more hospitable to women doing "men's work." Winning admiration and respect as they swept into town, Kate Goelet and her detecting sisters were rare in both fiction and reality; their behavior challenged prevailing codes and disoriented society's expectations of men as well as women. Naturally, their authors showed them paying a price. None was portrayed as a complete detective and a complete woman simultaneously; in particular, each was set up to prove her femininity—or be branded unnatural. Readers' approval of such a double standard for judging women is encoded within the structure and characterization of all these stories. The young men who were prime audiences for these early paperback books might have been intrigued and entertained by the fast-paced adventure and excitement of these novels but also would eventually have been reassured that society and their own privileged masculine position in it faced no real threat.

Like the police-notebook novel discussed in chapter 1, the dime novel is a genre fixed in historical time; both their beginnings and ends can be identified. These two forms, along with the sensational and gothic novels, were precursors of the formula usually defined as beginning with Poe. Their status is more contributory than sequential; elements from all were funneled into the narrower perspective which developed into detective fiction. The genre's shape rejected its early elasticity, as John Reilly indicates: "The framework [of detective fiction], however, is a genre historical in origin but now autonomous to the point where it can be bent and adapted but not fundamentally altered unless the author ceases to write detective stories altogether" ("Classic and Hard-Boiled" 334). Whether the introduction of women protagonists is an adaptation the genre can allow is the subject of the following chapters. As the form took shape, it served many societal purposes; like dime novels of heroic national growth, detective fiction—especially as the genre codified with rules and patterns—reinforced public values and political ideologies.

Notes

1. Durham claims that the dimes deteriorated in the 1880s with the introduction of the detective, gamin, and bootblack stories. This conclusion is based on his analysis of the dimes as stories of the frontier which were moral, exciting, adventurous, and reporting history as it was being made.

2. It is impossible to know whether or not this figure would hold throughout the industry, but it seems likely.

3. Naturally, these seven dime detective novels are only a representative sample. Many novels whose titles seem to suggest women detectives as protagonists have not survived; few are easily accessible. It seems unlikely that there are any serious challenges to the conclusions reached here. In a useful 1981 article which does not overlook women detectives, J. Randolph Cox briefly describes two novels I have been unable to obtain. Harlan Halsey's *Lady Kate, the Dashing Female Detective* (1886) is much like *The Lady Detective* as Kate Edwards (like Kate Goelet) falls in love with her suspect and ultimately chooses marriage over investigation. However, the protagonist of *Lady Kate* compounds her acquiescence to the female role by first resigning from the case and then the profession which forces her to suspect the man she loves. Edward L. Wheeler's hero in *Denver Doll, the Detective Queen* (n.d.) matches ruthless ability with her reputation as a "respectable woman of the world" (9).

4. Barrett's notion of "what is given with one hand is taken away with the other" might serve as an epigraph for this entire analysis of the conflicting messages about women detectives (82).

5. Questions about women's purity are implicit in most of these early works; the worldly experience from their professional activities seems directly contradictory to their continued sexual innocence.

6. Aiken spins an 1882 tale of a lost heiress, an impersonator, kidnapped relatives, duped police, and a detective persistently in disguise; novelty is added by his setting the story in Paris among French aristocrats. The novel is a typically convoluted one for the tabloid-like publication, ignoring chronological order, narrative reliability, and fictional unity.

7. This novel differs from those set in urban areas in its development of the typical dime novel version of the frontier, the code of Western versus Eastern behavior and expectation, and an intense nationalism and capitalism. Aiken is thus able to detail the codes of the Wild West and to insert an extraordinary amount of physical action including several gun duels, boxing challenges, and fistfights.

8. Like Lawrence, Wilkie Collins's Marian Holcomb in *The Woman in White* has a visible mustache; she too is caught by conflicting definitions of "woman." Her unfeminine appearance keeps her from being the romantic heroine while her gender limits her ability to be the detective hero.

3

Britain's Turn-of-the-Century "Lady Detective": 1891–1910

Two publications in 1887 marked the popularity of detective fiction on an international basis. Fergus Hume's Australian novel, *The Mystery of the Hansom Cab*, was a success previously unmatched in England, where over a quarter of a million copies were sold to individual readers and the rapidly growing subscription libraries in only eighteen months (Murch 141–42).[1] However, this is insignificant when compared with the phenomenal creation of Arthur Conan Doyle, whose first Sherlock Holmes detective adventure, *A Study in Scarlet*, was published the same year. Holmes's appearance revolutionized the detective story, and his popularity in both England and the United States kept Conan Doyle writing the four novels and fifty-six short stories of Sherlock Holmes for forty years, long beyond his own inclinations and interest. The works of these two best-selling authors met at a point where detective fiction was beginning to turn away from one and definitively toward the other. The sensational fiction of Fergus Hume, like that of the more important writer Wilkie Collins, was to be replaced by the cooler, more intellectual puzzles of Arthur Conan Doyle.

Despite other varieties of detective fiction, the form of the genre popularized by Conan Doyle assumed center stage for more than forty years and maintained its status in the field through *A Study in Scarlet*'s centenary year. In many ways, this style is far simpler than that of its predecessors; here, the detection plot and the detecting protagonist intersect. Often developed as a series character, the prominent figure of the lone detective intelligently and unerringly picks his way through clues left by a limited group of suspects to find the villain who has killed, robbed, or blackmailed. As he uncovers evil, the detective is always able to provide an explicable motive for the crime. The fixed formula of the plot requires a three-part ending: capture of the criminal, explanation of the crime, reestablishment of the social order guaranteed by the removal of the criminal from society. In its ability to create order out of chaos, the power of the detective intersecting with the plot is just short of godlike even if his personality does not always match.

If it is a commonplace that the detective novel, as opposed to the mystery story, could not have been written until there were detectives in real life to demonstrate the role, it is equally true that the advent of the woman detective depended on social conditions and changes which allowed readers to conceive of women in this role. The "daughters of educated men," as Virginia Woolf identifies the Victorian women who had no inherent identities of their own, initiated and reacted to a new image of themselves in the last thirty years of the century.

Women of the Victorian middle class were expected to have primarily domestic lives; in the separation between public and private spheres, theirs was the latter. Marriage was the only acceptable position for women. Yet the surfeit of spinsters in both fiction and society of the late nineteenth century challenged the truth of this conventional attitude (Delamont 139). Employment for women—the ladies, gentlewomen, daughters of educated men—was an economic necessity not to be met by private governessing or fine sewing and needlework. Their needs to be educated beyond drawing-room accomplishments and domestic management, to be self-sufficient and yet to remain socially acceptable ladies, were partially responsible for the magnitude of change in women's lives and roles in the last third of the nineteenth century.

Opportunities for paid employment gradually expanded for middle-class women (Holcombe 10). While the prospect of a career was widely considered only for the spinster beyond marriageable age, a job—naturally to be abandoned upon being married—was a distinct possibility for more women. They had then only to contend with the dual obligation of being good employees as well as perfect ladies, still almost a complete contradiction in the Victorian mind even as these changes occurred. However, societal accommodation to the unmarried woman's need to earn money for her support did not extend to married women until the Married Woman's Property Act of 1882 finally gave them the right to own property after marriage, including the right to retain their wages (Brittain, *Lady into Woman* 15). This legal change made significant differences in the options available to women and affected almost every household in England.

The greatest opportunities for all women came through education. The country's need for more teachers and women's need for economic survival required more than the simple education formerly given to middle-class girls. Despite many developments, in the press and in the public mind the most notorious change in women's educational status came with the establishment of women's colleges at Cambridge (1869) and Oxford (1879) and the pressure to admit women to the same final examinations as men (McWilliams-Tullberg 60; Brittain, *Women at Oxford* 53, 59, 66). In the popular image of the early Girton girl, society was presented a new and revolutionary picture of educated women (Crow 326).

The most emphatic arguments against women's education and employment were based on claims that a lady would not and could not manage anything so indelicate. Her nature would shrink from such coarse activities and demands while physical limitations would restrict her activity. The Victorian woman was seen as fragile and incapacitated—the conspicuous consumptive, an inevitable invalid (Duffin 31–33).[2] In response, early leaders in girls' education judiciously blended study with physical activity and a strong concern for the students' health (Atkinson 93). Later, young women who had walked decorously with their companions as well as those who had swung from ropes in their school gymnasiums found a new physical energy and greater mobility in the newly perfected safety bicycle which was enthusiastically adopted (McIntosh 129, 133). Whether increased sports and games for women resulted in dress reform or vice-versa, less hampered women found themselves able to participate in more activities without fatigue or fainting (Crow 330–31). As a result their opportunities and sense of their own abilities to accomplish increased.

In the same year Girton was founded, John Stuart Mill published *The Subjugation of Women* (1869), providing logical and reasoned descriptions of the historical, political, and personal enslavement of women. Even before the more militant feminist agitation by the Pankhursts and others, the question of women's right to vote was strenuously debated in Parliament, the specialized journals, and the popular press; the average citizen could not have been unaware of this pressure for a crucial change in women's status (Strachey).

The antifeminists, antisuffragists, antieducationists, and antireformers invariably buttressed their arguments by citing women's clearcut moral superiority over men and emphasizing the predictable loss of this virtue because of changes in women's condition. The purity of the chaste and innocent female, safeguarded by her nature and society's protectiveness from the evil embodied in sexuality, was thought to be threatened (Banks 108–9). In fact, although social pressure to mask their knowledge remained strong, by 1890 middle-class women had been exposed to sufficient information about contraception, childbirth, and "female disorders" and nostrums to contradict notions of their childlike and restrictive innocence (Smith, "Sexuality" 189–92). While no single event of legal or social consequence altered the daily lives of all women and societal attitudes about women, they jointly formed a climate in which the "daughters of educated men" and even some of their mothers could begin to free themselves from rigid and limiting social structures (Davidoff 67). The "lady detective" was the popular press's fantastic composite of this new image.

The influence of this climate upon the stereotyped genre of detective fiction permitted the appearance of Loveday Brooke and her sister detectives as detective fiction writers in the wake of Hume and Doyle's successes consciously sought ways of attracting increasing numbers of readers (Maugham 131). They employed the woman protagonist initially as little more than another sensational strategy for gaining readers' attention. Between 1891 and 1910, five such figures appeared in twelve novels; five of the titles included the woman's name, two announced the "lady detective," one simply said "detective" after her name, two more promised "her case" or "her adventures." Thus, the publishers informed the reader immediately of the books' unique feature, hoping to capitalize on two phenomena of the end of the nineteenth century—the rise of the detective novel and the emergence of the "new woman."

Detective fiction, like popular fiction in general, follows rather than parallels social change. The conservatism of the genre can be seen from its beginnings: structurally, the successful stories depended on a regular and familiar sequence of events; thematically, they reinforced a capitalistic, traditional, moralistic, and nostalgic world view. Widely adopted by writers and increasingly expected by readers, these consistent characteristics assumed the force of rules (aptly demonstrated in the 1920s by the Detection Club). In the chapters which follow, it is possible to trace how authors who introduced women detectives used and tested the boundaries of the genre—a pattern only visible now that the genre has endured longer than police casebook or dime novel examples. A three-way tug of war for the author's loyalties emerges among the demands of the genre, changing social reality which acknowledges women's new opportunities, and a nostalgic defense of traditional sex roles for women. These authors' presentations of a woman detective as protagonist seem to suggest a liberal attitude toward women in new public roles; however, there is a disjunction between that expression and the basic structural designs of the works, their plot form, and numerous telling incidental episodes which undercut and undermine this apparent liberalism. Furthermore, this disjunction, which manifests itself in the diminution of the protagonist, is at odds with the demands of the formula. Emerging from this contest among genre, reality, and nostalgia is a clear vision of the authors' challenges to the dominant form in order to defend explicitly the submissive, secondary position of women. In these works, readers are entertained and reassured by fantasies which encapsulate fictionally a vision of the world as it never was. Competing with the supposedly dominant detection plot is a powerful sub-plot showing woman in her supposedly rightful place; the detective script and the woman script clash because the necessary conditions for each are the inverse and contradiction of the other.[3]

The example of similar double-voiced discourse in nineteenth-century women writers' sensational fiction clarifies the process of simultaneously telling two stories. Elaine Showalter insists that sensational fiction formed part of a subversive tradition of women's fiction. Acknowledging that the novels apparently told stories of crime and violence, she argues that through a covert solidarity between readers and writers another, politically charged version of reality was shared among women (*Own* 159). These writers manipulated the popular genre in which they wrote to tell attentive readers a second, very different story criticizing "monogamy, the marriage-market, and the obstacles placed in the paths of intelligent women" (*Own* 161). Detective fiction written by both women and men reverses the outcome of this subversive process. Maintaining a stronger alliance with traditional, restrictive views of women's sex- roles, detective novelists undermine their genre—not, as might be suspected, by replacing male protagonists with women, but by undercutting the definition of the detective hero. This is achieved by their reestablishing in her traditional place the woman whom they have created for that new role.

As might be expected, with strong signals of approaching change at the end of the century, authors and readers found the old plots for women preferable to possible new ones. Rejecting the implications of the so-called new woman and her role, four of these five authors (M. M. Bodkin, George Sims, Milton Danvers, and Marie Connor Leighton, but not C. L. Pirkis) plot their works' true conclusions around the marriage plot or its sequel. The apparently submerged woman script comes to dominate the more obvious detection plot.

Despite the disclaimer that "there was certainly nothing of the New Woman, or for that matter of the old" about Dora Myrl, M. McDonnell Bodkin's *Dora Myrl, the Lady Detective* and *The Capture of Paul Beck* clearly describe the archetypal New Woman of fiction (*Myrl* 1). In appearance, education, occupation, and recreation, Dora Myrl corresponds perfectly with the Girton girl whose independence so challenged her countrymen.

The protagonist's background is not unusual for a detective but markedly different than most women's in her time. Daughter of a Cambridge don who originally wished for a son and a mother who died giving her birth, Dora was raised to be a lady and a scholar. Improbably, she succeeded in both. At age eighteen when her father died, she was a Cambridge wrangler about to enter medical school since she had "no taste for the humdrum life of schoolteaching" (*Myrl* 6). However, when a practice didn't materialize quickly enough, she chose not to wait patiently, taking positions in a single year as "a telegraph girl, a telephone girl, [and] a lady journalist" (*Myrl* 6). She worked briefly as a companion until she became intrigued by crime, having her new cards printed with "Miss Dora Myrl, Lady Detective"

(*Myrl* 19). Like her prototype, Dora has "the slim, agile figure of an athletic out-of-doors girl" (*Beck* 74–75); in her first golf game "she swung her driver with a free sweep, hit the ball a clean sweet smack, plumb center, and sent it sharp and low a good hundred yards straight for the hole" (*Myrl* 91)—and then decided to give up golfing. When the wind blows her short skirts, it reveals "slim ankles and neat feet cased in tan cycling shoes" (*Myrl* 2). She is able to keep up with a crook at 12 mph and is faster than a hansom cab in crossing London: "She found herself in a rushing stream of vehicles and went through it zig-zag, like a darting trout in a stream, finding an opening to the right or left, and shooting through before it closed again. It was perilous work for eyes less quick or nerves less steady than Dora's. With the cunning speed of a footballer, who carries the ball at a run, safe from the pressing crowd from goal to goal, writhing clear of collisions by an inch, she got safe from Victoria Station to Westminster" (*Beck* 147–48). Dora's talents even include being a steady shot with a "six-shooter."

As a conventional detective working within the formula, Myrl succeeds primarily by noticing a small, easily overlooked clue—sometimes recognizing its significance more intuitively than logically—to build an entire case around it. She often obtains information or verifies her case's direction by adopting disguises; she is always unrecognized. The recapitulation of her thoughts conclude the short stories in a Holmesean manner. The clues and investigation, sometimes a product of luck, are attributed to the ratiocinative process. But Dora and her clients are always confident of her success; only the criminals foolishly challenge her. When the suspected Dr. Phillmore mocks her " 'somewhat incongruous—I won't say comical—profession for a charming lady,' " she defends herself:

> "You think us women all weak and foolish?" she said smilingly.
>
> "Oh! It's not that," he answered, with a deprecatory wave of his strong white hand. "I would not harbor such a thought for the world." But all the time it was plain that that was precisely what he did think. "You, of course, are the exception, Miss Myrl. But do you think that women can fairly pit themselves in mind and body against cunning and strong men, and the so called criminal classes as a rule are both?"

"Women are clever and men are confident; their confidence betrays them."

"Well, let us put cleverness out of the question for a moment. How could a charming young lady like yourself for example, arrest a powerful desperado who had not the least respect for her sex or her beauty?"

"Oh! I'd manage it somehow." (*Myrl* 72–73)

This conversation's irony is revealed as Dora offers a solution to the hypothetical criminal problem the doctor poses and later uses it to capture him. Even though warned of her approach, he is outwitted; all the criminals are.

More of Dora's success as a detective is claimed than demonstrated in the two volumes. She solves twelve cases, is the "famous lady detective, whose subtle wit had foiled the most cunning criminals, whose cool courage had faced the most appalling dangers" (*Beck* 75), is a "tracker of criminals, unraveller of mysteries" (*Beck* 115–16), a "clever girl," "a wonder," and "an astute young lady." Yet the effect of these claims for her professional successes is consistently undermined. She is regularly referred to as a "girl" or "a slip of a girl"; she calls herself a "little busybody." Over and again she is described as "dainty"; combined with "lady" or "ladylike" it is the most frequent description of her and her activities. Detailed descriptions of lovely pastel tea gowns and dresses are used to overemphasize her femininity. Most of the time it does seem that "pleasure, not business . . . [was] her mission in the world" (*Myrl* 170). All of this emphasis serves to distract and deny the professional competence which the stories would seem to claim for her.

In the 1910 novel *The Capture of Paul Beck,* Bodkin explicitly introduces the marriage plot; quickly it dominates his detective novel. As the narrator reveals only Myrl's feelings, her growing split between being a detective and a woman can be easily followed. Beck's multiple roles are not explained for they do not exist; he suffers from no divergence between detection and male scripts. Meanwhile, throughout this novel, Dora is alternately overconfident and nervous about her abilities. She promises to be a friend's "bloodhound" and enjoys outwitting the famous Beck. Disguised as a parlormaid, she removes a clue directly under Beck's gaze, later giving way to "the temptation to startle him out of his placidity"; but he is not startled, remaining "complete master of the situation" (*Beck* 129). Dora becomes "frightened at the man" because she "can't hold a candle to him" (*Beck* 133); the reason, of course, is that "she solemnly swears that he's the only man she ever loved" (*Beck* 160). When Beck does not take her detection seriously and refuses to give in, Myrl's buoyance over bicycle chases, marked cards and fingerprints, and decoding cyphers evaporates instantly. Determined, but less confident, she continues on the case, while still erroneously believing Beck in league with the criminals. She relies on Beck's reputation as "Don Quixote of detectives. He has never yet been known to be rude to a woman" (*Beck* 230). Structurally, Bodkin demonstrates how the female detective's professional success is increasingly less important to her as she worries over her romantic plot, despite being unconscious of what really disconcerts her.

Instead of having to reconcile his life between two poles, Beck recognizes that he must persuade Myrl to accept his proposal despite her distrust of him. Astonishingly, Bodkin solves Paul's problem by making him the successful detective and Dora the failure. Although she has been the novel's protagonist, Bodkin shifts her position to hero(ine) of the marriage plot; without explanation, he fills the vacuum left in the detection plot with Paul Beck. Ironically, the author then returns his original detective to the investigation plot, as Beck selectively lets Myrl join his investigation at the end. At the same time, Beck assumes control of the marriage plot; having waited so long for a wife, he is "in a hurry" to achieve his vision of married life (*Beck* 312).

Paul's eventual success leaves the lady detective in tears, "even lovelier in sadness than in laughter" (*Beck* 269). She acknowledges defeat; he proposes; they are immediately married. Dora Myrl smiles "radiantly" once more (*Beck* 311). When she marries the opponent who had outwitted her and apparently retires from detecting, the novel's title seems only too clearly to identify the real case. Ellery Queen unjustly accuses her of "doing anything to get her man—be he criminal or husband," for she does not chase Beck (*Queen's Quorum* 41). Nonetheless, she gladly solaces herself with marriage only while Beck gets both criminal and wife as his share. Bodkin's subsequent publishing history reinforces the stereotyped rewards which his woman detective could expect. She trades her career for husband and child. Paired with additional novels featuring Paul Beck is *Young*

Beck; a Chip off the Old Block (1912) starring Paul Junior. No doubt Freud could have made much of this other Dora living an unfettered masculine life through her male child, reliving—quite explicitly—the pursuits of earlier years before she was limited to the roles of wife and mother. But when she reproduces, it is Paul, not Dora, whose image is perpetuated.

Dora Myrl's marriage to Paul Beck transforms her; she is well and truly caught. No longer the detective, she becomes an adjunct. The difference in their ages—his forty-one to her twenty-five or six—and experience only emphasizes the note of authority he has over her. Her tearful capitulation to his detecting skill reinforces the atmosphere of inequality. The novel is set up to reinforce old stereotypes: male success in men's professions, female success in women's only profession. For him the marriage and detection plots can coexist; the discourses of the author and the narrator are simultaneous and similar. For the woman, the two plots are established as contradictory. However, Bodkin does not admit that the presence of two scripts offers his female protagonist a choice; instead, her capitulation to the marriage plot alone is portrayed as her inevitable destiny. The novel's conclusion must have been as satisfying to Bodkin's male readers as Gilbert and Gubar surmise Jane Austen's endings were to her enthusiasts. They would have been flattered to see how a rebellious, imaginative woman was amorously tamed by a perceptive, experienced man (154). But if male readers envied or identified with Beck, women might have been reluctant to read themselves in Myrl's narrower sphere. Or, they may have been carried along by their own fantasies, Bodkin's promises, and society's reinforcement.

The sequel to marriage plots, the happily-ever-after of fairy tales, is seldom as predictable as courtship sequences. Many writers have demonstrated the truth of Tolstoy's perception of family life. Two of only five married women detectives in this entire study were created in late-nineteenth-century Britain. Beginning their detecting careers while married women, both face the difficult task of simultaneously upholding their reputations and their public/private images.

Married to a blind artist, Dorcas Dene works as a professional detective not because she chooses to, but because she must support her family. Although her social status as an artist's daughter and an actress had effectively removed Dorcas Lester from respectable middle-class society in George R. Sims's *Dorcas Dene, Detective: Her Ad-*

ventures,[4] she remains determined to demonstrate all the attributes of a lady: "I accepted—on one condition. I was to see how I got on before Paul was told anything about it. If I found that being a lady detective was repugnant to me—if I found that it involved any sacrifice of my womanly instincts—I should resign, and my husband would never know that I had done anything of the sort" (6). Fortunately, her reluctance was unwarranted; so she investigates a case her employer has described as one "in which an angel could engage without soiling its wings" (6).

Dene ranks herself with the best known fictional detectives and follows their methods. She is clearly determined to solve her cases. Despite her early protests at unwomanly behavior, she does not balk at illegality. Clients are protected; in one case she explains: "As I was employed by one of the guilty parties, it would have been unprofessional of me to give them to justice" (21). When Saxon, her male assistant and the narrator, protests at associating with the guilty, she shrugs her shoulders, " 'If everybody did the legal thing and the wise thing, there would be very little work left for a lady detective' " (22).

This kind of self-confidence hardly matches a description of her womanly apprehensiveness: "When the flyman had deposited me at the house, I made my way up the porch with a fluttering heart, for in spite of my profession, I have still that feminine weakness in moments of excitement" (17). This and Saxon's continual references to the womanly woman at home with her husband awkwardly contradict the description of the "famous lady detective." However, it is in terms of her family relationships, particularly her marital relationship, that Dorcas Dene is reduced as a detective. Paul Dene explains to Saxon how Dorcas shares her problems, " 'In all her difficulties, my wife comes to me, and generally we hold a council of four' " (9). Equal to Dorcas, who has investigated and gathered clues, are her blind, housebound husband, her tart-tongued mother, and even Toddlekins the dog. Paul Dene's blindness is supposed to limit his susceptibility to distractions; Mrs. Lester's matter-of-factness balances Dorcas's "looking about in every direction for something that lies close to their hand all the time"(10); the dog's special contribution is unspecified. Making no differentiation between Dorcas, two limited counselors, and a dog as participants in the solution of difficult cases clearly mocks and diminishes the detective's ability.

Unlike the use of similar physical handicaps for Charlotte Brontë's Rochester or Elizabeth Barrett Browning's Romney, Paul Dene's blindness is not Sims's device for undercutting the advantages of being male in a patriarchal society. Paul's limitation neither leaves him equal with Dorcas nor makes him capable of recognizing that he needs her help. Instead, Sims holds his married couple to the traditional pattern; his female protagonist must work hard to persuade her husband of his masculine superiority despite his blindness. She is doubly secondary and submissive as she bolsters his self-confidence by deliberately minimizing her own independence. Her self-effacing behavior, however, is taken for granted by the narrator and author as though a natural and reasonable attribute of married women.

Although to the lawyers and police she is a successful and respected detective, she is not given credit by the author for knowing or doing her own job. Her husband alternately expresses confidence in her judgment and insists that his overrule hers. When Saxon protests her midnight watch and appeals to Paul for agreement, Paul replies, " 'That's for Dorcas to say, old fellow. She knows her business better than we do' " (66). But he doesn't believe it. Soon after, he presses Dorcas: "There's a little invitation I should like you to give our guest tonight . . . I'm sure he'd like it, and I'm sure he deserves it . . . Mrs. Dorcas Dene requests the pleasure of Mr. Saxon's company at 11:45 for midnight underneath the lamp-post . . . in Berkeley Square' " (69). And like a womanly woman, despite her earlier protests, Dorcas acquiesces, " 'Of course, if you wish it, dear' "; she changes her view and agrees with this assessment of her need: ' "Honestly, I shall be glad of your company' " (69). On demand, she abandons her independence, her judgment, and her conclusions. The functions of both the detective as formulaic character and the protagonist as one of the novel's structuring elements are reduced in this novel as Sims replaces them with the combined presence of the male team—narrator and husband. Dorcas Dene, woman and detective, is submerged within the confines of patriarchal marriage.

Evading George Sims's problem altogether, Milton Danvers resolves the problem of the marriage plot and its sequel by marrying his amateur woman detective to the professional male sleuth. In the transformation from Miss to Mrs., Rose Courtenay is not the protagonist of the novels in which she appears; even in Danvers's *The Fatal Finger Mark, Rose Courtenay's First Case,* Robert Spicer is the principal detective and she is the helpful amateur, an orphaned governess-companion able to aid her accused friend.[5] In five subsequent novels as she becomes Mrs. Spicer and the "principal lady detective" for Robert Spicer's firm, she occupies an anomalous position. On the one hand, she investigates cases independently and successfully; on the other, her cases and Spicer's invariably coincide so that she assists him or occasionally is removed from the scene. This dismissal happens despite Spicer's loud praise of her abilities. Her special talent, perhaps the one to which Spicer alludes when he speaks of Rose's superior ability in some areas, is her gender. Merely by being born female, she has the benefit of "a woman's intuitive faculties . . . far more delicate and subtle than a man's" (*Grantham* 22). Her advice is viewed as especially valuable in delicate cases: " 'As a lady, she naturally understands the ways and peculiar feelings of one of her own sex, much better than a man would, however skillful he may be; and she will conduct the investigation with a woman's tact and delicacy' " (*Bride* 13). So Rose Courtenay is allowed tact, delicacy, and "peculiar feelings" while Robert Spicer is credited with skill. Her ability comes neither from training nor experience; it is simply a feature of her woman's nature.

Even so, what training and experience may have led to Rose's successes are not to her own credit. She has been Robert Spicer's pupil in the detective business; he has "brought her out" (*Doctor's Crime* 145). With love, "joy and thankfulness," Rose recalls her training: ". . . gradually and almost imperceptibly, he had cultivated her intellectual faculties, and drawn her upward towards his own level" (*Honeymoon* 20–21). With clients, "he gladly gave her the opportunity to prove . . . that she was really a clever lady detective" (*Grantham* 25). Naturally, he is quick to claim the credit. Acknowledging that she is a born detective previously wasting her talents, Robert insists that he can take credit for having discovered her abilities, joking that the laws unjustly discriminate against his right to patent this discovery. But he points out, " '[W]hat the patent laws did not provide for, the ecclesiastical laws did. . . . I have at last, by the aid of the Church, secured the sole and exclusive monopoly of the benefit of my discovery' " (*Honeymoon* 106). He made her; he owns her; he displays her. It is, perhaps, appropriate that Rose Courtenay uses a variety of professional names; her identity seems to be recreated for Robert Spicer's needs.

By this explicit acknowledgment of the covert purpose of marriage, ownership of a valuable commodity, Danvers strips the courtship, marriage, and marriage-sequel plots of the benign aspect they assume in Bodkins's and Sims's novels. By refusing to create a female protagonist, by not conflating the detection and woman scripts, he more clearly displays his loyalties to both the nostalgic tradition of women's secondary position and to the readers' expectations of detective stories. In this context, the denial of a marriage proposal to Marie Connor Leighton's character, Joan Mar, is an implicit denial of her desirability as a valued person.

Unlike her three sister detectives—Myrl, Dene, and Courtenay Spicer—Joan Mar is not set up by Leighton to need male assistance in outwitting brilliant criminals; she is herself a deductive genius in *Joan Mar, Detective*. However, all of her success is minimized also in the last dialogue between the two lovers she has saved: " 'Beautiful, clever Joan! We owe everything to her,' Lorine said enthusiastically. 'I wish she would marry someone worthy of her who would make her happy' " (306). The first assumption, that Joan could not be happy while unmarried, is less devastating than the second: that someone else, specifically a husband, will do for her what she is judged incapable of doing for herself—make her happy. The reader may infer that she has no control over the state of her emotions—a man does. Lorine's new husband, Brian Charlton, emphasizing Joan's professional interests, responds: " 'She does not want to marry. . . . She does not want the sort of happiness that we have. She wants to be free—free to work at her profession and get more and more famous in it, till the whole criminal world shall tremble at the name of Joan Mar, detective' " (306). This narrative's calculated division between happiness and freedom, between marriage and professional growth, is as effective in putting Joan Mar in her place as was Dora Myrl's retirement from detection when she married Paul Beck. What women are allowed to do must be limited; unlike men they cannot have marriage *and* a career, happiness *and* freedom. Their restrictions are obvious; they must choose only one script. And the happiness of Brian and Lorine in the final lines of *Joan Mar, Detective* implies that Joan has chosen wrongly.

This romantic, sentimental conclusion emphasizes Leighton's decision to undermine her protagonist. For Joan Mar has also fallen in love with Brian Charlton and is overlooked by him in favor of the more helpless ingenue who needs the detective's assistance. The novel is structured to allow two possible readings of Mar's unmarried status. She may be perceived as the "other woman" who has improperly fallen in love with an engaged man and then is rightfully punished by being denied love; her choice of an unwomanly profession would bolster this negative assessment of her character. Or, the author may show her avoiding emotional entanglements by having her fall in love with an unavailable man; she then appears either self-centered or cold-hearted. But, whichever the case, this novel reinforces (as will Leighton's *Lucille Dare, Detective* later) how society demands a single script for women's lives but denies them the ability to effect this respectable end. Every woman's essential inability to control the outcome of the marriage plot is a submerged message of Leighton's as well as Danvers' double-voiced discourses.

Like Joan Mar, Loveday Brooke—also the creation of a woman writer—is unsought; unlike Mar, she is not identified as a seeker. As such, she is different from the other characters in this chapter. This omission of both courtship and marriage defines the misnamed Loveday; past thirty years old and still a spinster, she has both the maturity and experience to succeed as a detective, but these qualities limit her opportunities to be seen as a potential wife. The physical, psychological, financial, and social circumstances of Loveday Brooke are described within the first two pages of C. L. Pirkis's *The Experiences of Loveday Brooke, Lady Detective* as though to orient the reader not so much to the crime, adventure, or detection as to the detective herself. Older than any of her late-nineteenth-century counterparts, Loveday is well established in her profession: "For five or six years she had drudged away patiently in the lower walks of her profession; then chance, or to speak more precisely, an intricate criminal case, had introduced her to the notice of the experienced head of the flourishing detective agency in Lynch court. He quickly enough found out the stuff she was made of, and threw her in the way of better class work" (7). The change in her social status with the decision to enter this profession is rapidly clarified. Her familiarity with Oxford and Machiavelli's writings suggest that she is one of Woolf's daughters of educated men; she is without "marketable accomplishments," despite her clear need for them when "by a jerk of Fortune's wheel, Loveday had been thrown upon the world penniless and all but friendless" (7). Rather than work as the nursery governess whose disguise she adopts in one case, Loveday "forthwith defied convention, and had chosen for herself a career that had cut her off sharply from her former associates and her position in society" (7). But she continues to maintain the ladylike air and manners which probably had resulted from her youthful education.

Appearance, manners, age, and gender all provide Loveday the anonymity her profession requires. Personally, she is indistinctive enough to attract little notice:

> . . . [She] could best be described in a series of negatives.
> She was not tall, she was not short; she was not dark, she was not fair; she was neither handsome nor ugly. Her features were altogether non-descript; her one noticeable trait was the habit she had, when absorbed in thought, of dropping her eyelids over her eyes til only a line of eyeball showed, and she appeared to be looking out at the world through a slit, instead of through a window. (6)

Her plainness renders the detective virtually invisible as does her gender; her employer insists: "[women] are less likely to attract attention" (96). As an older spinster, Loveday also does not draw men's sexual attention. She is doubly unnoticed; as both a detective and a woman she can expect to be overlooked by a society which has clear but restricted ideas of her value. Clients share society's confusion; although they know her place as a woman, some are confused by her professional stance. Ebenezer Dyer, chief of the detective agency, responds to queries about her professionalism with a catalogue of her talents:

> "Too much of a lady, do you say?" he would say to anyone who chanced to call in question those [Loveday's] qualifications. "I don't care twopence half-penny whether she is or is not a lady. I only know she is the most sensible and practical woman I ever met. In the first place, she has the faculty—so rare among women—of carrying out orders to the very letter; in the second place, she has a clear, shrewd brain, unhampered by any hard and fast theories; thirdly, and most important item of all, she has so much common sense that it amounts to genius—positively to genius. . . ."
> (7–8)

Loveday's actions as a detective justify her employer's lavish praise. She successfully represents herself as an unemployed nursery governess, a casual lodger, and an amanuensis; her portrayal of the last role is good enough to deceive others in the servants' hall, enabling her to obtain important information without revealing her professional interest.

Brooke's talent for disguise is shared by most of her nineteenth-century counterparts, both female and male. However, for women detectives, disguise is a more complicated matter. Unlike the straightforward masquerades of male investigators, the women resemble Shakespeare's boy actors playing roles of women who disguise themselves as young men—double deceptions. The woman employed as a professional detective is already in disguise, for she is playing a part different from the particular one established for her by society. When she adopts another costume, a false mustache, or a different profession to accomplish her job, she unwittingly magnifies her cover and increases the distance from her recognized self.

Having transformed herself from the person she was raised to be, Brooke is adept at recognizing suspects' efforts to appear as other. She sees through others' attempts to disguise themselves: ". . . he wore a bowler instead of a journeymen's cap, and he no longer carried a basket of tools, but there was no possibility for any one, with so good an eye for an outline as Loveday possessed, not to recognize the carriage of the head and shoulders" (110). She recognizes the substitution of a short-haired girl for her purportedly ill brother, their "strong likeness" improbably confusing even the attending physician (94). She even employs a burglar, posing as a helpful newspaper reporter, to carry a message in invisible ink to the police who trap him and his misled gang. Loveday is also adept at assessing groups of strangers to determine their reliability: ". . . Loveday made her way through the throng in leisurely fashion, and not a man but what had keen scrutiny from her sharp eyes" (125-26). And although a police investigator takes an unattractive woman's criminality at face value, Loveday is not so easily fooled: " 'I have seen female criminals of all kinds handling children, and I have noticed that although they may occasionally—even this is rare—treat them with a certain rough sort of kindness, of tenderness they are utterly incapable. Now Sister Monica, I must admit, is not pleasant to look at; at the same time, there was something absolutely beautiful in the way in which she lifted the little cripple out of the cart, put his tiny thin hand round her neck, and carried him into the house' " (140). Despite the stereotyping evident in her statements, her perceptions and intuitions about suspicious characters are inevitably accurate.

Loveday is clearly alert and careful about her conclusions. Determined to assess situations herself, she wisely ignores the advice of the police to discover a crucial clue and an additional victim. The inspector who claims he does not try to bias her gets Loveday's approval: " '[I]t would be rather a waste of time to attempt such a thing,' thought Loveday" (283). The inept police are always suspicious of the wrong person, forced to call in Loveday to gather the critical evidence, and finally proved wrong by her success. On one occasion, having taken a policeman's advice, Loveday behaves somewhat carelessly and finds herself being watched as she is watching the house of a suspect. She recognizes this and later also determines by the sound of footsteps that she is again being followed. Rather than abandon the case, she turns the pursuers against themselves and successfully outwits them: "I . . . allowed the fellows to think they were making a fool of me" (143). On another case she feigns knowledge which the criminal unwittingly verifies, putting her life in danger but also solving the crime. In short, Loveday uses her years of experience to outmaneuver both the police and criminals.

Her profession seems to be her only interest; she is incapable of taking a vacation from it. Deeply engrossed in newspapers, memoranda, and books of reference at the seashore, Loveday confesses to a visitor: " 'No sooner . . . do I find myself in full view of that magnificent sea and sky picture than I shut my eyes to it, fasten them instead on the daily papers, and set my brains to work, *con amore*, on a ridiculous case that is never likely to come into my hands' " (232–33). The detective's distance from an ordinary woman's life is clearly implied in this behavior. With obligations to no one but herself and her profession, Brooke chooses how she will spend her time. She has neither marital, parental, nor familial obligations to hinder her movements or thoughts; she does no conventional women's work. Because of this exclusive commitment to her profession, Loveday is irritated when circumstances limit her chances of solving the crime. Assigned to a case ten days old, she agrees to go—"If I'm to go I'm to go, and there's no end of it. . . . I only say it would have been better, for the credit of the office, if you had declined such a hopeless affair"

(279). She is not sanguine about finding clues. She is not in the best temper either, having a case forced upon her under such disadvantageous conditions. Nevertheless, where others have failed, she succeeds.

Loveday's style of detection is similar to that used by Sherlock Holmes. She makes careful observation of visible objects and, without really giving valid reasons, eliminates all but one possible conclusion. She carefully examines rooms, furniture, fireplace ash, and grass in the lawn; she identifies what she sees and knows its value in solving the case. She does not mistakenly overlook important clues or improperly overvalue apparent but irrelevant items. Like Holmes, she seldom acknowledges that clues might have several interpretations. Operating ratiocinatively, she announces, usually in a summation after the conclusion of the case, both her observations and what she has decided because of them. Because the case is already solved, the reader is not inclined to challenge her deductions any more than Watson would seriously disagree with Holmes. Unbiased by police suspicions, she draws different conclusions than the police do from the evidence they have assembled; she ignores their mistakes and fastens on their omissions. Frequently she challenges the police with questions whose point they cannot recognize. Throughout her detection, Loveday displays an imaginative intelligence rooted in common sense.

This extensive list of deductive talents, solved crimes, and similarities to the master detective Holmes would seem to imply that, although a woman and therefore unusual in the detective profession, Loveday Brooke is positively and approvingly presented, that a woman detective's competence is recognized. Unfortunately, this is not so. After clearly demonstrating Loveday's ability, Pirkis sabotages the effect of this positive portrayal by subordinating each of Loveday's successes against criminals to male associates. The structural and formulaic pattern of the genre is sacrificed to a gender-linked undermining of the protagonist. In seven cases described, Loveday concludes her own investigation only in the three noncriminal cases which result in marriage plans; in the others she is shown incapable of handling the criminals. The cases and their outcomes are clearly grouped by sexual stereotyping: as marriage is the appropriate occupation for a woman, Loveday can properly assist in forwarding these marriage plots. Her role is not central: although unmarried, she is not the object of a proposal; as a woman, she cannot control the process. Only as a detective can she participate by removing obstacles the wicked hope would impede these socially acceptable marriages. Loveday's activity is reversed when the crimes and cases involve men's traditional territory—murder, violence, and theft. Even though as detective she still solves the cases, as a woman Brooke is retired to a safer position as adjunct to the men or even completely removed from the scene. Trapped in the study at Troyte's Hill by a homicidal madman, Loveday just barely manages to divert him from killing her, though her indiscreet questions have brought him to this point, until she can be rescued by "three pairs of strong arms"—Police Inspector Griffiths and his men (91). When restricted in her movements by spies whom she is attempting to deceive, Loveday must sit quietly during the conclusion of another case while the police, the homeowner, and his two sons apprehend the criminals. Although she has solved the puzzle and instructed the police, Loveday is quite effectively kept from the final scene.

Although the apparent protagonist of the stories and clearly the detector of the criminals, Loveday Brooke is not given the opportunity to carry her cases through to the final capture; this is left to the men, presumably stronger and more capable than the Lady Detective. In choosing to subvert the genre, Pirkis nonetheless maintains a guarded stance toward the usual ramifications of the woman script. Not going so far as to establish a romance or marriage for her protagonist, she only minimally displaces Loveday from the detection script.

Clearly, each of these five women detectives has been created to meet her author's need for satisfying popular demand and mass imagination while reinforcing a conservative ideology. In externals the five form a varied group, yet essentially they are the same. Of different ages, marital status, and levels of social background, they are all more than minimally educated, compelled to work by economic necessity, and reliably ladylike in their behavior. Yet, each character's successful functioning as a woman and a detective is challenged. She is faulted as a detective by failure or inadequacy in capturing criminals or by abandoning her independence for marital harmony; or, she is minimized as a woman who cannot love or define her own identity. Most outstanding in all the novels is a determined insistence on the characters' ladylike behavior and appearance. Recent cultural anthropological studies have commented on the awkward bind of middle-class Victorian and Edwardian women. Their "new" activities were, by definition, unladylike; yet they persevered in trying to hold onto their only security—a good reputation— while grasping for new opportunities. They constantly demanded two difficult sets of standards from themselves. Some succeeded, at great personal and emotional cost; others inevitably fell between the known and the new, losing both in the struggle to retain both. The lady detective of popular fiction exemplifies this paradox; she searches dead bodies in an attractive white-collared, blue gown. And she usually solves her cases. Nevertheless, her successes are presented as subordinate to her traditional female roles and responsibilities. The underlying message of the novels insists that women stand to lose by wanting both opportunity and respect. They are put in their place, which is secondary. Even the first women writers creating lady detectives—Catherine Louisa Pirkis and Marie Connor Leighton—do not succeed in altering the pattern. Dishonestly, the authors entice readers with prospects of women's active participation in adventure, intellectual activity, and public roles only to validate the oppressive tradition (real or desired) when it is too late for readers to withdraw safely. The unsuspecting woman reader, unaware that she must adopt Judith Fetterly's strategy to become a resisting reader, finds herself in the protagonist's position—undercut at the end. Thus, the detectives and the readers of the books in which they appear are continually reminded not to go too far, not to ask for too much.

Notes

1. Although *The Mystery of the Hansom Cab* was first published in 1886 in Australia, the 1887 publication in England led to its real fame (Haycraft, *Murder* 63).

2. Still, it is important to remember the very real fear of death in childbirth experienced by Victorian women. Cynthia Huff cites 1870 statistics: "3,875 women in England and Wales died of either childbirth or puerperal fever" (67).

3. DuBois et al. have reaffirmed feminist conclusions that both the activity of women in circumstances of recognized oppression and the effect of oppression on a conscious human being fully capable of activity need to be taken simultaneously into account (40). Neither the detective script with its activity and suggestion of agency nor the woman script

with its recognized power of oppression can be slighted in criticism inasmuch as they coexist within the novels.

4. These conclusions are based only on the first volume.

5. Like Mrs. Gladden and Mrs. Paschal, Rose Courtenay Spicer does not fit exactly the pattern defined in the introduction; however, the number of women detectives at the turn-of-the-century is small and although she is not the protagonist, she plays a major, professional role in the novels.

4

The Lady Detective's Yankee Cousin: 1906–15

American detective fiction at the beginning of the twentieth century was influenced by several significant factors. Naturally, the British imports had a powerful impact; Sherlock Holmes and the deductive methods which he practices fascinated the United States reading public. Julian Symons insists on the primacy of the short story in those years before the golden age with its heroes divided between supermen reminiscent of Holmes and inconspicuous, ordinary men who solve cases by common sense. These latter often look and sound like the police despite owning their own agencies, a "fashion of the times" in fiction (76). However, Americans also claimed the mother (or grandmother, as some insisted) of mystery fiction as their own; Anna Katharine Green's *The Leavenworth Case* (1878), which preceded Conan Doyle's first contribution to the genre, was enormously popular, staying in print almost continuously until 1937 (Hayne 153). Unlike the distinctively American stories of Melville Davisson Post, Green's novels were also widely read in England. Finally, the dime novel, although well past its prime in production and popularity (also quality, some critics would argue), provided an example of action and adventure to contrast with Conan Doyle's and Green's styles. The most significant innovation of this period may be Green's creation of two female detectives—the amateur Amelia Butterworth in 1897 and the professional Violet Strange in 1915. Butterworth is by far the more imaginative creation, serving her male counterpart without minimizing herself. Still, as a wealthy, fiftyish spinster, she receives far more respect in fiction than she would in reality. Neither of Green's detecting women exhibits the ridiculous "had-I-but- known" tendencies of Mary Roberts Rinehart's young amateur heroines.

General public opinion about women in the U.S. underwent three major shifts from 1870 to the 1920s: it favored virtuous womanhood until the end of the nineteenth century, educated motherhood at the turn of the century, and wife-companionhood beginning in the 1920s (Rothman 5–6). Around the turn of the century, housekeeping and childrearing became full-time vocations. Almost every technological innovation between 1870 and 1900 significantly altered the daily routine of middle-class women. These included plumbing, sewerage, hot and cold running water which also permitted washing machines, and electricity (Rothman 14). However, the technological advances which freed women from menial home tasks did not free them from the responsibility for the home. In many ways, the shift to a servantless household (one of eight households in 1870 had at least one servant whereas the ratio dropped to one in fifteen by 1900) left middle-class women more rather than less occupied (Rothman 17). Meanwhile, the increasing importance attributed to marriage and maternity left growing numbers of women out of the mainstream. Between 1860 and 1890, 10 percent of American women surviving to the age of forty-five were unmarried, the highest figure between colonial times and the 1960s (Smith, "Limitation" 223). This may be due to death of eligible men in the Civil War and, especially, the westward expansion. Many of these single women were responsible for their own support.

Statistics on women's employment for the period from 1870 to 1910 are questionable because until 1910 enumerators were not told to ask women their occupations but were allowed to assume that women at home were unemployed (Rothman 87). Therefore, only the minimum employment figures for 200 occupations are available. In 1870, 1.8 million women were employed with 14.8 percent as breadwinners; 12.9 percent of the total were married. In 1880, 2.6 million women were employed; in 1890, 4 million; and in 1900, 5.3 million with 18.3 percent as breadwinners (Kennedy 70). By the late nineteenth century, there was nearly universal agreement that the expanding participation of women in the labor force was an unfortunate necessity that should not be allowed to interfere with domestic responsibilities and that the workplace should not hinder the capacity of working women to return to domestic work. Therefore, women were hired at the poorest levels to discourage their continuing employment or to match its supposedly temporary nature (Kessler-Harris 142). Nonetheless, by the 1890s the office had become women's workplace and by 1900 women were 75 percent of all stenographers and typists, 16 percent of clerks, and 90 percent of telephone operators (Kennedy 107). By 1900 they also held 29 percent of the clerking jobs in the U.S. Treasury Department. These employees were overwhelmingly middle-class, as many as 70 percent were single, and the majority had professional or white-collar fathers (Aron 836–37). As might be expected, these women were regularly exposed to charges of incompetence and rumors of sexual promiscuity.

Despite negative messages from public and private quarters, women increasingly sought educational as well as employment opportunities. The 1890 census revealed that 42 percent of fifteen-to-nineteen-year-old white, native-born women were in school (Aron 838). By 1900, 2,500 women had B.A. degrees; 250,000 were teachers; and 4,500 were physicians, surgeons, and other medical workers (Flexner 179). At the turn of the century a new educational and professional field opened for women: home economics. College training for housekeeping looked like an opportunity for women to have education with the approbation of society; in fact it turned out to limit them more severely than the lack of a college education might have done. Fueling the persistent criticism of antieducationists were the findings that college-educated women did not marry as young or as often as other women. Twenty-five percent never married and most who did had fewer children than the average because of later marriages (Degler 314).

Between 1895 and 1915, almost every group in the new middle class had grown toward self-consciousness; for women this awareness involved social reform. Women's clubs were organized into the General Federation of Women's Clubs in 1889, which had over a million members by the early twentieth century (Chafe, *Women and Equality* 28). Even women's suffrage movements shifted their emphasis at the turn of the century from an assault on the family and women's proper place to seeing suffrage as a way of bringing women's natural purity

and spirituality to government (Chafe, *Women and Equality* 29). Ironically, the antifeminists were also active in promoting the importance
of women's spiritual purity.

The dominant influences of both society and the literary genre
are clearly reflected in six detective novels published in America
between 1906 and 1915.[1] Fictionally, Madelyn Mack, Frances Baird,
and Violet Strange owe their style of detection and their professional
development to the model of Sherlock Holmes. Baddie Pretlow and
Balmy Rymal more obviously have their counterparts in the exploits
of Nick Carter or Old Sleuth. But marriage and social respectability,
not detection, are their looming concerns. Their views of social acceptance are strongly conditioned by class; in fact, in no other period
is it such an issue. Clearly a member of the moneyed class, Violet
Strange believes that even though her career and earnings serve justice, her activities are socially unacceptable. The reverse is true of
Baddie Pretlow and Balmy Rymal (and Frances Baird, to a lesser
extent); they are determined to prove themselves responsible members of society and become reinstated as members of the middle class
through the socially redeeming work of detection. For all of them,
the moral worthiness or debasement which accrue to their short careers is related to their hopes for marriage. Feeling socially although
not personally disgraced, Violet Strange (like Kate Goelet) worries
that her behavior might make her unacceptable to her lover. Rymal
and Pretlow explicitly believe the redemptive qualities of their work
will raise them to middle class, making them socially acceptable marriage partners.

M. M. Bakhtin insists that plot cannot serve as the organizing
force of adventure novels. Instead, they are usually shaped around a
"flickering, fading idea of the hero under test" (390). While Bakhtin
sees one example in the hero's "faithfulness to his calling," which
would seem to be detection in these novels, these characters demonstrate their true testing grounds in playing out the marriage plot
(389). More than surviving the usual varieties of conflict and confrontation in romance novels, these detectives meet the demands to
prove their respectability through detection and thus justify their worthiness for marriage. When they have successfully passed the test,
their prize is marriage. Ironically, while the narrators and the protagonists may see the women as having validated themselves through
work, the men for whom they make these efforts assume without

question that the women's detecting careers will end upon marriage. And so they should, for the point of their becoming detectives was never to stay detectives. Unlike romance novels which persistently subordinate independent women to the demands of the genre, these novels sacrifice both independent women and the genre to reinforce traditional sex roles. Less important as detective novels, these works function as cautionary tales for readers about the importance of middle-class respectability and its rewards. Catherine Belsey comments on the correlation among text, ideology, and readers: "The argument is not only that literature represents the myths and imaginary versions of real social relationships which constitute ideology, but also . . . 'interpellates' the reader, addresses itself to him or her directly, offering the reader as the position from which the text is most 'obviously' intelligible, the position of the *subject in (and of) ideology"* (45). In particular, the increasing number of working women, especially the growing pool of single women, among the reading public were being warned how easily the wrong kind of employment—whatever their motives for choosing it—could damage their entire future. As didactic examples, these detective novels reinforced other social pressures which sought to limit women's alternatives.

Like Rymal, Strange, Pretlow, and their textually encoded readers, Reginald W. Kaufman's Francis Baird fantasizes a courtship and marriage plot for herself; unlike them she is unsuccessful in her first appearance. By the second novel, she has apparently abandoned all romance. Any reader might be forgiven for not recognizing this turn-of-the-century American detective because of the changes which Kaufman makes between her 1906 and 1910 appearances. In *Miss Frances Baird, Detective: A Passage from Her Memoirs,* the detective herself is the first-person narrator and the focus of the novel is on her investigation of the Deneen diamond theft and related murders. In the second, *My Heart and Stephanie: A Novel,* the first-person narrator is a male newspaper reporter who assists Baird in a spy case which eventually turns into a romance with the reporter as the male lead and one of the characters in the spy case as the female heroine; both detection and Baird fade into the background quickly. More important, in the novel where she figures as the main character, the structural hero, the narrator, and the protagonist, Frances Baird is shown by every measure imaginable to be a very poor detective. In 1906 Kaufman thoroughly and emphatically develops a new type of

female sleuth; prior to this novel, characters were competent investigators either abandoned to the marriage plot or the rescuing arms
of men, or cited as unwomanly. Although Baird is eventually the agent
through which the crime is solved and the criminals caught, this
success is not the pivotal moment of the text. Instead it is sandwiched
between her earlier failures as an investigator, which are detailed at
length, and the conclusive evidence of her failure in the marriage
plot.

Although the preface identifies seven cases by name and refers
to a dozen others which she has solved, the "memoirs" open with
her being castigated for her recent failures by the chief of the Watkins
Private Detective Agency. Perhaps this reprimand is not surprising;
she attributes her previous successes to good fortune rather than to
her talent. Like the subjects of Matina Horner's research, she avoids
being the agent of her success (159). Unaware of her self-sabotage,
Baird refuses to recognize the skills and insights responsible for her
earlier achievements. Crediting luck leaves her no resources or fund
of knowledge on which to draw when she encounters problems. Kaufman goes beyond creating a modest, womanly hero to presenting a
self-deprecating young woman who attempts to assert herself by vacillating between agonies of self-reproach and bouts of arrogance.
Reinforcing her flaws, the chief is severe in his criticism: " 'You
started off so well . . . that I had begun to have high hopes of you. . . .
this last year you have more than undone all that you did at first. You
let Donald Dugan get away with a three days' start of us and it was
no fault of yours that he was ever nabbed at all. You were all wrong
in the Durham robbery. You botched the Van Hamburgh jewel case.
You were really worse than useless in the matter of old Eben Stoner's
divorce. And—Well, I don't suppose I'll have to go over the whole list,
but it seems to me that you've about finished off matters with this
affair of Bella Bringhurst' " (3–4). Even as he acknowledges her abilities—fearlessness, poise, youth, attractiveness—he questions her capacity to function in any but the least important cases. Knowing that
a detective ought to behave bravely, quickly, and intelligently, she
sets off to regain her reputation and assure her professional existence:
"[D]uty may not amount to much in this world but business certainly
does, and I've found it a pretty good substitute for the rarer article"
(41). She also recognizes her economic need; two months behind in

her rent and overdrawn on her current salary, Frances needs this job for financial as well as psychological survival.

No evidence points to how this twenty-five-year-old woman came to adopt a profession for which she seems to have mixed talent. Nothing in her background, which included finishing school and several years abroad, nor her good looks, wit, and poise would have prepared her for this choice. Despite her experience in previous cases, she times herself to see how long she can stay in the room with a corpse and when she runs out after seven minutes attributes it to natural impulses. "Nobody, I protest, could have put up with it—not even a man—and so at last I slunk out and into Bromley Deneen's room and crouched down by the far wall" (59). Later, she decides that she is not cut out for strenuous and emotional murder cases. The only clue to her choice of a profession comes in a truncated recollection: "[J]ust because you were once a little fool, nothing ahead but—detective work" (27). Undeveloped is the inference that inappropriate behavior has effectively removed such alternatives as the conventional woman's script with courtship and marriage or even opportunities for social respectability. Passing as a guest at the wealthy Deneens' house party, Frances contrasts her appearance and background with those of other guests; her exclusion from their company except because of duty, she concludes, is "a pity" (27). Kaufman's refusal to name Baird's foolish behavior describes how large the range of women's unacceptable actions can be; it could as easily be a venial error as a mortal one which has barred her from full-fledged social respectability.

Frances Baird's own reservations join forces with her errors and problems, her chief's criticism, and the novel's romantic conclusion to limit any positive signs a reader might have about her competence. Her mistakes are legion. She allows the original diamond necklace and the substituted paste version to be stolen while she is in the room watching the thief; later when the corpse is discovered, she tries to control her shivering by sitting down on the bed—which destroys clues. She allows herself to be won over by women's intuition and love to dismiss the chief suspect but bungles her testimony at the inquest so that he is held for the crime. Her initial solution is to cry: "After all, I was a woman before I was a detective! Facts are convincing enough when they stand alone, but they are nothing when they are confronted by a feminine conviction to the contrary" (133). Separately confronting two suspects, Baird is routed by the one's innocence and the other's cynicism. Turning to another angle of investigation, she lets her guard down and on two separate occasions is seen by the man she is tailing. Even the briefest recital of her slip-ups leads the reader to agree with the criticism leveled by her boss: "[W]ith logical precision, he checked off upon his fingers each and every one of the mistakes which I had made in my conduct throughout the case and through which I had brought such discredit upon his firm. . . . 'I fancy the humourists will not need a fresh subject for the next couple of months' " (85–86). Again Baird cries, and "even as I spoke, I felt my weakness and was conscious of my failure" (87).

Finally, it is the element of romance which completes the undermining of the detective—for herself, for other characters in the novel, and for the reader. She recognizes and acknowledges the problem: "To the ideal detective, the scientific attitude of mind is indispensible. He—or she—must work, not in defense of a theory, but for the determination of the truth. . . . [But] in the Deneen case I stood, for obvious reasons, otherwise committed" (208). This romantic impulse almost keeps Frances Baird from solving the case at all. When she finally does so, no deduction or rationale is given for her conclusions; they are merely stated and attributed to her gender's intuitive knowledge of other women. When her elaborate theories come undone, the detective is saved by a "lucid interval," and then the "white light of inspiration" (220, 239). Like an epiphany, the solution appears. Frances Baird's success in clearing a man she's come to love is only briefly acknowledged; in the end, she does not win his love. Like Marie Connor Leighton's romantic detectives, she falls in love with the suspect, vacillates among love, duty, and revenge, and loses the man who had long since chosen another woman. Like both Mar and Dare, she loves a man she cannot hope to have; the narrative undermines her by firmly upholding social conventions. The novel's conclusion announces wedding plans which do not include her and notes poignantly that Baird is left only with a small ring which had belonged to the mother of the freed suspect.

The language of the final paragraph insists again on the primacy of the romance novel over the detective story: ". . . I, for my part, have told enough of this event in my adventurous history to explain why Lawrence Fredericks was married to Evelyn Bladesdell . . . and why I always—somewhere—carry, set with a ruby and two diamonds, a certain pretty but old-fashioned ring" (269). The narrative subordinates the investigation to the victory and defeat in the marriage plot, insisting that the telling of the former is less important in itself than as a function of illuminating the latter. Thus not only is the detective herself undermined as both sleuth and woman, but the genre itself is relegated to secondary status.

The powerful contrast between Kaufman's two novels arises from the mode of narration. In the 1906 novel, first-person narration by the female reveals her weaknesses, charts her emotions, and details her limitations; in that respect it is a psychological novel. The 1910 work uses the male protagonist as narrator in the way an epic might, to relate adventure and moments of glory; there is little failure here to prod the narrator to psychological investigation.

In *My Heart and Stephanie*, the real detective hero, first-person narrator and reporter Sam Burton, is also in love with one of the suspects in a spy case. He manages to solve the case, save the woman, and win at romance simultaneously. Baird is a secondary figure whose detecting talents are legendary but largely undemonstrated. Nonetheless, as the narrator notes, she still has her limitations and as before they are set by her gender: "There are times when I sincerely admire the manner in which Frances Baird, through all her strange career, has preserved those traits which are essentially feminine. . . . The average male detective would at least have given me some word of apology. . . . But the woman detective remained a woman" (88). Later Burton attributes her intense interest in the case to a woman's hatred for the ambassador who had tricked and deceived her during the case, as though her motivations could only be understood if personal rather than professional. In the end, the novel is really about Sam Burton falling in love with Stephanie and how the mystery must be solved to aid their love. More a spy story than a detective novel, it is transformed into a romance by the conclusion. Sam Burton is the protagonist while Frances Baird is barely a secondary character. In the concluding pages, she arrives at the scene only after Burton and Stephanie have shot their way to safety. In both the spy plot and the romance, she is clearly superfluous. Where she has failed in both detection and marriage plots, the male amateur succeeds at both. *My Heart and Stephanie* lacks conviction as a demonstration of Baird's redemption from her earlier failures. Although present, she occupies a secondary position as both character and detective; Frances Baird is so effectively relegated to minor status that she might as well have stayed home.

To a great extent, staying at home is exactly what Violet Strange does. Unaware of being trapped by her socioeconomic status, Anna Katherine Green's protagonist is the most unlikely of the six American detectives of this period. She hints throughout at a special reason for undertaking this unsavory activity but does not reveal her praiseworthy motives until the final chapter. She keeps her activities secret from family and friends, leading one potential client to exclaim, " 'That yon silly little chit, whose father I know, whose fortune I know, who is seen everywhere, and who is called one of the season's belles is an agent of yours; a—a—' " (1). The word he cannot pronounce is "detective," and despite his reservations, Violet Strange does solve five cases of murder, two of lost property, one of theft, and one of a missing person in *The Golden Slipper and Other Problems for Violet Strange.*

Although claiming to take only cases which interest her while avoiding the sordid ones altogether, she can be intrigued, coaxed, or challenged into undertaking any which is proposed by her employer. When she protests his choices, reminding him of their agreement that she would join him in such "matter where a woman's tact and knowledge of the social world might tell without offense to herself or others" (68), his flattering response eventually carries weight: " 'You are by nature, as well as by breeding, very far removed from everything of the kind [low-down crime]. But you will allow me to suggest that no crime is low-down which makes imperative demand upon the intellect and intuitive sense of its investigator. Only the most delicate touch can feel and hold the thread I've just spoken of, and *you* have the most delicate touch I know' " (68). Violet Strange hopes to maintain a self-image which matches her public facade of innocence and unworldliness; by her own admission, however, she also gains satisfaction from the work. Like Dorcas Dene, she seeks and receives public male approval for choices she has already made. Although she readily admits that her motive for becoming a detective is mercenary, she will not accept cases merely for money; her employer is relieved by this inasmuch as so simple and sordid a motive does not accord with his image of the lady detective. In fact, he even describes as idiosyncratic what he alleges is her "theoretical dislike" of the work (3). Her transparent hesitation reaffirms Violet's demeanor as a modest young woman, reassuring her and her employer that she knows the rules which govern women's behavior in society. A similar hesitancy in responding to a later marriage proposal confirms Strange's adherence to the code despite her immodest investigation of low-down crimes.

Because Violet is frequently described throughout the volume, no reader could fail to be aware of the incongruity between her appearance and her activity. As a detective, Violet Strange is always in disguise. Not only is her public behavior different from her professional behavior, but she is also sheltered by her usual appearance as one of society's debutantes. She chides a client who misreads her talents: " 'You regard me as unfit for practical work, and so credit me with occult powers. But that is where you made a mistake. . . . I'm nothing if not practical' " (148).

When Violet falls in love with a stranger she sees across a room in her fourth case, she would rather keep him in the realm of fantasy; instead he becomes a client. She refuses to become emotionally involved with the gambler Roger Upjohn, but helps him prove his father's innocence in the death of Roger's wicked wife. Nonetheless, the reader knows that romance will eventually triumph.

Detection becomes a metaphor for courtship as Roger's and Violet's lives intersect in a third of the cases. In the first she solves the mystery of his marriage but rejects the cautionary message which it offers about the institution. In the last, he solves the question of her marriage, also rejecting the knowledge gained by his previous experience. Green establishes a testing ground for their permanent union in setting up these three temporary alliances.

In the final story, romance joins the revelation of Violet's motive for becoming a detective to vindicate her decision and her behavior. All she has done was to aid a wrongly disinherited sister to establish her musical career. Weighed down with guilt at having kept such a secret from her stern father, Violet Strange confesses it to another man—the one she will marry. Although both her siblings, her employer, their clients, victims and suspects, and the police know of her activities, she sees the secret, her "natural sense of guilt," and her reluctant confession only in relation to these two men, one who has authority over her life now and the other who will soon accept that role (56). Upjohn assumes the power of a father substitute as confessor and spouse.

Titling the story "Violet's Own," Green conflates the detection and marriage plots; Violet's search for her sister is only the ostensible case. But it is embedded in an explanatory letter to Upjohn just before their marriage. This is her criminal's confession, description of extenuating circumstances, and plea for mercy. The framework for the letter, a second case of Violet's own, is the successful conclusion of her marriage investigation. Despite the purity and goodness of her motives, Strange fears that Upjohn will find her too socially debased to esteem her; however, he responds by reminding her of his own tarnished reputation. In so doing, he does not challenge her assertion that detective work is unacceptable for a lady, but only assures her that he accepts her nonetheless. Still insisting on her inferior position, Violet relays her father's warning that she has begun to lose her social position. This announcement is accompanied by a smile as though the two were engaged in a game of one-downmanship. But the author's message is a sobering one: women, it seems, must always contrive to be their husbands' inferiors. In this final episode, Violet Strange makes clear that her reasons vindicate her actions, her plan to leave the work as soon as she sees her sister established has been realized, and her romance has validated her womanly inhibitions and reluctance. She has dabbled, however successfully, in detection and is now free to return to the social, marital, and familial life for which she was born. The profession for which she seemed so suited has merely been a guilty episode in an otherwise blameless life.[2]

The triumph of the marriage plot introduced by Anna Katharine Green for Violet Strange is taken to extremes by Arthur Stringer in two detective novels which owe more to the legacy of the American dimes than the influence of Sherlock Holmes. Despite detective Balmy Rymal's extremely active career for the Jewelers' Protective Alliance, most of *The Diamond Thieves* is dominated by Winfred "Winkie" Ealand. From the prefatory letter to "my Winkie" to her final capitulation, first-person narrator Rymal cannot free herself or the novel from the implications of love and romance, her unworthiness of this special man, or the fear that her profession will repulse him. Her conviction that she is morally inferior is shared by the narrator and Winkie; later, she is absolved of that charge to be considered only naturally inferior, as a woman.

Her attribution of hoped-for success to luck rather than skill and her tendency to self-recrimination challenge the reader's confidence in any version of the woman detective's superiority. That Balmy Rymal can be frightened or impulsive does not strongly discredit her; but, she is reckless because she has nothing to live for in the absence of Winkie and a "softer byway in life to tread," which diminishes and undercuts her (36). Her failures—being deceived by a pair of con artists, allowing a criminal to evade her, being tied up by another—are errors which she can overcome; her professional abilities are sufficient to correct these mistakes and to keep her functioning successfully. However, she continues to define herself as a woman unworthy of her lover.

When Winkie signals his willingness to trust Balmy (having had proof of her lawful behavior) and comes to her rescue in the final case, he is not the all-powerful knight she had persisted in imagining. She has to save both of them. Unaware of the danger in which he and Rymal stand, Winkie bluffs, lies unconvincingly to a criminal, and reacts with horror to scenes in which she must continue to function; again he has misjudged her motives and her actions. Her generous understanding revolts: "I didn't feel a shred of pity for him. I even resented his soft and sheltered channels of life which had always led him away from ugliness. . . . [I]t would do Winfred Ealand good . . . it would wake him up to some of the things I'd had to wade through" (412–13). Still, when he masterfully announces that he is taking her away from both the horrors and the rewards of her profession, Balmy Rymal acquiesces to his protective demand. The reader has been prepared for this conclusion by her repeated announcements of her desire to leave the force as soon as she accumulated enough money to live well and learn enough to make her worthy of Winkie. Then, at least, one can believe that she would join him as an equal on her own terms; this way, she is merely a beggar maid raised from the gutter by a wise and generous benefactor.

The Pygmalion motif is repeated in Stringer's second novel, *The House of Intrigue*, as three strands to the narrative of Barbara "Baddie" Pretlow are told by the woman detective herself. The reader is introduced to her life before she was a private eye, briefly acquainted with her detecting talents which do not come into use here, and follows her when she resigns from the Locke Agency after two years employment, believing that the agency's head is making a pass at her. Actually, she's being set up. In Baddie's name is her past.

Approached by a pair of elderly crooks to participate in a con scheme after her hasty resignation, Baddie Pretlow agrees because she is sure she can outwit them. In fact, having been one herself she is adept at spotting criminals. Evading her elderly employers; caught up in a house-to-house chase and near escape, toting a bag full of stolen jewelry; encountering two apparent ghosts, several likely killers, and Wendy Washburn, Pretlow feels surfeited by crime, evil, and chicanery. Washburn turns out to have had a hand in this disillusionment.

What Pretlow and the reader discover simultaneously is that Wendy Washburn, or "Hero Man" as Pretlow thinks of him most of the time, has been manipulating her life since their first meeting four or five years earlier. His reason—love; his intentions—honorable; his purpose—marriage. This romance comes as a shock less to the reader than to Pretlow who has been thinking of him as a criminal like herself and a possible partner on whom she can depend, sharing her burden of theft and guilt. However, in proper fairy-tale style, he is actually a wealthy man who has been playing Pygmalion because he recognizes her potential: " 'What I mean is that you've never lived up to your potentialities. You've never given yourself a chance. You've never really risen to your opportunities. You've wasted your time on the small caliber things of life. Instead of conquering, you've merely fretted. Instead of using that restless brain and body Heaven gave you, for one big end, you've let them blow like a leaf in the winds of chance! . . . I mean that you're too clever a woman, yes and too fine a woman, to be doing the things you have been doing' " (282). So, finally, in this non-detection crime and mystery story, the "Hero Man" saves the heroine by providing her with an overdose of excitement to demonstrate how unhappy it could make her compared to doing nothing in his company. Apparently the heroine agrees as she sobs her surrender and acknowledges in the final paragraph that she has found her "Hero Man." Having given up two lives of crime, one life of detecting, and any hope of controlling her own life, Baddie capitulates to his greater insistence on who she is and what she wants. But, she never realizes that his decision reflects what will be best for him, not necessarily for her.

The presence of an acknowledged hero-man means that the formulaic hero of the detection plot must be transformed into the heroine of the marriage plot, which already has its proper male hero.

Displaced by the fictional structure and the social reality in which gender, age, experience, wealth, and moral rectitude give Washburn (like Ealand) power and position, Pretlow is trapped into marriage. Washburn's behavior parallels her employer's apparent sexual harassment; both use her disadvantaged position as criminal and woman to benefit their status. Her employer hopes to catch a criminal; Washburn hopes to catch a wife. Baddie would be merely their tool if she had not absorbed society's values as her own; she can repulse the overt harassment but is blind to similar implications in a marriage proposal.

Standing apart from these examples is Madelyn Mack; her cases follow a more cerebral, less emotional route like those of Conan Doyle's Sherlock Holmes. No other woman detective is so clearly modeled on her masculine ancestor as Hugh C. Weir's protagonist. The comparison seems to take little account of their different genders. Madelyn Mack resorts to cola berries as a stimulant, relies on music to assist her thinking processes, and becomes quickly bored when no new or interesting case is available. Like Holmes, she pays careful attention to tobacco ash (and "nicotine addicts") and claims to deduce logically and ratiocinatively as she reconstructs her methods and insights at the conclusion of each case in *Miss Madelyn Mack, Detective*. In addition, Mack has her own Watson narrating these five cases; reporter Nora Noraker is Mack's acknowledged "lieutenant" (70) with a "card-index brain for newspaper history" (13). Like Watson, she suffers from hero-worship.

In their first encounter, Noraker had expected to find a stereotypically masculine-looking detective but discovered instead "a young woman of maybe twenty-five, with red and white cheeks, crowned by a softly waved mass of dull gold hair, and a pair of vivacious, grey-blue eyes that at once made one forget every other detail of her appearance" (4). Occasionally, Noraker describes her gowns and smooth golden hair; only once does she get carried away with metaphor. She sees Madelyn in her own sitting room "lying flat on her back on a tawny leopard skin in an attitude strongly suggestive of Cleopatra reposing on the trophies of her royal huntsmen" (260). With a sort of fame altogether different from the Egyptian queen's, Mack's success in her profession has been well established by the time of Nora's first interview; Madelyn Mack is a household word, "the woman who had made so conspicuous a success in a man's

profession" (4). However, her start as a detective had been less auspicious. Dropping out of college to earn her own living, she applied
at a department store hit by a rash of shop-lifting cases. When refused
employment, she took the case freelance and solved it. The reward
from a second success gave her the capital to open her own office.

Her methodology, as she defines it, is quite simple: hard work
and self-confidence. Noraker finds her aggressively sure of her conclusions. Mack claims to treat cases as exercises in mathematics,
substituting human motivations for figures; her adoption of this masculinist style reinforces the comparison with male detectives and distinguishes her from her female counterparts. Madelyn rejects the
Holmes version of uncommon sense in favor of common business
sense and imagination. She boasts that "a woman . . . always has a
more acute imagination than a man!" (5); but except for Nora she
still employs an all-male staff, which raises questions about her preference for imagination. When working on a case, she ignores questions about her investigation, methodology, or suspicions; but, like
Holmes, she often asks questions which do not make sense to her
sources. Frequently, she shuts Nora out of the room where she's
checking for clues or contemplating the suspects; as Nora is the narrator, this leaves the reader and other characters ignorant of her
deductions. Only when she has solved the crime does Mack startle
and amaze all with her results. But she is easily bored and usually
emotionally flat after a case; so it is easy to understand that she would
find it "a relief to cross wits with one who has really raised murder
to a fine art!" (193). She fits the formulaic pattern exactly—except
for her gender.

It follows then that despite her reputation, the police are seldom
complimentary about Mack. A detective is amazed to find himself
apologizing to a "petticoat detective" (93); another sarcastically describes her as "Miss Sherlock Holmes at work!" (181); a third refers
to her "pink tea wisdom" (83). Only one gives her credit openly; but
even he hedges the compliment: "I was wondering how long you
would wait for that question. It is when we drift away from the ear-
marks of the professional criminal, where the card-index methods of
headquarters are of no avail, that the lack of imagination in the police
department is evident" (323). The same lieutenant later credits her
solution of a crime to her being a woman, a repeated claim which
Nora had earlier disputed: "It was nothing less than genius in the

final analysis" (298). This rejoinder unfortunately suggests that genius, like investigative ability, is not a female characteristic. Like Nora Noraker, clients and suspects are sometimes surprised to find Madelyn both attractive and competent, using masculine logic and feminine psychology to solve cases.

All five of Mack's cases involve murder; four are meshed with romance as the solution of the crime also reunites young lovers. In the final case, "The Purple Thumb," a racist tale of murder and detection, the beneficiary of Mack's investigation is her own Watson's romance. The detective, like Holmes, is virtually immune to the attractions of the opposite sex.

Seen through the eyes of a female narrator, Madelyn Mack really is "Miss Sherlock Holmes." As an American she may not shoot the queen's initials into the wall; but she is whimsical enough to name her dog Peter the Great. Financially successful, she separates her "221B Baker Street" into town office and country home but she still furnishes the latter with fairly gruesome souvenirs of her profession. Easily bored, she travels widely, disappearing for long periods although unlike Holmes she is never presumed dead at the Reichenbach Fall. Mack's investigations begin with apparently irrelevant questions which confuse suspects, police, and even her faithful Watson. No clue is ever trivial, she insists; failure comes only when thoroughness is abandoned.

Mack is so totally another Holmes that it is often difficult for a reader to remember her gender except for Noraker's occasional urging "you are a woman, even if you are making your living at a man's profession! What you need is a good cry!" (141). Still, like Nora's remark about genius, this comment unconsciously reifies sex-role stereotyping. The woman's touch claimed for her hair, dress, and house decor is more stated than demonstrated; her femaleness is not strongly emphasized.

One way Weir seems to avoid undercutting his female detective is by dividing the role between two players: Madelyn Mack plays out the detective script and Nora Noraker adopts the female script. Both are self-supporting, professional, working women; each seems successful at what she does although Nora is neither widely known like her friend nor as well rewarded financially. While Madelyn is alternately bored and engrossed in her work, Nora alternates work and romance. She agonizes over Thorndyke Preston's apparent interest in a chorus girl, hides her feelings by snubbing him, and agrees to his demand that they marry immediately. The more beautiful, clever, and mercurial Madelyn Mack is free to continue her career; unlike Marie Connor Leighton's Joan Mar, she does not have a pair of ingenues bemoaning her unfortunate, single status after she has rescued them from suspicion. This alternative conclusion, however, does still leave Mack categorized as a detective, like Holmes, rather than as a woman. Certainly both scripts do not have equal status in her characterization.

Weir's treatment of a split female protagonist in a single novel parallels Kaufman's achievement with two protagonists—female and male—and two novels. The male success of Sam Burton is matched with Miss Sherlock Holmes, Madelyn Mack; the bumbling of Frances Baird with the unseeing Watson, Nora Noraker. But the romantic successes alter the pairs: Sam and Nora succeed; Madelyn and Frances are left unwanted and unmarried. More explicitly than Bodkin's demonstration of the choices for Dora Myrl and Paul Beck, Kaufman and Weir portray the range of alternatives: Burton dominates detection and marriage plots; Mack, detection; Noraker, marriage; Baird, neither despite unproven claims for her sleuthing abilities.

Detective fiction, especially in its action stories and even in its classical form, encodes gender-based structures of power; these inscribed messages resonate through narrative, character, and plot to address the readers. Annette Kolodny insists upon the impact these models of significance have for characters, readers, and writers alike (162). Believing that "[w]omen who write are not only capable of appropriating myths, genres, ideas, and images that are 'populated' with patriarchal meaning," Patricia S. Yeager proposes Bakhtin's theory of the novel which "offers the woman writer a dynamic and preformed (but not preformulated) structure for the deconstruction of patriarchy as an ideology" (955, 957). This potential generic openness is narrowed considerably by the formula which transforms fiction into detective novels. Gradually authors of this sub-genre abandoned its elastic form, narrowed the alternatives, and codified their options. No less than the male writers Kaufman, Stringer, and Weir, Anna Katherine Green was both author and follower of these formulaic developments. Her professional woman detective shares her counterparts' characteristics, their fictional limitations, and their structural fate. Violet Strange's author shares her male counterparts' phallocentric view of the world: pretty young women (or their convenient substitutes), whatever their professions, are best suited by ladylike behavior, respectable social positions, and advantageous marriages. All the novels reify a standard of male position and power contrasted with female inferiority. Double betrayal of class and gender marks all the characters including the neatly divided Mack/Noraker; recovery is defined by the marriage plot. In these endings, all five authors rejected the generic formula in favor of societal imperatives. The reader's contradictory expectations of detectives' active behavior and womens' passive acceptance were resolved in favor of the older, established bias. The generic newcomer fell by the side as female and male authors bolstered the male hegemony which seemed inevitable as well as right. The consistent and unassailable ease with which the nostalgic view of sex-linked traits dominates these detective novels testifies to the strength of gender-linked stereotyping and the satisfaction readers found in having their unrecognized prejudices reinforced.

Notes

1. Set at the turn-of-the-century, Teona Tone's 1980s novels about Kyra Keaton McMasters sharply illustrate the pervasive conflict between being a respectable woman and a private detective. On the second page of *Lady on the Line,* Senator Gerald McMasters, Kyra's client and future husband, links her most disreputable acts: "[I]f the rumors were correct, she had done some things that would have ruined an ordinary woman's reputation forever. Like living openly for six months in Paris with an impoverished French artist. Or running a private investigation agency out of her home in Philadelphia" (2). The submerged accusations of other early novels are explicitly answered here in narration as well as rumors. Kyra is sexually harassed, threatened with rape, protected from rape; she recalls her first sexual experience in detail and then relies on that initial partner for assistance. Most tellingly, however, she and McMasters share a number of fully described sexual encounters, both before and after marriage, beginning at only their third meeting since their introduction during her childhood. Although Tone borrows plots freely from ninteenth-century sensational and dime novels, the freedom with which she details her woman detective's sexual activities is clearly modeled on late-twentieth-century erotic romances. These contradictory styles do not work well together, and the reader is continually

forced to shift between the two. Finally, however, Tone choses the conventional marriage plot for her primary narrative focus: at the end of the first novel, Kyra Keaton marries her client-lover and promises to "limit" herself "to finding missing jewels and locating runaway sons, and leave matters of national importance to Pinkerton" (277); in the second novel, she has disbanded her agency and investigates the apparent death of a neighbor as any amateur might, worrying occasionally about her three children at home with their nursemaid. Even the pride her husband takes in her ability and his apparent similar attachment to domestic matters do not compensate readers for the undermining of her position. Gerald advances in his political career while gaining a beautiful wife and family; Kyra abandons her career to be that wife and provide the family while, at best, sharing in and promoting his career. Like both British and American women detectives of the period who marry, she exchanges one script for another with no more than a quickly abandoned suggestion that she might choose both.

2. Barrie Hayne successfully challenges John Cornillon's claim that Violet Strange is " 'engaged in the positive act of rejecting patriarchal domination' " (174). He recognizes that in this novel of sensation rather than detection, Strange stays class-bound and, therefore, safe. Discussing the retelling of an Ebenezer Gryce story as Violet's problem #7, Hayne charts the limitations of Green's female creation: Gryce's rationality is triumphant but Violet's emotions and intuition hold sway, leading to a "scarifying failure" (175).

5

How Golden Was the Golden Age? British and American Sleuths between the Wars

In the period between the two world wars, detective fiction flourished. This flowering may have begun as early as 1914 with *Trent's Last Case,* or in 1920 with the appearances of Hercule Poirot and Reggie Fortune, or in 1926 in America with Philo Vance (who deserved "a kick in the pance"). But it is clear that a new style and a new breed of authors were in control. The Detection Club enforced—mock seriously—an oath which bound writers to an intellectual puzzle which allowed readers to believe they were participating at the side of the great detectives. Murder became the required crime. As a convenience to increasing numbers of devoted readers, libraries and reviewers began categorizing mysteries separately from other forms of fiction (Watson 95). On all fronts the genre was becoming more self-conscious.

Critics differ somewhat in their assessments of this golden age although none challenges its preeminence in establishing still-current definitions of the classical detective novel. Howard Haycraft contrasts the new fiction with its predecessors, finding it more natural and plausible, using less "hokum" and fewer attempts to startle or amaze. The novels are better written and follow rules of fair play. The detectives are eccentric, human, and fallible; they seem "more ordinary" (*Murder* 121). Nonetheless, Haycraft also finds them flawed, overly static and mental in reaction to their excessively physical predecessors (*Murder* 140). More recently, LeRoy Panek emphasizes how deliberately readers are distanced from the novel (19); this helps Agatha Christie and her colleagues create a world in which justice is served, crimes are solved, and murder cancelled out by a competent, almost business-like hero (Watson 173). According to Ernst Mandel, the classical detective novel also supports the forces of bourgeois society by reducing crime and human problems to solvable mysteries (16). Although women writers dominated the period—in addition to Christie, Dorothy L. Sayers, Josephine Tey, Ngaio Marsh, and Margery Allingham were well reviewed and widely read—their detectives were all men; so were the heroes of the male writers. The glittering and glamorous world of the golden age novel easily acknowledged women as wives and mistresses, murderers and victims, assistants and troublemakers, but seldom as detective heroes. Haycraft himself is comfortable with blind, armchair, or dilettante detectives but assumes that women or boy detectives violate "probabilities if not the strict possibilities" (*Murder* 230).

Although the lived experiences of middle-class women in Britain and America offered concrete evidence of their ability to perform in traditional male roles, detective fiction followed the widespread postwar attitude which supported subordinate female behavior. Readers who were dismayed by the appearance of working women still encountered them in detective fiction—Troy Alleyn paints, Lady Amanda Campion designs airplanes, and Harriet Vane writes mystery novels. Nevertheless, readers were also reassured by the familiar image of a male detective, home from the war and once more in charge.

Because national military and economic need had put women in previously unacceptable jobs during World War I, British women's attitudes about working began to change. Young middle-class women felt themselves entitled to work; working-class women who had done men's work questioned female subordination on the job; and the number of women in trade unions rose (Rowbotham 110). These attitudes caught the government off-guard. Expecting that new women workers would gladly abandon their jobs in peace time, the government made no provisions for those who wanted to continue working; their calculations misfired as only about 50 percent of these workers voluntarily left after the war (Braybon 179). Still, public opinion was hostile to women workers who were keeping men's jobs instead of keeping house; they were seen as leeches and bloodsuckers for wanting decent wages and not being willing to go back to domestic work. This animosity went beyond the consistent hostility toward women working during the war when their usefulness was acknowledged (Braybon 86). Publicly and privately, the postwar period of the 1920s in Britain was a time of antifeminism.

The British government's postwar policy to "divide and rule" set against each other male and female workers, different social and economic classes, and the young and old. This divisiveness was highlighted when the 1918 approval of the vote applied only to women over thirty years old; not until 1928 did women vote on the same terms as men (Rowbotham 120). In 1932, Harold Laski was quoted as saying that the Woman Suffrage Acts of 1918 and 1928 merely registered in law the social change which had taken place; this statement is not entirely accurate (Harrison 16). Certainly some changes were evident. In 1919, the Sex Disqualification Removal Act passed: no one could be legally disqualified from public office, civil or judicial post by sex or marital status (Rowbotham 120). The 1923 Matrimonial Causes Act allowed adultery as grounds for divorce by the wife as well as the husband in a period when divorce was becoming more respectable.

Having succeeded in winning the vote in 1920, the Women's Suffrage movement in the United States turned to an Equal Rights amendment in 1923. Introduced by the National Women's Party, it stated: "Men and women shall have equal rights throughout the United States and every place subject to its jurisdiction." Support for this movement and other women's issues was divided over increasing protective legislation for women and children.

When Margaret Sanger founded the first U.S. birth control clinic in 1916, it was used primarily by middle-class women and encouraged later by the popular marriage manuals of the 1920s and 1930s which promoted a wife's companionate, rather than exclusively maternal, role. By 1936, a Gallup poll revealed that 63 percent of those interviewed favored the teaching and practice of birth control with contraceptives widely and easily available (Ware, *Holding Their Own* 7). During the twenties, health care shifted from trained women to professionals, usually men. The Sheppard Towner Act of 1921, which funded maternal and child care health clinics, was disbanded in 1929 at the encouragement of physicians who saw their practices threatened (Rothman 142), and midwives were almost totally eliminated by 1930 in a so-called triumph of scientific medicine (Ehrenreich and English 88).

The twenties and thirties were affected by two major economic factors: the aftermath of World War I and the Great Depression. For women, the postwar period changed their attitudes toward job choice and good wages (Greenwald 219). However, most Americans agreed with the Women's Bureau that wives belonged at home; both traditionalists and reformers accepted women's employment before marriage but believed that after marriage they would and should return to the home (Scharf 17). During the twenties and the Depression, there was a two-pronged attack on married working women: they were accused of abandoning their social responsibilities and competing economically with men (Scharf 44).

Legislative restrictions were passed against married women's employment. When labor, government, and mass media joined in urging women to refrain from paid work, the majority of citizens agreed (Chafe, *The American Woman* 135) In short, the Depression forced rearguard defensive action rather than forward movement on women's (especially married women's) right to work. This situation may not have been what Eleanor Roosevelt referred to in her 1933 book *It's up to the Women* when she urged them to carry heavier burdens in weathering the crisis than men (33). But, it surely is related to Margaret Mead's perception that a woman had two choices: to proclaim herself "a woman and therefore less an achieving individual, or an achieving individual and therefore less a woman" (Chafe, *Women and Equality* 15).

As the flapper caught the public eye in the 1920s, so too did the Miss America pageant, first held in Atlantic City in 1921, draw attention to apparently emancipated women and, especially, to their bodies. Fashion also changed women's lives: the cosmetics, the bobbed hair, the silk stockings, and the clothes which were one-tenth the weight of Victorian women's outfits visibly marked the sexual defiance which was a style for young middle-class women (Rowbotham 124–25).

In the Hollywood films of the 1920s the intelligent woman could be seen but not heard; independence for women in silent movies was announced by posing them with satin gowns and cigarettes, not by showing them at work (Haskell 76). The working heroine of the 1930s was less a liberal development than a response to prohibitions against sexual explicitness legislated by the Production Code and enforced by the Hayes Office as well as the rise of Depression-related films. Nonetheless in films as in life, women's work was seen as provisional—not part of her life's commitment or her self-definition (Haskell 139).

The strength of gender-based biases held by filmgoers extended to other mass-produced entertainments as well. The ironies implicit in authors undermining their women heroes in detective novels assume increasing force, parallel with the stricter definition and codification of the genre. Although Eric Bentley showed Trent pursuing false lines of reasoning, and Sayers provided Wimsey with the after-effects of war trauma, and Tey forced Grant to wade through evidence about Richard III which had long since been disproved, readers were eventually left with no doubt that these protagonists solved crime successfully. Although lucky or imaginative readers might work out the puzzle before the detective announced his solution, they felt themselves in league with a great mind, not in a contest with an inferior intelligence. Readers could choose any of the novels published in this period with the certainty that the conventions would be met—unless, of course, the detective were female. Then, as though there were a separate set of rules for women and men (like separate public bathrooms), the detectives were allowed to fail. The failure took many forms but implicit in the pattern was the authors' and readers' need to reify the traditional view of women. The flawed analysis and narrowness of this perspective parallels limitations Gayle Rubin finds in Freudian theories about women. She contrasts Freud's acceptance of the divergence between his findings and conventional morality with his determination to prove that the feminine personality corresponded with traditional, biased views of women (202). She continues, "The extent to which these rationalizations of femininity go against the grain of psychoanalytic logic is strong evidence for the extent of the need to suppress the radical and feminist implications of the theory of femininity" (203). As psychoanalysts ignored the implications of their own theory and replaced them with formulations which would reinforce their existing assumptions, so too did detective novelists substitute restrictive but socially approved views of women for the successful sleuth demanded by their theory (or rules of the genre). Conservative descriptions of women's nature reinforced equally conservative ideologies about women's positions; they proved far stronger than the conservative genre which experimented with but finally rejected a standard of equality for women and men.

Perhaps nowhere are the conflicts of the detective's script and the conventional woman's script so explicitly articulated as in Mrs. Sidney Groom's golden age novel *Detective Sylvia Shale*. The protagonist, a "baby face[d]" woman of twenty-five, is convinced that she will win an international reputation as a great detective until her goals and extraordinary self-confidence are overthrown by romance (5). Here, the intensity with which the detective claims, abandons, and reclaims the extreme limits of both scripts makes it difficult for the reader to take her prospects for success in either very seriously. In the novel's final page, the author validates this inference.

Groom begins by giving prominence to the detecting career which Sylvia Shale has outlined for herself. The first sentence announces: "Sylvia Shale's one ambition in life was to establish the identity of the elusive and terrifying master-criminal . . . under the *nom de guerre* of "Notorious Nick" (5). However, the narrator immediately hedges this confident statement by advising readers that "the most astonishing thing" was that Shale did not think herself incapable of achieving this goal despite the limitations of her age and gender (5). Sylvia's appearance is the first apparent contradiction to her career plans. At Pemberthy's famous New York detective agency as the youngest and prettiest woman on the staff, she is "an underpaid girl-detective who had nothing to her credit beyond the fact that she was considered sufficiently intelligent to occupy a place" (8). Even the experience she gained by associating with her father, a famous Scotland Yard detective, is not sufficient to win her an important assignment in her first year. Nevertheless, she is impatient and ambitious: " 'I adopted my father's profession because I was more or less brought up in it. My mother died while I was still at school, and from then up to the time of my father's death, I was always helping him in some way or other. It seemed quite natural that I should. But even if I had taken up any other sort of career, I shouldn't have been satisfied until I had risen to the top of the ladder . . .' " (12). As a result, she has left London for New York where she feels opportunities for success and reputation are greater. The only foreshadowing of the romance which is to play such havoc with these goals is Sylvia's assurance that "[l]ove, marriage, the joys of home life" were unimportant beside the fame she meant to have, "cost what it might" (15).

The intersection of these conflicting scripts begins on an ocean voyage where her official assignment is to find children kidnapped by their father and her ever-present private plan is to capture Notorious Nick. Despite their dramatic nature, subsequent events are never more than backdrop for the two central issues of Shale's life. On board, she falls in love with Philip Traymore whom she comes to suspect is Notorious Nick; he saves her when the ship sinks and she is initially presumed the only survivor. She discovers that Traymore and others have survived and that the sunken ship is being looted of its valuables; Sylvia's suspicions of Traymore continue, but she can get no assistance from Britsh authorities. Eventually, she discovers a secret plot, learns the identity of Notorious Nick, and loses her lover.

Both onboard the ship as she is falling in love with Traymore and later when she discovers him in London, she is always uncertain whether he is innocent or criminal. Then Sylvia Shale vacillates wildly between the cooly rational detective and the emotional woman. Time and again she harshly drags herself back from a lover's commitment and acceptance to face her detective's growing doubt and strident accusations. Repeatedly she castigates herself for these lapses, never acknowledging that conflicting emotions, like conflicting scripts, can mesh in a single person: "A week ago, all this [conclusions of her investigation] would have filled her with excitement, elation. Every pulse in her would have been throbbing with enthusiasm and her brain would have been teeming with speculations, with plans for the capture of the man who might prove to be—Notorious Nick. But to-night she was only a weak, vacillating woman who shrank from incriminating the man she loved" (60). Her responses and the language in which she states them only validate her earlier image of herself as a romantic novelette heroine pinned into inaction by her emotions.

This emotional trauma seems to overset all Sylvia's previous abilities as well as her self-reliance. Unable to win assistance from Scotland Yard which has not received an official request to investigate from her New York office, she lapses into thinking which takes her from the plausible explanation of sex discrimination (the Yard doesn't value her information because she's female) to the self-pity which accepts the inability of "one poor weak girl" to outwit Notorious Nick and his gang (204). It is true that Nick's ability to anticipate her actions, to see through her most clever disguise, and to reduce her to tears and anger make him seem unnaturally prescient. Nonetheless, his success backfires as she obtains a revolver, reestablishes her courage and autonomy, and confronts her lover despite her emotionally rocky state. These actions do not help Shale capture the gang but do keep them from further looting and also verify her claim that the ship had been sabotaged.

The final chapter brings the evidence of both the romance and the mystery to a conclusion which involves Sylvia Shale centrally and yet keeps her an observer rather than a participant. Called to the bedside of the dying Philip Traymore, she discovers that the criminal she has sought is his brother. Traymore acknowledges his love and devotion; he wills his estate to Sylvia Shale. The second visitor to the deathbed is Notorious Nick himself, revealed now as James Pemberthy, Sylvia Shale's employer who has also been in love with her. Like his brother, he dies acknowledging his love and devotion for her. He also leaves a legacy—a warning that only the brothers' love had protected her from the gang; their deaths will eliminate that safeguard.

This deathbed meeting between Shale and both her tormentors climaxes the manipulation which Groom has used both explicitly and implicitly throughout the novel. Pemberthy is more obvious: as her employer, he directs Shale's professional career, refuses to assign her important cases, and exercises "friendly concern . . . [to] hesitate to expose you to any unnecessary risk" (12). His romantic inclination is more muted; emphasizing the conditional tense, he reflects, "Now if I were a marrying man, she'd be the ideal wife for me" (15). His disguise as Notorious Nick conflicts with both of these stances; he and Shale are supposed enemies. Directly challenging her professional ability, he uses several notes and a telephone call, the arrogance of which immediately excites Shale. One message reads:

> Dear Sylvia,
>   So sorry you didn't see, but cheer up—better luck next time. Look out for my colossal coup across the herring-pond, coming shortly.
>   Yours, with the greatest of respect,
>   N. N. (18)

She responds immediately and directly to the insolent mockery of the note, setting her plans to capture the criminal without revealing her leads to anyone else. These more explicit attempts to control Sylvia's thoughts and movements are matched by the unspoken but often hinted inducements of love and romance offered by Philip Traymore. Like a puppet, Shale can be moved to action by either man. In her, Groom creates a character whose motivations are so transparent that she can be easily used; her views of the world and herself are neither complex nor individuated. They are based on commonplace models: Shale's version of detective success is based on a male model (her father) and her view of romance is drawn from widely read popular novels.

When Shale reviews her moment of triumph—"[H]er name would be famous as the girl-detective who had revealed Notorious Nick's identity to the world, and she would be a woman of wealth"—both she and the author acknowledge the unsatisfying nature of this apparent victory (247). She has failed as both a detective and a woman. As an investigator, she had no clue to the identity of Notorious Nick and only discovered him accidentally as he came to his dying brother's bedside; she could claim no credit for his capture. As a woman in love, she had lost the man for whom she cared. Concluding that she did not expect to ever marry, she chooses to be a pseudo-widow. At the novel's end, she can only announce in a "low and dreamy" voice that she has chosen the new goal of capturing Nick's gang; the reader is left to conclude that if this venture takes the same kind of luck that capturing the gang's leader did, Sylvia Shale is doomed to yet another failure (255).

Describing the feminist critique of nineteenth-century women writers, Elaine Showalter uses the terminology of object/field problems which explains how the reader keeps "two alternative oscillating texts simultaneously in view" (266). Unlike George Eliot or Charlotte Brontë who submerge the unacceptable plot beneath a conventional one, Groom and other detective fiction writers with woman protagonists submerge and then restore the acceptable story—the traditional woman's script—and sink the unacceptable, more radical presentation of a woman professional. In *Sylvia Shale*, the reader's task of juggling two texts is simplified by the lack of subtlety with which the conventional structure of the woman's script is presented; it is both easily understood and readily accepted, drawing on formulas from romance and romantic gothic novels of women who fall in love unwisely.

Like Sylvia Shale, Olga Knaresbrook juggles scripts while her cousin-companion Molly Kingsley eventually abandons her professional career for a domestic one. But, author Hazel Campbell leads the reader on as wild a chase as detective Knaresbrook leads her Watson, Kingsley, in *Olga Knaresbrook—Detective*. The result is a convoluted tale in which the professional detective, the amateur/professional detective, and the criminal are all failed women. As the final chapter reveals, a bored and drug-addicted Olga Knaresbrook has committed the crimes which she pretends to professionally detect, using as her secretary-assistant Molly Kingsley, who is actually a professional investigator disguised as a reporter. In a plot reminiscent of *The Moonstone*, the two detect at cross purposes: Olga tries to shift the evidence of her crime onto Molly who finally uncovers her insane cousin's secrets.

As the putative detective, Olga Knaresbrook is a collection of personal and professional contradictions. Although looking the part of the "Modern Woman," she describes herself as attractive but unsexed, capable but unhappy; ". . . she cherishes deep down in her inmost soul a desire to be a domestic paragon" (24). Even so, she seems to enjoy her battle of wits with the male detectives who are challenging her conclusions. But she resents their hostile response to her carefully reasoned arguments when they offer amazed approval for her assistant's girlish intelligence. She claims to have chosen this profession because of her "well-known talent for deduction and sleuthing," her boredom with small-town life, and the chance opportunity offered by a recent burglary (31). She announces that she will model herself on the great Sherlock Holmes. Kingsley is among those who are amazed how well Knaresbrook can imitate the ratiocinative methods of the master; they do not know that she has committed the crimes and is planting the clues.

However, Olga's arrogance leads to her own capture: "Her nerves wouldn't let her leave well enough alone. She was always foreseeing new holes in her stories and trying to be the first to call attention to them and provide a false solution" (285). Her mercurial temperament plus her alternately alert and languid behavior are carefully attributed to womanish fears or a desire to imitate the famous Holmes (as she imitates Lord Peter Wimsey in her decision to sport a monocle). Readers who do not yet know the plot twist are suspicious of her sincerity and dedication as a detective. Olga whines, " 'I'm sick of sleuthing . . . it's a sordid business. Horley was right, I suppose—no job for a woman. But I wouldn't mind the sordidness so much. It's feverish work. Keeps you always on the jump for what's coming next' " (86). When she is finally revealed as the criminal, Knaresbrook's behavior is attributed to insanity, both her mind and her body destroyed by drugs. Her abilities are conveniently ignored by the narrator: she has been clever enough to smuggle drugs, murder two people, blackmail several others, and lead astray three qualified professional detectives despite her drugged state. While hardly estimable behavior, it does suggest that she is neither as limited nor as transparent as the simple diagnosis of insanity would suggest. But despite Olga's cleverness, the novel's structure labels her a failure—a woman who is unhappy with her choices, a detective who is deluded in her profession, and a criminal who is unsuccessful in her machinations.

The legitimate but unrevealed detective Molly Kingsley spends much of the novel sitting quietly with a notebook in the corners of rooms where her cousin is conducting her own investigation. Molly's pose as assistant-secretary-Watson means that although she occasionally offers ideas or bits of minor information to her cousin, her actual detection is carried on outside the purview of the third-person narrator and remains secret from the reader until the final chapter. Campbell plays on stereotypes to keep this dual identity hidden; Kingsley is described as the quintessentially feminine young woman whose appearance is thought to signal marriage and maternity. Her desires are at odds with her appearance, just as Olga Knaresbrook's are. This leads her to problems: ". . . to her it seemed that the many and various hopes of a career which she had entertained during those years had been frustrated not so much by any lack of ability on her own part as by the firm conviction on the part of the world in general, but prospective employers in particular, that a height of five-foot-three and naturally wavy hair, coupled with soft brown eyes and a rose-leaf complexion, necessarily precluded the possibility of brains or business acumen" (14). In another reversal at the novel's conclusion, it appears that the employers may be correct. Eventually, the reader learns that Molly Kingsley has been recommended for this job by her fiancé whom she will not marry until she can " 'feel I could stand on my own feet' " (270). But she never does. She is kidnapped by Olga Knaresbrook who penetrates the disguise and plans to force her cousin into confessing to murder before killing her; she has to be rescued by Scotland Yard and her fiancé, himself a detective. Finally, Molly rejects her fiancé's offer of a detective partnership after their marriage in favor of domestic bliss. Little can be made of Hal Barnard's willingness to encourage Molly Kingsley's professional aspirations; he accepts them only so long as she refuses to marry him and welcomes her eventual decision to abandon these earlier goals. In the end, the woman who had always aspired to "the more masculine professions" (12), wanting to be a doctor or a lawyer, quickly rejects her announced aims: " 'Hal, I'm never going to do one more bit of sleuthing as long as I live,' she declared. 'I'm going to take Dad's advice. I'll be a cook—but in my own home. I don't want to carve a career anywhere else' " (288). Although Molly is clearly more successful in achieving women's traditionally approved goals and marginally more successful in investigating crime than her cousin, she too is undercut by the other characters' attitudes and by the fictional structure. Her professional goals are insubstantial and easily abandoned; her final career choice is domestic and limited.

Much is made of the job of detection itself in this novel overloaded with four detectives who have varying degrees of professional qualifications. Scotland Yard's Detective Inspector Macdonald is the most fully credentialed, followed by Hal Barnard, a former police officer in India now assigned to this drug case. Behind them comes Molly Kingsley, who is employed by a little-known and somewhat shady detective agency, and all are trailed by Olga Knaresbrook with her three-room office in town and a nagging mother at home. The diminishing professional status of the four is matched by the gender shift from the top to the bottom half of the list; the women are seen as little more than amateurs and their professional status nominal. Even Molly Kingsley agrees with this negative assessment: "Not for the first time, the absurd nature of their venture struck her, and she almost laughed aloud. The thing was farcical. How could Olga possibly hope to make good? To set out, in these days of specialists and scientific appliances, armed with nothing more—so far as Molly knew—than her native wit, and with the apparent hope of solving murder problems in a tiny country town, seemed nothing short of lunacy" (34). A young woman whom Olga high-handedly questions puts the issue more succinctly and baldly, " 'Why should I be cross-questioned by a mere amateur with no qualifications except her own swelled head?' " (199). The derogation of the women continues until the case and the novel end. Even as Molly is explaining how she uncovered the truth, Inspector Macdonald is caught between admiration and incredulity because "[l]ike many of his sex he could not associate brains with that brand of cream-and-roses prettiness" (275).

Structurally, Campbell has organized the novel's conclusion in such a way that a sequence of reversals thoroughly undercuts the idea and the practice of a woman detective. The traditional detective novel focuses all its attention toward the final chapters where the criminal is caught, the crime solved, and the solution revealed to the reader; its conclusion is a detective novel's ultimate moment. Clearly, all these criteria are met in *Olga Knaresbrook*; yet they are not the point of the final chapter. Murder and drug smuggling are quickly settled; the real focus of these pages is the disposal of the women detectives. The ostensible detective is revealed as a phoney who planted the clues she then discovered; she is doubly discredited by being made the criminal and, to insure her undercutting, a drug addict. The undercover woman detective is acknowledged, immediately retired by her own choice and, for good measure, married off. In this chapter, ordinarily the detective's moment of recapitulating the entire crime and investigation to display his own powers of deduction, both of these detectives are removed from the center of the formula; their placement in the narrative at this point in the structure reconfirms their minimal positions. By contrast, Molly and her fiancé dominate the final paragraphs of the novel; the marriage plot triumphs. Unlike her cousin, Molly is worthy of this victory because she rejects the unwomanly identity of detective or criminal (whose simultaneous adoption by Olga suggests that the two are conflated; for a woman to be a detective is, perhaps, criminal).

Like these two exceptionally clear-cut examples of the contradictory scripts provided for a woman detective, other golden age novels pit investigation against the marriage plot. Half a dozen demonstrate the permutations chosen by authors who vacillated between the two scripts, persistently undermining their protagonists by this pattern. There is an incompetent detective who gets married off, and one who is rejected; a competent sleuth who gets married off, and one who doesn't; a reformer who gets married, and one who won't. In each of these cases of the unmarried detective, the formulaic elements of the marriage plot are as important as those of the detection plot; marriage is not ignored but unachieved. In an age so rigorously committed to the genre, the dominance of the detection formula is subordinated in these novels to another imperative; it looks like romance, courtship or marriage (whether achieved or only desired), but is actually societal tradition. Like the Shakespearean comedies where love is secondary to social reintegration and reproduction through marriage, romance in these detective novels is a cover story for reinforcing conservative ideologies about women's sphere.

As a consequence of these underlying motives, it is irrelevant that, like Olga Knaresbrook, Lucie Mott is both flawed and culpable; what matters is that like Molly Kingsley, she plans to give up independence for marriage. In fact, it is fair to say that Lucie Mott, advice columnist and proprietor of Mott's Enquiry Agency, is no detective at all. In the ten cases described by E. Phillips Oppenheim in *Ask Miss Mott,* she solves only two—finding a missing woman locked in her own house and recognizing that an apparently philandering husband was actually out thieving—and in a third helps rescue her uncle. In five stories she is saved from her own folly by a supposed criminal known as Violet Joe with whom she immediately falls in love. Her behavior is naive, reckless, and even morally culpable although the formula would identify her as the book's hero. Three strains of action are interwoven throughout the volume: the romance of Lucie and Violet Joe, the maniacal attraction of the criminal gang leader Meredith for Lucie, and Miss Mott's investigative career. All are neatly tied up in the final case.

The most serious of Mott's errors is her involvement with Boss Meredith who kidnaps her, fakes a marriage ceremony, and tracks her despite Violet Joe's numerous rescues and Scotland Yard's protection. At the novel's end, she suggests that Meredith safeguard himself by getting rid of the informant who betrayed him to Scotland Yard. No democrat, Miss Mott apparently values the thoroughly evil Meredith, now revealed as the aristocratic Earl of Westerleys, over the common-born informant who has offered to share the reward with her. By this behavior, she is directly responsible for the informant's death although it is arranged by Meredith. Lucie shows no remorse over this killing. At most she admits that "[s]he was not sure, after all, whether crime appealed to her so much" (275). This dilettantism characterizes both her behavior and her attitude. It allows her the pleasure of playing detective without having to take responsibility for her actions. Whatever apparent risks she encounters are merely paper tigers, and she is the illusion of a professional detective or newspaper columnist.

The only plausible connection between Lucie Mott's actions and the rest of the novel lies in the unrealistic world of romantic novels. Nothing in Meredith's treatment of her can have appealed to Lucie except his unyielding determination to marry her. This motive seems to have expunged all his wrongdoings. A similar motive and aristocratic connections have also expunged all the crimes of The Honorable Joseph Chilcott, alias Violet Joe. Even Superintendent Wragge can then give his blessing to Chilcott's marriage proposal, noting that his niece has " 'taken a partner into the business' " (281). Just as Sylvia Shale panics over her conflict of roles as detective and woman, Olga Knaresbrook slides from criminal to detective and back, and Molly Kingsley matches professionalism against domesticity, Lucie Mott juggles competing scripts. But in her case, she's failing at both from the beginning. She is an ineffective detective without any ethical code and a romantic fool with a craving for excitement.

Sylvia Shale's conflict between detection and romance reappears as both the plot and the characters of Marie Connor Leighton's second novel replicate those of her earlier volume, *Joan Mar, Detective*. Coming to the assistance of an innocent young woman involved in a murder, the detective discovers that she herself has fallen in love with the ingenue's fiancé. Inevitably, this misjudgment clouds her professionalism in *Lucille Dare, Detective;* error and a plan for vengeance follow. In this novel of love gone wrong and only finally put right, the elements of romance—here glorified as sacred and divine love—predominate.

In inverse proportion to the little said about Lucille Dare's detective methodology is the excess devoted to her romantic attachment to Rev. Brian Havelock, whom she names beloved, suspect, accused, and vindicated in sequence. Sensible enough to know that he is not responsible for her feeling of betrayal because he is engaged to another woman, she nonetheless decides to punish him for the pain she has felt, "a work alike of justice and of revenge" (87). Over and again the limits of her thwarted passion are dissected: had he loved her, she would have shielded him; should he promise to marry her rather than his fiancée, she will work to clear him. She is more an avenger than a detective. She lays her passion before Havelock: " 'You became the star of my life—of my brilliant, agitated, successful life. . . . I thought that when we met, Lucille Dare, the detective, would give way to Lucille Dare, the woman, the lover, the beloved. But it was not to be so. . . . For the sake of my love for you I might have spared you; but I chose instead to listen to the voice of duty' " (156–57). Of course Dare is wrong on two points: she has let duty be overcome by personal revenge and she has reacted only as a wronged woman, not a professional detective.

Although this sabotage of the detective by the emotionally untrustworthy woman in love and the substitution of vengeance for fairness are reversed in the second half of the novel, Leighton makes it clear in the final pages that little has actually changed. The angry detective, deceived by the real criminal and not merely by her own emotions, saves the wrongly accused man and for her pains is critically wounded by the criminal. But, as in *Joan Mar, Detective*, the young lovers marry and the detective vanishes to pursue her career. The dichotomy between professional success and romantic fulfillment is made clear as the lovers offer "a prayer that some day the great detective might find and welcome Love" which they define sentimentally, through their own marriage, as " 'a lamp through which the light of God's truth shines on . . . the world' " (320). Against this background, mere detection and the woman who has lost love and settled for detecting cannot compete. Twice a failure, Lucille Dare has loved and lost, detected and been deceived; although she is able to redeem herself in one area, she is branded a failure by the new Mr. and Mrs. Havelock in the more important one. Their justified happiness clearly illuminates Lucille's failed and misdirected life; as a woman rejected in the marriage plot, she can hope for little more than compensatory activities.

Unlike Mott and Dare, the protagonist of E. Phillips Oppenheim's *Advice Limited* succeeds in both detection and marriage plots almost without exertion. Never fully developed as a character beyond her aristocratic marriage and entrée into socially prominent circles, Baroness Linz solves eleven cases without revealing much of her method of deduction. Four cases of ten end in reconciliation of engaged or married couples, like her personal case.

Three of the Baroness's cases are brought by a Spanish duke with whom she gradually becomes romantically involved. In the final case of the volume, she saves his lands and fortunes from an unscrupulous estate agent, leaving him free to propose marriage from a position of wealth and strength. But even here, Clara Linz makes the first move: " '. . . [Y]ou do need someone to look after you' " (318). She names a restaurant, suggests a taxi, and announces that she had always thought a marriage proposal in a taxi very romantic. He obliges. Unlike Lucie Mott who is charmed into marriage and out of detection by her loving fiancé, Clara seems to dominate her own proposal. But this power is illusory; actually, she abrogates her independence. Oppenheim has her set the stage, relieve the duke of any uncertainty about his reception, and then withdraw to allow him to take the more prominent, central position. Like a cliché of the clever woman behind the powerful man, Clara reassures Rodrigo that she will step aside for him.

Akin to the Baroness Linz in her elegance, her flair, and her entrée to society, Madame Rosika Storey is distinguished from Clara by her unmarried status. Hulbert Footner's five novels and thirty novelettes or short stories published between 1925 and 1937 are narrated in the first person by her secretary and admirer Bella Brickley, also her sometime assistant detective. Like Madelyn Mack's Nora Noraker, this Watson *is* a woman, openly amazed by her employer and determined to record Madame Storey's many successful cases.[1]

Rather than define herself as a detective, Madame Storey considers herself a psychologist who specializes in the feminine because women are more realistic and more interesting than men. Originally she had no interest in crime but hoped only to straighten out people's problems, but she discovers that wrongdoers do not usually want to be saved.

These novels and short stories are atypical in fiction of women private eyes for the close personal and professional relationship between Rosika Storey and Bella Brickley. Although they are not partners, they do work together in solving cases. Bella frequently shrieks or faints or interrupts at exactly the wrong moment; but neither she nor her employer is really troubled by this lack of professionalism which is never evident in Madame Storey's principal male operative. In several cases, notably *The Under Dogs* and "The Viper," Brickley operates with a minimum of supervision and assistance from the absent Madame Storey although the information she locates is transferred to the principal detective for action. But on other occasions when they discuss cases, this Watson is seldom able to offer any independent information or deduction; frequently she cannot even follow her employer's train of thought.

Only once, early in the series, does Madame Storey reveal any deception in her role as cool and self-possessed sophisticate, describing "my tragedy": " 'I have yet to meet a man bold enough to face me down. How could I surrender myself to one whose soul was secretly afraid of mine? So here I sit. You know that the Madame I have hitched to my name is just to save my face. No one would believe that a woman as beautiful as I could be still unmarried—and respectable. But I am both, worse luck!' " (*Madame Storey* 25). Despite an ironic tone, Rosika reveals her awareness of a world in which a woman without a man is perceived as incomplete. Nonetheless, she has constructed a personal legend as a defense against criticism and perhaps also against herself. She is willing to use her sexual attractiveness and her femininity both to vamp and to hide her intelligence and skills.

So, what can be made of this intrepid detective? Despite foolish mistakes, she solves her cases and seems to earn her investigative reputation. Yet her private life is designed to evade the commitment she associates with marriage. Moreover, her criteria for a husband are remarkably restricted—he must be not only unafraid of her but also bold enough to face her down; the latter seems to suggest that she secretly wishes to be dominated. So long as she receives proposals from men who accept rejection, she can bemoan her unmarried virtue without challenge. Even if she is searching for an equal partner in marriage, her defenses are too well-established to allow anyone but a bully to succeed. If this is the case, then Footner has left her in the classic double bind to choose between being either unwillingly unmarried or unhappily married. In either case, in personal and societal terms her private life does not match her successful professional one; this conclusion, like the happy ending of the marriage plots in other novels, reinforces society's pressure on women to choose between available scripts rather than to merge them.[2]

More naive than Madame Storey about both her own and criminals' motivations, London shop investigator Millie Lynn wants to transform her job description. She prefers to bring criminals to confession, repentance, and restitution rather than to the police. Inasmuch as her cases involve everything from lovesick, jealous secretaries to major thefts, she is not always in control of the outcome.

Her determination—" 'You may shoot me first. I shall never give in' "—
ordinarily leads to success (156). But in Millie's final case, the success
is different; although shot by the thief and hospitalized, she does not
regret the obstinacy which had led her into this difficulty. Wounded,
she watched Scotland Yard lead away the criminal. Resting safely on
the shoulder of the man she has fallen in love with, she reassures
him, " 'It's nothing—really—Ken. I—I—kept my promise [to capture
this particular thief]—' " (173).

    This position between the criminal and the lover in Cecil L.
Bullivant's *Millie Lynn, Shop Investigator* symbolically illustrates the
difficulty of the woman detective caught between the investigation
and marriage plots. Bullivant resolves his character's dilemma in the
most conventional way. Although Ken Rawson has worked with her,
shared cases, and recognized her abilities, what he wants most is to
stop her from being a detective. Although he has not criticized her
occupation earlier, he cannot find it compatible with the other career
he plans for her. In wanting to "get the girl" who has gotten the
criminal, Rawson plans to make it impossible for her ever to get
another criminal. Millie's heart, much in evidence earlier, dominates
the conclusion of the book; like the repentant criminals, an unre-
pentant Ken Rawson appeals to it. In fact, he makes demands and
issues orders: he insists that she not return to work. Her gasp of
surprise and question is silenced with the inevitable romantic kiss
and his offer—" 'Come with me to try and solve the greatest mystery
of all . . . the mystery of love' " (174). Thus Lynn's talent for mystery
solving is turned in a single direction and devoted to him as Rawson
continues to be free to solve both sorts of mysteries—crime and love.
Only the woman is expected to narrowly confine her life and activities
while the man proportionally expands his.

    A woman detective's retirement into marriage with her profes-
sional counterpart makes explicit the different cultural norms for
female and male behavior. Historically, society encourages men's
marriage and employment, legally requiring financial support for their
wives and families; it virtually prescribes women's marriage and maternity while roundly criticizing their paid employment. When the
partners are equally qualified for marriage and the same career, only
socially reified inequality could describe the results as being to her
advantage. His options—to control the marriage proposal, determine
the level of family support, and decide his own profession—are not

matched in her lack of alternatives. Like Paul Beck, Hal Barnard, and
Robert Spicer, Ken Rawson holds all the cards and plays them to his
advantage, adding marriage to his already satisfactory professional
life. Millie Lynn joins Dora Myrl and Molly Kingsley in being able
only to exchange one role for another, never to take both simultaneously. Even Rose Courtenay, who seems to achieve the masculine
advantage, holds only a shadow of her husband's position, and only
at his discretion. When women exchange their detecting careers for
marriage to men who can have both, they are not choosing among
marriage, career, or both but following an approved sequential pattern
which tolerates paid employment for spinsters but defines marriage
as both women's life and their work.

More successfully than Millie Lynn or Rosika Storey, New York-
based detective Millicent Newberry redefines her profession from
investigator to social worker or therapist. Like them, she prefers to
reform rather than punish criminals. In this respect, she also redefines herself as a non-detective. She would prefer to be married and
might be described as sublimating her disappointment through maintaining an unusual view of her official profession.

At the opening of her golden age series Jeannette Lee withholds
a vital clue from her readers. Although Lee describes her protagonist;
shows her going into her own agency office; has her dust, arrange
flowers, and take out her omnipresent knitting, she does not reveal
until page 9 of *The Green Jacket* that Newberry is a detective. It is as
though the protagonist's womanliness is being established before her
independent, more masculine career is acknowledged.

The uniqueness of Millicent Newberry's detective agency, the
reader learns, is that she does not hand criminals over to the police,
believing that official justice is often wrongly directed. Instead, she
insists that clients give her the " 'chance to say what shall be done
with the criminals I catch . . . I decide whether they are to have
another chance—or to go to prison' " (*Jacket* 40, 42). She believes
that crime is a manifestation of sin, a curable or preventable disease;
like a missionary, she has undertaken this work as a moral responsibility. Clients and confessed suspects see her as both absolute authority and a kindly, encouraging woman. As such, she is the all-
powerful maternal figure of their childhood dispensing moral education and love simultaneously. Newberry flourishes in this atmosphere of needy people relying on her for their growth into well-

behaved adults. This role allows her to reject her acknowledged loneliness and turn aside romance.[3]

Despite her consistent rate of success, Newberry is regularly
troubled with one admiring disbeliever, her former employer, Tom
Corbin. This split attitude continues as he magnanimously urges partnership in insulting terms: " 'You have a good mind for details, but
you need me to handle the case as a whole' " (*Jacket* 50). He credits
her success to luck rather than talent. Incapable of understanding her
refusal to merge their offices and wanting to make a dent in her calm,
he challenges the heart of her agency's principles: " 'You're a disgrace
to the profession, Milly! It's all right, dabbling in juvenile cases and
effeminacy. But this was deliberate theft' " (*Office* 26). This attack
is made in the context of his regular marriage proposals, couched in
terms of her need for him and, occasionally, his need of her. Ignoring
the insults, Newberry responds to the need, never agreeing to marry
but often thinking about her loneliness and Corbin's lack of anyone
to care for him, darn his socks, or brush his clothes. She sees him
as a "big, blundering, protecting dear who would never quite understand that she could take care of herself . . . " (*Dead Right* 1). So,
despite his condescending offer to share a case she has already accepted directly, Millicent considers marriage if only he would not
unromantically link that proposal with a business merger. In her need
to be needed, she becomes an ambivalent womanly woman who deflects insults and rude challenges to her dedication and talent rather
than the competent professional who can use a person's need to reform him.

Nonetheless, it is only the peripheral cases—the clients who
show up for their probationary appointments, those whose parents
lavish praise on Newberry, those who are seen living honest lives—
which have been solved by Millicent Newberry the detective rather
than Millicent Newberry the social worker or priest. She consciously
claims that her business is to help people out of their blunders and
mistakes, not to catch criminals. Had the healing professions of the
post-World War I period regularly included women psychotherapists,
social workers, or priests, she probably would have chosen a different
career. Rejecting the usual demands of her announced profession for
the more supportive behavior of the helping professions, she denies
the "successful masculine career" of Tom Corbin which might have
also been hers for a successful but feminine one (*Jacket* 327). Her

decision implies gender distinctions which make this choice more than simply plausible; it becomes almost inevitable. In the end Corbin's initial assessment of the public's bias against a woman detective seems justified, and Millicent Newberry has evaded rejection by not really being a detective.

Late in the golden age, two U.S. writers—one female and one male—created forward-looking, modern young women who choose detective work from a range of other possible employments. Kay Cleaver Strahan and Rex Stout join Jeanette Lee and Canadian Hulbert Footner in creating American protagonists, but vary the model noticeably. In several respects, their characters seem to anticipate the early female hard-boiled detectives.

Although best known for his creation of Nero Wolfe, Rex Stout is also responsible for Theodolinda Bonner, the female detective—an oxymoron Archie Goodwin is loathe to imagine—who appears briefly in several Wolfe works and also in her own novel, *The Hand in the Glove*. This latter, narrated in the third person, gives a more unbiased view of the protagonist than when she is filtered through Goodwin's first-person narration.

At both the beginning and end of the novel, Dol Bonner has a partner in the heiress Sylvia Raffray whose funds, friendship, and personality Bonner values. As egalitarian partnerships between women who choose to become professional detectives are otherwise unknown, this novel moves in new directions. However, the partnership comes under fire on the first page because of the objections of Raffray's guardian, is watered down by the principals, and then is dissolved by page 22. Bonner is angry about Raffray's "submissiveness" to a man but realistic about ending the association (*Glove* 21). Her primary concern is financial, but she looks forward to the independence of working alone, though in a cheaper, dingier office. On the final page of the novel with her guardian now dead and her fiancé under indictment, Sylvia announces her willingness to return to the partnership and a somewhat embarrassed Dol agrees. Raffray has done no investigation or consultation; indeed, she has criticized rather than encouraged her "partner." The idea of two detectives working together is not developed, and the more unusual vision of two women detectives functioning together is abandoned without any effort to show it in action.

Having decided to be a detective on fairly flimsy grounds, Dol Bonner keeps reminding herself of her professional commitment throughout the murder investigations. Acknowledging that she could as easily have chosen to be a hairstylist or secretary, she explains: "... I made a long list of all the activities I might undertake on my own. They all seemed monotonous or distasteful except two or three, and I flipped a coin to decide between detective and landscape design" (*Glove* 21). A combination of police indifference to her investigation, friends' accusations of cold-heartedness, and an awareness of her lack of experience keep Bonner from resting securely on her credentials as a detective: "She was proceeding on the assumption that she was a detective. ... She was aware of the picturesque incongruity of an attractive young woman ... undertaking such a career, but since the first week in the office of Bonner and Raffray it had not been prominent in her thoughts. She was a pretty good realist, and it was obvious that she must either seriously endeavor to establish herself in the profession she had chosen, or be prepared to admit to herself that she was a phoney. The latter, for Dol Bonner, was not likely" (*Glove* 82–83). Were her only cases lost dresses and dogs, this self-scrutiny might not have been necessary; but Dol later finds two bodies. She bolsters her courage to examine the first body and surrounding clues by remembering that although veteran and even famous detectives might investigate this case, she also is a detective and already on the scene. This recognition shocks her.

At first glance, it would seem that Dol Bonner is quite a successful detective. She solves the crimes when the male detectives and officials in the case hardly cover themselves with glory. Her uncertainties or errors can be laid to her youth, inexperience, and lack of training. Even the description of her previous cases and the acknowledgement of a $1164.35 agency income put her career into perspective; she is a beginner, entitled to a few misgivings and problems. But if Stout has set up his woman detective in a way that limits her opportunities for full-scale failure, he has used the same evidence to restrict her chances for full-scale success. She is squeamish about observing bodies, inordinately proud of her elaborate and as yet unused scene-of-the-crime bag, has only practiced and read about taking fingerprints and shooting her gun, manages to shoot the ground as well as the criminal when he is about to attack her, and faints after she has shot him. None of this behavior is surprising in a small-time detective who stumbles on bodies accidentally as an amateur might; none of it is expected in a calm, professional detective who uncovers a mentally ill criminal in the face of others' failures. But all is true of Dol Bonner; in the very contradictions of the detective's behavior are the challenges to her authority as a professional. In the end, her limitations are more believable than her success. Undermining her competence here, Stout validates Archie Goodwin's suspicions of women detectives; even though Bonner's success is apparent in her brief, subsequent appearances, this first impression establishes readers' limited expectations of her.[4]

Like other authors included in this chapter, Kay Cleaver Strahan uses generic conventions as well as structure and character development to minimize the position of her female detective. Although all seven of Strahan's mystery novels feature red-haired "crime analyst" Lynn MacDonald and advertise her on the dust jackets, MacDonald plays a much smaller role than might be expected of a series detective.[5] In four of the novels narrated by a folksy, on-the-spot suspect, she does not appear until the final quarter of the book; in another she is introduced early but lost as chapter after chapter reprints old letters from the victim's family; only in *The Hobgoblin Murder* with its limited third-person narrator does she play a visibly important role.

All six of the narratives are constructed so that only an external view of the detective is available; until she chooses to reveal herself to other characters, nothing of her thoughts or theories is known to the reader. The novels claim to be based on the rule of fair play and, as a result, spend an extraordinary amount of space on the suspects' descriptions of events and their responses to MacDonald's often puzzling questions. Again, these factors repeatedly cause her to fade into the background, allowing Strahan to evade the problem in creating a working detective and woman. Because the novels demand fair play, MacDonald's methods are fairly straightforward; she does not detect so much as make both useful and misleading information available to the reader. The detective's personal and professional stories are secondary.

Despite her success and reputation—one ex-con furnishes her references from San Quentin—Lynn MacDonald is constantly faced with problems which arise because she is a woman. Her gender-neutral first name leads one client to assume that he has hired a man and her failure to solve the crime as quickly as this client would like makes him openly threaten to replace her with several male detectives; he is mollified only by remembering her help in the kitchen. Lynn pleads against her dismissal to avoid an unstated humiliation, but she is reluctant to compromise by agreeing to work with others he might hire: " 'Consciously, or unconsciously they work against me, because I am a woman. You don't know them as I do. You don't know their methods, as I do. If you feel that you must have others here, working on the case, allow me to send, at my own expense, for my own assistants; the girls whom I have trained' " (*Moon* 275). This tantalizing hint of an all-woman office is never developed; the client doesn't " 'need any more girls around here' " (*Moon* 275). Two subsequent encounters with male detectives, one fool whom she easily vanquishes and another who betrays her trust, verify the accuracy of MacDonald's reluctance to work with her male counterparts. Otherwise, she never speaks of being a woman in a typically male profession nor describes herself as different from other professional detectives.

Strahan sets Lynn MacDonald off from her male counterparts in other novels by having her bewail her failures just at the moment when she is ready to announce her success. This repeated private and public self-castigation is both unnecessary and demeaning. Dwelling on the job yet to be done might be a way of motivating herself and tamping down overconfidence, but it contrasts with the detective's otherwise collected, professional behavior. It diminishes the detective without adding to the dimensions of her character, advancing the plot, or drawing sympathy from the reader. Her attitude corresponds with that of Matina Horner's female research subjects who feared their own success; MacDonald is set up by Strahan to accept her limitations and undermine her strengths (Horner 173).

Although all these characters are products of the golden age, only Stout's novel of Dol Bonner comes close to the typical game-and-puzzle oriented novels of the period with their cerebral emphasis. The others break most of Ronald Knox's and the Detection Club's rules (especially if Olga Knaresbrook's Indian suspects are allowed to substitute for Knox's proscribed Chinese). Half the characters are neophyte detectives, working on their first cases; they are at least as interested in love and marriage as in detection. Dorothy L. Sayers's critique of young women detectives seems aimed directly at them:

There have also been a few women detectives, but on the whole, they have not been very successful. In order to justify their choice of sex, they are obliged to be so irritatingly intuitive as to destroy that quiet enjoyment of the logical which we look for in our detective reading. Or else they are active and courageous, and insist on walking into physical danger and hampering the men engaged on the job. Marriage, also, looms too large in their view of life; which is not surprising, for they are all young and beautiful. Why these charming creatures should be able to tackle abstruse problems at the age of twenty-one or thereabouts, while the male detectives are usually content to wait till their thirties or forties before setting up as experts, it is hard to say. Where do they pick up their worldly knowledge? Not from personal experience, for they are always immaculate as the driven snow. Presumably it is all intuition.

Better use has been made of women in books where the detecting is strictly amateur. . . . But the really brilliant woman detective has yet to be created. (Sayers in Haycraft 79)

The false dichotomy between career and marriage, between professional success and personal happiness which affects these characters is not typical of their male counterparts. Ngaio Marsh's police detective Roderick Alleyn claims both his professional stature and his wife despite her reluctance to share the details of his work. Sayers's Lord Peter Wimsey saves and then wins Harriet Vane by his detecting ability. And Margery Allingham's Albert Campion gets his wife and "lieutenant" when Lady Amanda Fitton reaches marriagable age. Just as male protagonists are seldom forced to choose, female protagonists are rarely allowed to decide for themselves. Society hands them their proper script. Women's professional lives are stopgaps until or in place of marriage.

This undermining of women detectives did not grow out of the requirements of the genre. Creators of the American hard-boiled novel also writing at this time criticized the elegant and intellectual detective novels as unrealistic and unbelievable. Although correct in their accusations, they were mistaken in their complaints' source; detective fiction only seems realistic, especially in the golden age where even the impression of mimesis is thin. The careful structure and sequence of the works makes them plausible but this, ironically, only makes them seem less real. Inasmuch as little fidelity to society's image occurs throughout the genre, the authors' undercutting of the unlikely woman detective is not necessary in realistic or generic terms. Instead, it is an attempt to control the parameters of reality, to retain women's position and activities unchanged. The golden age of detective fiction which codified so much of the genre's structure reaffirmed the old rules for women's behavior and kept its priorities firmly in place. Authors were willing to sacrifice the genre's usual form to the exigencies of controlling the reading public's perceptions of women. Even ordinarily imperceptive readers could not have failed to recognize how few golden opportunities women detectives—and similar, independent, professional women—really had.

Notes

1. See Rex Stout's parody of Holmesean scholarship, "Watson Was a Woman."
2. In an interesting and informative article, Robert Sampson places Storey in the context of other pulp and women detectives. He is insightful about both Storey and Brickley although succumbing to some stereotypes about female behavior. My own conclusions are based on reading eight of Footner's nine books.
3. Craig and Cadogan perceptively note that "Millicent stands for a very facile idea of moral goodness, and it is this that shapes the content, not the complex of interrelated facts and fabrications that came to characterize the detective story" (48).
4. Although Bonner is described as a successful detective agency owner when she appears briefly in other Nero Wolfe novels, Stout undercuts this (as Frances Baird's success was also minimized) through Wolfe's misogyny and Archie Goodwin's leering sexism.
5. These conclusions are based on my reading of six of the seven Strahan novels.

6

The Hard-Boiled Private Eye and Her Classical Competition: 1928–63

Although the hard-boiled detective was created in 1923 by Carroll John Daly for *Black Mask*, his true definition is Dashiell Hammett's Sam Spade in *The Maltese Falcon* (1930). In a thoroughly pragmatic definition, Michael Nietzel and Robert Baker clarify the basic characteristics: a worldly-wise private investigator who works at the business full time and derives most of his income from these activities; he functions "in the tough but sympathetic tradition made famous by Hammett and Chandler" (229). But many other critics have noted that the private eye is a fantasy figure—an urban cowboy, knight errant, all-American hero (Geherin 3–4). Engaged in a modern quest for truth and the eradication of evil (Grella 104), he is both tough and cynical while becoming ever more isolated from his corrupt society (Margolies 15). He replaces the deductive subtlety of golden age detectives with a sure knowledge of his world and a keen moral sense (Grella 106). As he always succeeds despite the personal cost, Robert Edenbaum finds him beyond the power of his enemies with "godlike immunity and independence" (81). Finally it has been said that he is "the apotheosis of the everyman of good will who, uncertain of his own values and certainly alienated by the values of his time, seeks desperately and mournfully to live without shame, to live without compromise to his integrity. He is everyman's romantic conception of himself: the glorification of toughness, irreverence, and a sense

of decency too confused and almost half ashamed to show itself"
(John Paterson quoted in Ruehlmann 73). Nevertheless, this is an
excessively romantic description of the new American private eye,
as improbable a detective or man or hero as were Poirot and Wimsey.
Indeed, some critics do not see the sharp distinction between the
hard-boiled and the classical investigative novel. John Reilly notes
that the difference is largely in the new stress on characterization
and milieu, but both detectives eventually reconstitute order ("Classic
and Hard-Boiled" 291). And Howard Haycraft balances the claims of
new realism by recognizing that those works are "sharply stylized
and deliberately artificial" (*Murder* 171).

The popularity of detective fiction, both the new American model
and the traditional puzzle, increased during the years of World War
II. The paperback revolution generated by Penguin's low-cost series
and Simon and Schuster's Pocketbooks matched that of the dime
novels during the U.S. Civil War, and for the same reason. The government required large numbers of easily transportable books for the
armed forces (Mandel 66). The civilian population sought its own
versions of escapism; at the height of the 1940 London Blitz, special
air-raid libraries were set up at the entrances to underground shelters
"to supply, by popular demand, detective stories and nothing else"
(Haycraft, "Whodunit" 536).

The war was responsible for many changes. By 1941, a shortage
of workers in Britain led to the demand for some form of national
service from all women and men between ages eighteen and sixty;
so-called conscription of women was also introduced (Calder 267).
Despite sweeping legal provisions, exemptions were numerous: married women living with their husbands and women with children under fourteen qualified (Marwick 291). Nevertheless, between 1939
and 1943, the percentage of employed women doubled; they constituted 27 percent of the labor force in 1939 and 39 percent by 1945
(Oakley, *Housewife* 58–59). Easing the burden of married women
with young children, including the two million added to the work
force during the war, the government established 1,535 day nurseries
for young children by 1945 (Oakley, *Housewife* 58).

In the British press, the housewife was the heroic figure because
she kept house, family, and community intact while also doing war
work (E. Wilson 16). Still, when women were allowed into men's
jobs, it was assumed that a woman's home and family were her first

responsibility; this acted as a brake on opening employment opportunities for women after the war (Penny Summerfield cited in Braybon 39). Wartime agreements to provide women with equal pay were easily evaded (Calder 402) and a Royal Commission established during the war's last year rejected recommendations for equal pay as not in women's best interests—although all three women on the commission dissented (Marwick 293).

As in the United States, military demobilization forced women out of the workplace and back into the home with little attention to their preferences. Family obligations were expected to dominate women's energies. It is not ironic that the Royal Commission on Population recommended that contraceptive advice be made available to married women in 1949 and to the unmarried in 1966. By and large, birth control was considered socially respectable around 1955 and approved by the Church of England in 1958 (Wilson 90). Attention to family size was seen to allow women to provide more and better attention to individual family members. In this context, the 1953 coronation of Elizabeth II was a reassuring symbol of the family and the security of the traditional order.

In the U.S., public attitudes during World War II about the role of women in wartime work established three conditions which set limits on social change: women were replacing men only for the duration of the war; they were expected to retain their femininity; and they were working for patriotic motives rather than self-advancement (Hartman 23). By 1944, for the first time in U.S. history, married women outnumbered single women in the female work force although the lowest participation rate was for mothers aged twenty-five to thirty-four (Anderson 4). In fact, 75 percent of all new women workers during the war years were married (Chafe, *The American Woman* 145). This change is reflected in the statistical shift of Americans approving women's waged work: although in 1938, 80 percent opposed it, by 1943 the number had fallen to 40 percent (Chafe, *The American Woman* 174). War work made other paid work increasingly acceptable in middle-class life by prompting a boom in white-collar occupations deemed respectable for these women (Chafe, *The American Woman* 183).

Neither labor unions nor the government were active in helping women keep their employment or wage gains after the war (Hartman 69). The National War Labor Board's equal pay principle was weak-ened with the assumption that married women would choose to return to homemaking and childrearing while many single women would choose to marry and stop working (Hartman 65–68). Instead, in 1945 75 to 80 percent of women war workers wanted to stay on the job. Despite this, women were pressured to relinquish their positions; between 1944 and 1947 women dropped from 35.4 percent of the labor force to 28.6 percent (Hartman 24).

In postwar years, social welfare and childcare experts called upon women to pay more attention to their maternal duties (Hartman 213). They were supported by the media such as *McCalls* and *Ladies Home Journal* which encouraged femininity and family togetherness, as even women's colleges trained their students to be good mothers and wives (Chafe, *The American Woman* 205–7). Tax deductions on home mortgages and the increasing sales of automobiles helped create suburbia which increased women's isolation from public life. Meanwhile women's gains in education declined: between 1940 and 1950 while their absolute numbers increased, women as a percentage of all college graduates fell from 40 to 25 percent, particularly due to the G.I. bill for which only 2 percent of those elegible were women (Hartman 105–7).

Between 1935 and 1948, a new Hollywood sub-genre developed: films about working women who gave up independence for love and marriage. Film critic Molly Haskell believes that the questioning of sex-roles in the thirties had been possible because of the security of the sexual and social framework. But, by the forties women became a serious threat to male economic dominance (132). This tension was evident as postwar films tried to urge women out of the workforce and into the home (222) while simultaneously knocking them off their pedestals with the dark melodramas of the 1940s (189). This dichotomizing is partially responsible for the prominence of the "professional virgins and teases" in the movies of the fifties (x).

The early female hard-boiled detective and her more classically styled colleagues faced the same tension between private, domestic lives and public, working ones which had been faced by "lady detectives" who preceded them and working women from both war eras. As women's positions in society jockeyed from one extreme to its opposite, so too did the opportunities for Gale Gallagher to walk down mean streets or Mary Carner to let her husband take care of the baby while she investigated murders. But, there were restrictions. Joanna

Russ has suggested that because most plots are male narratives, women cannot be protagonists in crime/adventure/hard-boiled fiction ("Heroine" 8–9). James Naremore agrees that the hard-boiled novel based on Hammett "speaks a masculine ideology" (52).[1] The repetition of "man" and the masculine pronoun in Chandler's essay on the subgenre is not coincidental; simple substitution provides no solution: "The story is this man's [woman's] adventure in search of a hidden truth, and it would be no adventure if it did not happen to a man [woman] fit for adventure. He [She] has a range of awareness that startles you, but it belongs to him [her] by right, because it belongs to the world he [she] lives in" (Chandler 533). Neither adventure, a range of awareness, nor rights are terms commonly associated with women and the world they live in; nor are they a feature of the texts women inhabit. Russ believes, by contrast, that women can star in more classical, puzzle-dominated novels ("Heroine" 8–9). She is correct, but also too hopeful. For some authors, re-visioning the text is possible; but others, socialized to hold conventional and stereotyped views of women, can only imagine a limited and traditional script for their characters. The latter dominate the field. Of Nurse Pomeroy, Flora Hogg, Miriam Birdseye, and the Beagle sisters it must be asked: "What if she were a man in the same circumstances?" Then it is possible to see just how little "material scope for choosing, women characters have" (Robinson 27).

Given Dashiell Hammett's famous model and Raymond Chandler's equally famous defense and definition of the new sub-genre, it is no surprise that the two novels in which the first independent woman hard-boiled detective makes her appearance—Gale Gallagher's *I Found Him Dead* and *Chord in Crimson*—are filled with mixed messages.[2] Not only must the protagonist simultaneously be a competent detective and a lady like her predecessors, she must also be, according to Chandler, "a complete man and a common man and an unusual man . . . a man of honor . . . the best man in his world and a good enough man for any world" (20). Although the end of the 1940s is late for the hard-boiled sub-genre, it is still early for such a change in women's roles, especially in view of the post-World War II message of re-domestication to leave jobs outside the home free for the returning servicemen. Thus, the novel is structured around contradictions. Gale Gallagher of Acme Investigating Bureau drinks bourbon or scotch and smokes but is reluctant to enter a strange bar alone. She neither judges emotion nor understands simple mechanics. Her background includes both police academy and nurses' aide training. Even her own emotional preferences are described in markedly disparate terms: on the one hand, she rejects the weak, defenseless, fragile, feminine appeal of spring in favor of autumn—"Autumn is mature and strong and able to take care of itself" (*Dead* 22). On the other hand, Gale is consistently caught off-guard by her developing romantic relationship with painter Bart Crane—"It's a bad sign when a man becomes your morning prayer" (*Crimson* 72). The character's own sense of contradictions and gender definitions is encapsulated in her description of New York's George Washington bridge: "That always seemed such a feminine structure, so obviously utilitarian by day, so deceptively fragile by night" (*Crimson* 22). Her version of feminine links not only the opposites of utilitarian and fragile but also the more subtle distinctions between the obvious and the deceptive. However, none of the permutations of these opposing pairs accurately parallels Gale's thoughts and behavior; the metaphor is a broken and incomplete one.

As a detective, Gale Gallagher's forte is finding missing persons with unpaid bills, not solving murders, kidnappings, or theft; nonetheless, she does all four both competently and successfully. Despite insisting " 'We're not police. We're for hire. We can pick our own trouble,' " and " 'Crime's out of my line,' " she encounters unexpected crime, trouble, and police problems (*Crimson* 33, 51). Early in the case when a client decides to cancel their contract, she responds angrily: " 'I'm sorry you won't go along with me . . . but actually, there isn't anything you can do about it. Since I've been on this case I've been spied upon, lied about, hit over the head, threatened by cops, and perhaps . . . offered a bribe in an odd sort of way. I'm right in to my eyebrows and I'm either going to drown or come up with the answer' " (*Dead* 96). She protects her clients and her information from the police even when the latter are old family friends who use emotional as well as legal and professional pressure to influence her.

Walking down the mean streets of Manhattan, into tenements or studio apartments, downtown office cubicles and westside abortionists' rooms, country estates and out-of-town alleys, Gallagher encounters the standard challenges of the hard-boiled detective. Corpses litter her path; she is shot at and shoots back; when she cannot bluff her way into a building, she resorts to breaking and entering, climbing down fire escapes or sliding through unlocked windows. Tailed, she eludes her follower; challenged by the police, she deflects their anger or their questions. She hides suspects, gets hit over the head, is threatened by innocent and guilty, is warned off cases. Clients and their families lie, withhold information, and mislead her. They try to withdraw from contracts, leaving her unprotected against police accusations of unprofessional or illegal behavior. Gale refuses to abandon either a case or a line of inquiry: " 'I had an uneasy feeling that I might be working against justice, if not actually for a killer. But working I was. I couldn't quit now. It would haunt me' " (*Crimson* 71).

Despite this catalogue of similarities with her male counterparts, Gale Gallagher is a different detective. Both the pseudonymous author and the first-person narrator conspire in this depiction; on this point they speak with a single voice. Clearly the most significant factor in her life is the memory of her father who died when she was eleven. Quoted over a dozen times in the novels is his wisdom about solving cases, assessing cops and criminals, and following leads. He is credited for both her style and her awareness: "All my life, I followed every big crime as if it were my own particular problem. Dad taught me that. He wanted a son who would grow up to make his mark on the Force. I was a girl, but he treated me as a boy . . . almost. Every big murder, every major crime—as long as it wasn't too bad—he'd tell me all the details and how he'd solve it if he were a detective instead of a cop" (*Dead* 14). Consistently, the recollection of what Dad would say or Dad would do determines how Gale Gallagher behaves despite the improbabilty of her having learned enough in her eleven years before his death. Yet, her father who said that women were too impatient to make good detectives might not have approved of her career. Hank Deery, his friend from the force, emphasizes this possibility: " 'A sweet girl like you in this dirty business, it's enough to make Jim Gallagher spin in his grave. You ought to have a home of your own and be raising babies' " (*Dead* 55). While she doesn't argue with him or with the remembered wisdom of her father, she does serve up coffee and breakfast, placating and pleading for a little extra time to prove her case. This kind of antagonistic behavior between police and detective is not unusual in the hard-boiled novel, but the context in which it occurs serves to undermine her independence, her own professional intelligence, and her credibility. When Deery compliments her detecting ability at the end of *I Found Him*

Dead, " 'Your old man would have got a bang out of this,' " she views this praise as "the Congressional Medal, the Croix de Guerre, and the Apostolic Blessing all rolled in one" (206, 207). The joint male approval of her father, Deery, and Crane is important to Gallagher who has no female colleagues or confidantes.

Introducing a female version of the hero who walks down mean streets, the author is careful continually to remind readers that Gale Gallagher has not lost her femininity by engaging in men's work. She falls in love with a handsome man whose access to beautiful models validates Gale's attractiveness; she is sufficiently angry to resent his missing a date in favor of a hunting trip and passive enough to feed his cat while he is away. She resists other attractive men, thinks about Crane when they're separated, and never declines his invitations, no matter how busy or tired she may be. Gratefully, she accepts his ministrations after finding a corpse: ". . . he hurried me in, like a parent dragging home a runaway child. Too heartsick and tired to resist, I handed him my key. . . . 'Put the chain on after I leave,' he instructed. I nodded meekly. . . . He tipped up my chin, kissed me firmly, then strode out, slamming the door" (*Dead* 130). This instructive male treatment parallels the conclusion of the second novel: " 'I guess I blew my top,' [Dr. Rob Hemming] said ruefully, 'but I grabbed her [his fiancée] up, rushed her out of there, slapped her rear, and sat her in the car. I told her I loved her but I wasn't taking any more of her damned nonsense. And gee,' he finished boyishly, 'it worked.' " (*Crimson* 184). Gale encourages him " 'don't forget the formula' " (*Crimson* 185) as though masculine assertiveness and feminine passivity were inevitable and unquestionable traits. Even more, her assessment validates the appropriateness of the men's behavior, both the right to act and the form which that takes. Both novels' persistent reinforcement of this conventional attitude about sex roles underscore their rejection of the genre's characteristics in favor of restating limited roles for women.

Sixteen times in the two novels Gallagher describes her clothing, hair, or make-up; makes a big point of how much a "girl's" self-assurance depends on her appearance; and longs for a wardrobe that is never rumpled, out at the cleaners, or needing repair. Only once does she relate her choice of clothing to professional concerns: "I had changed to my working clothes—the belted all-weather coat and the Knox hat. I have found it the perfect outfit for my purposes. It's so inconspicuous that no man gives you a second look and any woman assumes you're going to work—forgets she saw you. I could be any of the women who work through the night in a big city—waitress, telephone operator, nurse, small-time entertainer, or—from that look of the taxi driver—even a call girl" (*Dead* 113). Otherwise, her attire is deliberately and carefully chosen to attract attention, even the wrong kind. Early in the case when Crane makes a pass at her, Gale is insulted but later feels responsible and guilty. Her conclusion: "Being a girl is a full-time job; any other profession louses it up . . . and vice versa" (*Dead* 98). Clients and suspects both insist that she doesn't look like a private detective; she puts it down to her youth and slimness but certainly the beaver jacket, gabardine suit, silk faille dress, and mad hat do not add to her professional image.

Persistently, the author links the character's behavior as a detective and a woman. Believing herself followed in *A Chord in Crimson,* she narrates: "I stood still as the crowd would permit, took a cigarette from my pocket, lit it. Often I'd stood just like that while my escort paid a check. Apparently concentrating on my cigarette, I knew that quickening of my pulse when coming up to something strange" (90). Patience, close observation, and awareness are typical and necessary characteristics of a detective; however, here they are tied to the passive behavior expected of a woman being taken care of by a man. Ordinarily, the detective's watchfulness anticipates action but the woman's passivity simply continues; the difference in results arises from a contrast in motives. The same cross-attribution of female and investigative behavior is raised ironically when Gallagher jokes with a friend about being unmarried. "I guess," she says, "the boys figure the average girl is detective enough without marrying a professional" (*Crimson* 137). The pejorative attribution of detecting propensities to women here does not imply a corresponding ability; instead, it suggests a female style versus professional (or male) methods. Gale remains unmarried, the narrative suggests, because prospective spouses recognize that she is too much like a man. Not content with the extent of detecting attributed to typical married women, she defines herself as a professional, a term which is self-contradicting in this context.

Structurally, the conclusions of her two cases continue the mixed messages to the reader. In the first, Gale Gallagher solves the case and finds the kidnapped girl. However, she is trapped by the kidnapper/killer and, like the child she is saving, has to be rescued by the police officer who has been following her. Although she gets credited with solving the case, she clearly would have been right but dead without the assistance of her old family friend, Officer Hank Deery. The second case shifts the pattern: when the police officer is entirely wrong about the case, she sees through his errors and the suspects' maneuverings to solve it correctly. Then she steps back to give the policeman full credit when he unblushingly takes it. In each case, she manipulates the less competent officer. Both novels end with the reestablishment of her feminine priorities. She worries about choosing the right outfit, having her hair done, and canceling her other plans when Bart Crane calls.

However, with her reliance on Dad's wisdom and his old friends, her nonsexual relationship with Bart Crane, and her naive self-confidence, Gale Gallagher is hardly the tough and cynical loner suggested by her male predecessors in the tradition. The most striking and reiterated change in the hard-boiled detective characters who follow her is their acknowledged sexual activity; authors use this as a shorthand for worldly knowledge, cynicism, and experience as though ceasing to be a virgin were a woman's only initiation rite. Conversely, they often make sexual activity the women's only form of experience. The patterns introduced by G. G. Fickling and Henry Kane establish a model for the new hard-boiled hero which holds until the feminist challenges of the 1970s and 1980s. This attitude persists even though men's sexual behavior in hard-boiled novels reinforces rather than replaces all other aspects of their work.

For hard-boiled novelists in particular, parody is the dominant authorial stance. Unlike Jane Austen whom Gilbert and Gubar believe parodied the female gothic in *Northanger Abbey* to reinvest the form with authority, these writers undermine the genre, undercut their protagonists, and ridicule women's challenges to male dominance (135). Like the dime novels, these works clearly and unquestionably inscribe their readers as male. Regarding such encoding, Janet Batsleer and her co-authors distinguish between women's romances (the love story and the marriage plot) and men's romances (the thriller or detective story). Of women reading men's genres they surmise: "[T]hey are inevitably involved in an act of self-alienation, since the only way in which women can have access to popular codes of knowledge, endurance, physical and intellectual agility in these forms is through the mediating codes of masculinity" (73).[3] In reading a masculine genre which replaces the usual male hero with a female one and then diminishes her as both a woman and a detective, women readers have to adopt an antifemale as well as an antifeminist stance unless they become self-consciously resisting readers. Men would suffer fewer setbacks to their self-respect by identifying with the male cops, lovers, and even criminals rather than the exposed, mocked woman detective.

Despite the common base of the tough-guy sub-genre, in eleven novels published between 1957 and 1971, G. G. Fickling created an American detective as unlike Gale Gallagher as possible. The "sexsational private eyeful" Honey West is presented as the hard-boiled woman detective at work: on the one hand, each case provides her with an average of seven corpses and ten attacks where she is either threatened with a gun, shot at, or hit. On the other hand, in solving each case she manages to lose her clothes, five times winding up partially or completely naked both indoors and out. Actually, the numbers of corpses, attacks, and strips increase over the span of the novels so that in the final work, *Stiff as a Broad*, there are eight corpses, sixteen attacks, and seven strips. Given the latter statistic, it almost goes without saying that she winds up in bed with either a suspect, a killer, a friend, or a cop in each of the novels. Only in the final two is this bedding made explicit; otherwise, the reader is as teased with suggestion and innuendo as some of the men she leads on. Regular puns on "private eye" and "private parts" are enhanced for a Broadway production about her life:

> I'm a private eye,
> With a private list of parts,
> That you cannot buy
> In any stores or supermarts.
> My equipment is expensive,
> And sometimes quite recompensive,
> As you can see!
>
> (*Blood and Honey* 25)

Even the settings of the novels contribute to the steamy atmosphere. They include nudist camps, strip joints, beauty contests, movie and stage sets. Discarded underwear litters her office. Other women are unclothed as frequently as Honey West; and sex—sadistic, homosexual, masochistic, paid, transvestite, forced, and frenetic—is as common a feature of the novels as is murder.

The detective herself is described most fully in a dossier compiled for a neurotic who imagines himself Hitler in need of a perfect mate to populate the world. To the reader, none of the information comes as a surprise; in every volume her decision to take over her murdered father's detective agency and search for his killer is repeated. The same is true for her measurements, lack of a brassiere, appearance, attraction to men, etc. In all but the last two novels, the woman who offers, " 'Call me Honey. Call me any time' " engages in a stormy loving-adversarial relationship with Lt. Marcus H. Storm of L.A. Homicide (*Flesh*, frontispiece). He wants to marry her, to force her to give up her profession, to solve her cases before she does, and to rescue her from trouble. Excused as the responses of a man in love who is pushed beyond endurance by concern, his persistent insults are intense: " 'You'll never be able to fill his [her father] shoes! And don't think your body will ever open any doors—unless they're bedroom doors! You're just one flight up from the street as far as I'm concerned. Even a prostitute's got more pride in her profession than you have in yours. . . . Oh, you give me a big, fat bellyache!' " (*Gun for Honey* 33). Neither his attraction to her nor hers to him is plausible in any context except the clichéd caveman scenario or a verbal version of sadistic-masochistic flagellation.

Honey West's choice of a profession is considered inappropriate because she is female and beautiful. Lt. Storm acknowledges the first reason: she should be home raising kids and warming dinner for him when he's late. Several other characters jump to the same conclusion: female private eyes are characters for paperback novels but not real life. Most surprise about Honey's activities, however, is elicited from those who think that her physical attractiveness automatically precludes this type of work. They consider contradictory the combination of a conventionally attractive female with a dangerous and physically demanding job. She is even offered a number of jobs for which the prospective employers find her more suited: stripper, movie or stage star, beauty contestant, or whore as well as the predictable roles of wife and mother.

It is true that Honey West solves the cases she undertakes, frequently outsmarting even the police, although often the growing pile of dead bodies points to the murderer more quickly than her deduction. She uses judo and her .22 caliber gun in the approved manner of her male counterparts in the hard-boiled novel. She even subscribes to their knight-errant code of compassion and rescue: " 'I don't worry if I'm in trouble. But somebody or a lot of somebodies are in trouble and that does bother me' " (*Bombshell* 42). However, this posturing is really of secondary importance in all the novels. Three activities dominate: adventure, sex, and detection; the last never occupies more than a third of the novels. The books clearly have been written to satisfy readers' interest in the first two. Combining the traditionally male adventure story with the sexual focus provided by a female protagonist in a non-traditional profession creates a whole new package to tempt purchasers. That the traditional elements of crime solving either from the classical or the new hard-boiled novels get slighted in this product should be no surprise to readers: the books' covers and blurbs promise as much.

By the time Marla Trent establishes Marla Trent Enterprises in Henry Kane's 1959 novel *Private Eyeful*, using money left by her inventor father who died "stark nude, in the swooning embrace of a startled mistress in a *pied-à-terre* in gay Paree" (12), the nature of the female hard-boiled detective novel has changed almost beyond recognition from Gale Gallagher or Bertha Cool's adventures. The promise of the Honey West novels finds its reinforcement here. Having completed a doctorate in abnormal psychology at Columbia and inherited $600,000, Marla establishes a private detective firm as a way of using both specialized knowledge and specific interest in a lucrative business: " 'Lady private detectives are in short supply—comparatively unique—and there must be a demand for the more deadly of the species. If not, I'll create a demand''(13). Her conservative public relations firm dubs her "The Private Eyeful" in acknowledgment of her shapely figure and sensational blonde looks; the newspapers love both the story and the photos.

The second chapter of *Private Eyeful* introduces the combination of beauty and brains which characterizes the detective. However, while thirty lines are devoted to assessing her shape and the variety of male responses to it and ten are devoted to her short marriage, only three are allocated by the narrator to detail her intelligence and education. These proportions are directly echoed throughout the rest of the book. On 62 of its 160 pages, Kane describes Marla Trent's physical appearance, her sexual activity, or the responses of men to her attractions. One brief example is typical: "The taxi driver remained transfixed, staring, open-mouthed, at the long tapered legs, the slender waist, the full firm-swaying buttocks, as Marla Trent proceeded toward the revolving doors of the tall building. 'Dear God,' breathed the taxi driver, 'a rear end like that is like a benediction. I thank you for favoring me with this peek. Man oh man!' " (21).

Indeed, throughout this novel, both the author and the characters subordinate the investigation of the case to fascination with sexual exploits and descriptions. The ostensible case involves a false conviction, a false accusation, and a pair of murders; until the last thirty pages, however, the only detecting which takes place is her partner Willie's searching the apartments of several suspects. Otherwise, he follows two unimportant leads which allow him to spend most of his time with a nude model or an ex-stripper turned nude tableau model with the stage name of Lakme Good. Only some of their activities, covering over a quarter of the novel, are left to the reader's imagination. Meanwhile, Marla is busy promising and seducing the male suspects so that their attention will be distracted while Willie searches. Her tease-and-withdraw routine backfires once when her ex-husband, Inspector Andrew King of New York Homocide, rapes her on his office floor, claiming to teach her a lesson. Initially she struggles violently but does not scream; later she confesses: " 'In a weird, sick, crazy kind of way, I enjoyed it—I enjoyed every single disgusting second of it' " (37). This validation of rape as both a source of pleasure and a deserved punishment for the character's open sexuality gratifies the fantasies of readers who criticize her behavior or wish to excuse their own appreciation of sexual violence. The novel concludes in her seduction of the plastic surgeon whose testimony helped solve her case, reinforcing the reader's perception of her as a sexual object.

When the case is returned to court with Marla Trent acting as attorney for her client, her newly-purchased brassiere and girdle invite as much attention from the narrator as her unexpected appropriation of the role of legal counsel does from the prosecutor. The reader is shown nothing of Marla's detective ability and little of her legal knowledge. Except for the statement of the easily impressed other characters, readers might conclude that she had no role in the solution of the case. Kane's emphasis on Trent's sexual attributes, the absence of her detecting, and the improbability of her legal activity all serve to blur the image of her as a detective and to reify the reader's impression that the book's appeal is of an entirely different sort.

None of these three women bears much resemblance to Sam Spade, Phillip Marlowe, or the rest of their fraternity. Although gender is not the only contrast, sex-role stereotyping is responsible for most distinctions. Yet, the women are more akin to these men than to the classically styled women detectives of the same period. Their investigations are urban, potentially corrupting, and physical rather than cerebral. Unfortunately, in plot and characterization, the authors imitate the second- or even third-rate rather than the best of the hard-boiled. Not until the 1970s and 1980s does the female private eye match the style and characteristics of her male models. However, novels featuring traditional or classical detectives also directed readers' attentions to the genre's margins. Characters during this time are often improbable and unbelievable. Two who do not conform to the stereotype are striking for their originality in an otherwise lackluster period.

A number of series which flourished during the war years can be generously described only as escapist fiction unaccountably cast in the mystery formula. The employment of the eccentric English and American detectives Miriam Birdseye, Flora Hogg, and the Beagle sisters (as well as Petunia Best, discussed in the chapter on partnerships) is brief and unconsidered. They become detectives by accident or on a whim, knowing almost nothing of the jobs they propose to do.[4]

Nancy Spain's Miriam Birdseye is a British revue actress who, having encountered several murders, decides to open an agency, *Birdseye et Cie—detectives*, and promises to "detect *anything*."[5] But, Birdseye does very little detecting; she is too busy being clever and zany: " 'I am not supposed to catch murderers. I am employed here as a heroin-hunter. How do I know the Union of Incorporated Detectives would allow me to hunt murderers at such a cut rate? I shall write to Mr. Albert Campion. It is a perfect disgrace' " (*Voyage* 148). Whatever the narrator thinks of her having "one of the keenest and clearest brains in the world" (*Voyage* 22), the reader waits in vain for Miriam to solve the case. Perhaps this expectation is too much to demand of someone who hangs a neat black and gold notice, "OUT— GONE TO CRIME," on her office door and accepts a case by stating

" 'Jolly d. [*sic*] of you to ask us, I think' " (*Poison* 19) or " 'Isn't this fun?' " (*Voyage* 27).

The career of Austin Lee's Miss Flora Hogg is equally brief.[6] Although she is the daughter of a police superintendent, it is difficult for the reader to take Flora Hogg seriously as a detective. Called only "Hogg" by her frequent first-person narrator and Watson, she fits the stereotype of an eccentric fiftyish English spinster. A former school-teacher like Miss Silver, she wears a pince-nez, smokes a cigarette after breakfast, goes to church on all the proper days, and doesn't approve of the Inland Revenue. She expects to be paid but has a distinctly haphazard attitude about retainers. She speaks of detecting as "something like collecting stamps or taking up gros point" (*Last Case* 92); acknowledging that a detective ought not to be without a weapon, she suggests an umbrella. Without a car, she conducts her cases by walking or taking the bus, to the detriment of her investi-gations. Needing to follow a suspect, she commandeers two Cam-bridge undergraduates who are bored and have had a bit too much to drink; naturally, they treat the whole matter as a joke. But Miss Hogg is easily tripped up; once she even fails to negotiate a revolving door.

It goes almost without saying that Flora Hogg always solves her cases by a combination of good luck, trances, forced confessions, and intuition which she attributes to psychological insight from her years of teaching. She readily admits that guns, bullet trajectories, foot-prints, and other material clues are beyond her scope. Her vivid imag-ination overcomes the deficiency. In *Miss Hogg and the Dead Dean*, she explains her methodology: " 'My forbears had a very low opinion of episcopal clergymen. And, of course, I have a romantic tempera-ment. I was brought up to think all baronets were, *ipso facto*, wicked. Bold bad baronets figured in lots of the books my mother used to read, and which I read as a child. So Sir Andrew was my first suspect, naturally, and then when I saw the archdeacon with him in the Mitre, I moved the archdeacon up into first place' " (189). The police su-perintendent who is told that her intuition needs material to work on queries aptly, " 'Like compost?' " (*Bronte* 133). Results—upholding justice and capturing criminals—are certainly important to her; but she admits another pleasure: "In this job . . . you enjoy all the delights of not minding your own business with none of the feelings of guilt" (*Call In Miss Hogg* 65). This sort of frivolity pervades Austin Lee's novels; they achieve their humor through stereotyping and misogynistic mockery.

A pair of eccentric American spinsters created by Torey Chanslor parallels the British examples; neither country escapes the stigma of foolish women clearly out of their league trying to solve serious crimes. Inheriting the family business from their brother without ever having asked what it was, Amanda and Lutie Beagle of "The Beagle Detective Agency—Licensed Private Investigating Bureau" are the only functioning legal or contractual female partnership in detective fiction. In their sixties, the sisters and their Watson-narrator are the New England version of the eccentric spinster already seen in Flora Hogg. Lutie Beagle is bubbly, occasionally foolish, and serenely irrelevant whereas her sister Amanda is "full of prideful common sense" (*First* 5). The contrast between the two and the astonishment of their Watson is designed to add humor to Chanslor's novels.

When they set off for New York City with their obscene parrot and the household cat in a basket, the sisters have very different motivations for their new professional activity. For Amanda it is a duty and a responsibility left to them; for Lutie it is a dream of adventure. Amanda sets the business tone: no marital cases inasmuch as " '[w]hen people get married they get themselves into trouble. They can get themselves out!' " (*First* 29). But when a client calls about a decapitated body, Amanda assures the rest of the firm " 'the files contain a very complete and satisfactory record of Mr. Bynam's antecedents' " and so they take the case (*First* 33). Amanda, who is always efficient, logical, concise, and specific in her investigations and reports, is also always wrong; meanwhile, Lutie, who is apparently haphazard, chatty, and intuitive, invariably uncovers the murderer. Rightly enough, little is said by anyone in the novels about their detective skills except for their mutual self-congratulations. When the police and the reader unravel Lutie's convoluted notions about motive, suspicions, timetables, etc., of course, the plot holds together; but this convention is merely borrowed for an opportunity to write an amusing story of two lively elderly New England spinsters whose lives are suddenly and dramatically changed. Because another formula would have sufficed, detection is hardly the point of these novels.

In fact, detection has been virtually irrelevant in all these examples of classical detective fiction in the years following the golden age. Therefore, it is a surprise to discover that the period also contains two of the more interesting, cross-stereotyped characters covered in this analysis. They are unlike both their counterparts and each other: British and American, elderly spinster and young married mother, ex-governess and department store security staff. Miss Maud Silver and Mary Carner Whittaker challenge gender-role stereotyping in detective fiction over a span of thirty years. Their fictional strength is most noticeable during the fifteen years following World War II when women's traditional roles were being reinforced by both British and U.S. governmental and media propaganda.

Introduced in 1928, Miss Maud Silver, retired governess turned detective, does not appear again until 1937; the flood of thirty-three novels featuring her lasts until 1961.[7] Patricia Wentworth may have reestablished this reassuring figure deliberately in the pre-war years for readers who preferred escape to a safe and secure world. In her first appearance, *Gray Mask*, Miss Silver is already an investigator of some reputation who discovers facts which her client tries to conceal. But she does not solve the mystery; the client and his lover do that. Nor does she rescue them alone; instead, she has to be coaxed by their friend. Once involved, however, she accurately reads clues and even provides the "jemmy" for the rescue (317).

Miss Silver's appearance and gender pose problems for her clients, criminals, and the police. She is introduced in a way which suggests the difficulty even her admirers have in describing her: " 'A sleuthess . . . has old Sherlock boiled. . . not exactly what you'd call a little bit of fluff. . .' " (*Gray Mask* 69). The police are sometimes uncomfortable with her participation in an investigation. Only Detective Inspector Frank Abbott whom she indulgently regards as an impudent nephew is consistently pleased by her arrival—she is "Maudie the Mascot" to him (*The Key* 112). Others, including one whose governess she had been, suspect her of being a witch or having something up her sleeve or pulling rabbits out of hats. Nonetheless, they recognize her advantage: "He [former student] was thinking how thoroughly she looked the part [governess]—so thoroughly that no matter what she talked about or where she talked about it, no one would dream that her conversation could have the slightest interest for anyone at all" (*Danger Point* 151). Other characters have similar problems: combined with her own unquestionable personal authority and intelligence is the reminder she brings of their childhoods where a teacher, nanny, or other powerful figure could call them to task. Frequently, they respond to her as they had done years before with other authority figures. Miss Silver takes advantage of this reflected authority and the comforting reminder of a safer, less troubled time to draw them out. Some find this reassuring; others react far differently: "He became aware of a thought penetrating and illuminating whatever it touched. The prim, old-maidish manner which was its cloak began by amusing him, but before long the amusement changed to something not unlike discomfort. He felt a little as if he had picked up an old lady's work-bag and found it to contain a bomb" (*The Key* 103). Usually only criminals find her entirely negligible; this fact raises both her suspicions and the reader's.

As a detective, Miss Silver operates in a very subjective manner. Although she insists to clients that she will not undertake a case to protect anyone, but only to determine the truth, it is clear that among the raft of suspects in the typical country-house murder story she has her favorites. Her method is typically to discern some motive for the crimes already committed and to work backward through likely suspects to determine the criminal. Her investigations consist primarily of careful observation of people on their own territory, usually as a social visitor rather than a professional questioner; hardly anyone openly refuses to talk with Miss Silver. Her insatiable curiosity about other people's lives and her genuine interest in them is apparent. Additionally, as Frank Abbott notes, she finds the human race glass-fronted, unable to hide its thoughts and emotions from her. Like Agatha Christie's Miss Marple, she is adept at psychological analysis and often suspects certain characters based on stereotyped analysis of their characters.

Miss Silver is always aided in her investigations by her close, if sometimes unwanted, association with the police. They allow her to read transcripts of their interviews, to sit in on their questioning of suspects, and to check out situations where a policeman might not get answers from a suspect. Believing herself to be scrupulously just, she insists that she would not withhold information from the authorities; however, when she suspects that they would misunderstand or mishandle that knowledge, she does keep it from them. In fact, she notes that "[s]he did not regard herself as something to be kept handy [by the police], nor did she expect to be so regarded" (*Latter End* 159). Miss Silver's attitude is strongly at odds with historical capitalistic tendancies to use women as a surplus labor force, taking them up when needed and discarding them when the need had passed. It also contradicts the widespread perception of spinsters as surplus women, half of a couple which never materialized. Valuing herself equally with the male-structured and controlled police force, Miss Silver is clearly a force to be reckoned with. Indeed, she is quite satisfied with herself: "She took her new profession very seriously indeed. She was a servant of Justice and of the Law, she played her part in restraining the criminal and protecting the innocent, she made many devoted friends, and all her needs had been met" (*Deep End* 9).

Two factors which raise questions about her portrayal as a successful detective are related to her overall image. Several times in each of the novels her clothing and appearance are described: she looks like a relic from an old photograph album of Victorian times labeled "The Governess." Her tightly braided hair is secured in a net with only a fringe showing at the front; her dresses often look like those thrust on elderly ladies by strong-willed saleswomen. Her hats are old and dowdy; her coat merely old. Not until the 1954 novel, *Poison in the Pen,* is there any explanation which puts these persistent descriptions into the framework of her professional activities where she is, unlike the elderly ladies, competent and authoritative: "If Miss Silver's own garments were quite incredibly out of date, it was because she liked them that way and had discovered that an old-fashioned and governessy appearance was a decided asset in the profession which she had adopted. To be considered negligible may be the means of acquiring the kind of information which only becomes available when people are off their guard" (128). Similarly, the knitting which occupies her in every novel—each averaging twenty-four and reaching as many as fifty-three references to baby shawls, booties, coatees, and twin sets—becomes part of the frame of reference in which potential clients see her: " 'Her name is Maud Silver. Louisa says she has solved many difficult cases besides being an extremely expert knitter' " (*The Benevent Treasure* 236). Although this activity is also described as part of her professional disguise, allowing her to put suspects at ease by the homey sound of clicking needles, it has the effect of defining her. The novels eventually acknowledge these parts of her professional appearance; nonetheless, they also make it clear that both her style of dress and her constant knitting are continued when she is at home or in the company of the police whom she has no cause to deceive.

It may be to counteract this dowdy, out-of-date, spinsterish attitude that Wentworth mentions Miss Silver's ancestor Louisa Bushell, "[a] formidable pioneer of women's rights in an age which saw no reason why they should have any, since a gentleman could always be relied on to give a lady his seat" (*Pilgrim's Rest* 445). Miss Silver also recognizes the handicaps in being a woman so she will not allow the police or clients to deflect her from her responsibilities because their judgment as men is to be deferred to. Of this Wentworth writes: "Miss Silver had no dislike for the male sex. In their proper place they could be very useful indeed. She admired all their good qualities, and regarded their failings with indulgence. But occasionally she reflected, as she was doing right now, that they were too much inclined to believe in their own opinions, and too much convinced that these opinions must be right" (*She Came Back* 134–35). This entire quotation is laden with negatives and qualifiers; the specific criticism, when it comes, is couched in superlatives. The assessment is based on sweeping critical generalizations which are not minimized by her grudging acknowledgment of men's limited virtues. Her patronizing tone is not reserved exclusively for men, however. Although she thinks highly of women, she cannot "credit them with any abstract passion for justice" (*Pilgrim's Rest* 154). In this observation, Wentworth anticipates Carol Gilligan's research demonstrating that whereas men are concerned with an ethic of rights based on noninterference with others, women base their ethic on responsibilities to others. In fact, the detective herself alternates between the two modes of thinking; her passion for abstract justice is reserved for criminals while her sense of responsibility extends to the unjustly suspected. Fortunately, she never seems to confuse the two groups.

If, especially in the earlier novels, Miss Silver does not always identify the criminal from among a logical group of several suspects or solve the crime before a confession has been overheard or offered, in that she is not particularly unlike her counterparts in other detective novels. What sets her off from the successful male detectives is her sex, and what sets her off from the rest of her sex is her success. Police, clients, criminals, and even readers who are initially amused or unimpressed with the perennially dowdy spinster find the tables turned on them so that they are forced to regard her with respect and admiration.

It is unlikely that readers would have been as enthusiastic about Mary Carner, who does not relinquish her career with either marriage or maternity.[8] Although her behavior as a detective is fairly conventional in the early novels beginning in 1938, Zelda Popkin's protagonist occupies an anomalous position in the final three books. It is a position which, like Miss Silver's, has negative undertones in a generally positive image for women.

Carner's career develops gradually. With a background of five years in detection which includes working for hotels and private agencies, she is employed as one of the detectives in Blanchard's Department Store where her ability to look like another shopper is her best disguise. Her supervisor is her husband. Although she quits her job briefly, she is otherwise employed as the principal assistant to the head of store security throughout five novels, her marriage and honeymoon, and the adoption of a child. Despite this natural opportunity to investigate crime professionally, only Carner's first murder takes place on the job; in all others she is either a friend of the victim or brought into the case by propinquity. She works without pay, without clients, without legitimate professional status in the case much as an amateur might. This choice of plots on Popkin's part unfortunately replaces the female detective's career with a hobby.

Nonetheless, women's professional careers are seriously addressed here. In *Time Off for Murder*, a member of Carner's career woman's club/network is murdered. Recognizing the mixed messages which such women receive, the novel portrays the network members as cynical, fatigued, or "smart"; a man who addresses their meeting urges them back into home and motherhood. However, as Mary investigates the case, she can depend on their professionalism, their contacts, and their experience to help her succeed. Even the victim turns out not to have been killed in a foolish love affair but because, as an attorney, she recognized her lover as head of a racketeering organization. A different professional is also defended when Mary bitterly defines prostitution as a "crime [young girls] couldn't and wouldn't commit if men hadn't made the kind of rotten world this is" (206). In neither case does Popkin shrink from attributing at least part of women's fate to their attempts to survive in a gender-biased, stereotyped world which is controlled by those who do not wish to share their power or privilege with women.

This serious if not unmixed attention to women at her club is a provocative counterpart to the many public reactions to Mary Carner's profession. Initially she encounters disbelief and often both serious and mock-serious warnings to be careful or to keep her distance. The police react more strongly. Although one detective inspector considers her the best detective he knows, others are less impressed. Whenever she oversteps her limits in their eyes, the reprimands and rejoinders always take the form of gender-related insults: " 'Take a powder. Crime's no place for a woman. I always said it. I say it now. . . . Go join the Quiz Kids. That's your speed all right. That's what you can do' " (*No Crime* 214). One cop even describes himself as humble for merely being willing to talk with her about a case. The police seem to agree with the only criminal who ever outwits her, however briefly; he believes that it is dangerous for women to be clever because it gets them in trouble. Usually Carner's trouble is that she is the smartest person present. The combination of her independent status, her ability, and her gender elicits the same hostility found between cops and hard-boiled private eyes; but Carner is not a hard-boiled detective perpetually jabbing at the police, which makes their defensively motivated, offensive behavior seem like an automatic response to stereotypes.

Gender roles and societal expectations play a more pervasive role in these novels than mere woman baiting by clients, criminals, or truculent police officers. In describing the marriage and family life of Mary Carner and Chris Whittaker, Popkin turns conventions upside down. At the office, although he is the boss and she the principal assistant, they work as a team to solve their first murder case in the store. When Carner begins to solve cases off-the-job, Whittaker assumes the background position of supportive spouse ordinarily allotted to the woman. Ironically, no one challenges either his masculinity or his professional competence for this role reversal although his wife is insulted for hers. At every opportunity he extolls her professional virtues. When she is away working on a case, he keeps the household running; when their housekeeper is unavailable, he takes care of their adopted daughter. He even foregoes opportunities to share in an investigation because he is busy with their child.[9] When he could interfere, telling her what cases to accept or reject, he does not. When he might try to protect Mary by directing or controlling her actions during the investigation, he restrains himself. When he could assume her desire for his professional assistance in a case, he waits for an invitation. And when asked to help, he does so without taking over the case as though she were incompetent. In short, he treats her personally and professionally with respect. Even when he once comes—irritated and worried—to her assistance, his aggravation is more friendly than threatening as she refuses to placate him. Although their relationship is marked with occasional frustration, disapproval of some of the other person's actions, and a certain amount of meddling, they display affection and tolerance rather than possession or power seeking. Such behavior is virtually nonexistent in other novels about women detectives.

Zelda Popkin's reconsideration of male as well as female roles emphasizes how the cultural givens are obvious, unquestioned norms in novels from *The Lady Detective* and *The Capture of Paul Beck* to those published in the 1980s. To the extent that neither Carner nor Whittaker resembles the conventional stick figures of the typical marriage plot, Popkin's reversal challenges those inherited conventions for both her texts and her readers. In that respect, these novels contrast with the suppressed discourse of the other works in this study which eventually submerge the detective story. Using Macherey's theory of "gaps," Newton and Rosenfelt write: "What a literary text does not say, therefore, becomes as interesting as what it does say. The discourse suppressed tells us as much as the discourse expressed, for omission throws the margins of a text's production into relief, allowing us to see the limits and boundaries of what it posits as the real" (xxiii). In Popkin's novels there are no extended passages on role reversals, house husbands, or shared parenting; these terms and the practices they describe were unmentioned and probably largely unknown in America of the 1940s. Yet the concepts are present in these narratives despite the lack of a language to describe them. Similarly, earlier novels had left undiscussed the legal, financial, and social reasons why women would abandon their careers upon marriage; but their structures insist upon the strength of these unacknowledged imperatives.

A significant "gap" in the novels, however, is Popkin's silence on marriage as an institution. In a series of novels full of unhappy, discordant, and even brutal marriages, the cautionary tales implied by their messages are subsumed under the inferred heading of bad marriage, offering the explicit contrast of good marriage in the Carner-Whittaker alliance. The happiness, success, and satisfaction which Mary and Chris enjoy is attributed to their good luck in having chosen a compatible partner; the pain of the other marriages, Popkin implicitly suggests, results from poor personal choices. This markedly conservative view of marriage, putting all the blame for marriages which go wrong on the individuals involved, refuses to see marriage in its political, economic, and social setting. Governed by law, supported by custom, and validated by society, marriage is an institution which has weight and power far beyond the preferences and needs of the individuals involved. Attributing the Whittakers' happy marriage to their own efforts accords with the conservative nature of the genre but is out of line with Popkin's otherwise imaginative and unstereotyped variation on the standard.

No doubt the war years and their aftermath are responsible for the two varieties of detective novels discussed in this chapter. Escapism flourished: there was both the security of a familiar world represented by Grace Pomeroy or Maud Silver and the foolish, lighthearted gaity of Hogg, Birdseye, and Honey West, for the early hardboiled novels were no less frivolous than their classical counterparts. It is not surprising that the "war-relief" was gender-linked: security is represented here by the caretaking, nurturing women who protect their charges during vulnerable moments of childhood and illness; improbable adventures happening to types who could never be soldiers briefly kept painful wartime reality from intruding. Yet, this is also the era of Rosie the Riveter; more so than in the first world war, women competently took over "men's work." And, at war's end, the majority did not want to give it up. Unlike Nurse Pomeroy and the others, British and American women war workers did not welcome reinstatement in women's jobs or in the home.

Maud Silver and Mary Carner represent two ends of the spectrum of possibilities. One is the never-married woman who reared other people's children and is glad to be doing her own kind of work with adults for a decent income. The other is the young married woman who chooses her husband well so she does not have to make the more typical choice between career and family, ambition and love. Together, Silver and Carner provide alternatives for both female and male readers not satisfied with texts or lives which reduce women to sex objects or silly fools.

However, these novels are not the models taken up by subsequent writers. Instead, the hard-boiled detective story becomes the dominant mode; here, the emancipated woman is not defined through voting or supporting herself but by her sexual experience. Virginity is a metaphor for ignorance, and explicitly described sexual activity is supposed to signal equality with men in both society and fiction. By the late 1960s the split between the two sub-genres had become obvious; at least for women, the classical novel had become the refuge of the amateur while the hard-boiled story promised, however inaccurately, the gritty life of the professional detective.

Notes

1. Agreeing with Russ, Dennis Porter is far more explicit about women's exclusion:

   To be hard-boiled and to have retained heroic integrity was to be a man. The culture had generated no precedent for a tough-talking, worldly-wise woman, capable of defending herself in the roughest company, who also possessed the indispensable heroic qualities of physical attractiveness and virtue. A woman in the private eye's role would have been conceivable only as fallen comic, as Belle Watling or Annie Oakley.
     Thus the new ethos of hard-boiled detective fiction was not only anti-English and antielitist, it was also antifeminist. The equation that makes gentility equal femininity, and the civilized life a woman's estate, is a well documented fact of American cultural life. . . . A linguistic double standard operated, making such language [vernacular slang, cursing, bad grammar, etc.] in a female mouth the sign of a bumpkin or a fallen woman. In dominant culture the implications of such a taboo are far-reaching. Unusually attractive women in popular literature tend to be either ladies or whores, nature's slobs or sexually overripe dropouts. (183–84)

2. A. A. Fair's Bertha Cool, who predates Gallagher by eight years, is discussed in the chapter on partnerships. Women appeared throughout the thirties as hard-boiled detectives in the pulps but are not found in sustained, full-length works (Drew).

3. The same would be true if men read women's genres, but statistics suggest that they do not.

4. Introduced as faithful nurse and Watson in a more serious vein than Hogg, et al., Miss Grace Pomeroy joins the Keene Detective Agency

when the psychiatrist who employs her enlists in the service. But, like Millicent Newberry, she is uncomfortable in this unfamiliar guise. Throughout Anna Mary Wells's *Murderer's Choice*, the only novel in which she figures as the protagonist, Pomeroy vacillates between the roles of nurse and sleuth. Somewhat surprisingly, she sees both professions standing outside society's sex-role expectations despite the general public's usual assumption that nursing is a natural female occupation and detecting a logical masculine one. She reminds herself: "Neither a nurse nor a detective claims the traditional privileges of a woman" (97). Where the two responsibilities conflict, she opts for the nurse's role. Miss Pomeroy's feelings about this job are mixed. On the one hand, she apologizes to her employer at the Agency for her apparent lack of success with the case; on the other, she also believes that she doesn't care whether she keeps the job or not: "On the whole she rather thought she preferred to lose it if every case was going to prove as harrowing as this of the Osgoods" (230–31). It was easy enough for her to abandon detection as a career; the alternative was far more comfortable.

5. These conclusions are based on reading three of the six Spain novels.

6. These conclusions are based on reading four of the nine Lee novels.

7. Although Miss Silver was created during the golden age and the novels fit the definition of works favored then, she is placed in this chapter because it chronologically covers the period of the thirty-two other novels. The influence of the golden age on the genre was still strong in subsequent decades although that is not generally evident in the other novels considered in this chapter.

8. Like earlier authors whose protagonists are married, Popkin evades opportunities to show Carner as a sexual being; the inevitable inferences raised by childbirth are suppressed because this couple adopts their child.

9. There are parallels here with Katherine Hepburn and Spencer Tracy in *Woman of the Year* (1941) where Tracy, as Molly Haskell notes, was allowed to combine love and ambition in a way that Hepburn was not.

7

Modern Detectives: 1972–84

Detective fiction in the postwar period has been superseded by what the critic and novelist Julian Symons calls the crime novel.[1] The earlier emphasis on plot and puzzle is replaced by attention to psychological motivation and character development (178–79). Writers as distinctly different as Patricia Highsmith and Emma Lathen are included in this category although Lathen writes detection-oriented fiction having evident parallels with the golden age whereas Highsmith explores the motivations of apparently ordinary people who find themselves committing crimes.

A variation of the crime novel sometimes dated from Hillary Waugh's 1950s novels is the police procedural. Its protagonist is unlike the police-hero of the classical model such as Roderick Alleyn or Allan Grant; instead, she or he is caught up in the routine of police investigation, often checking on more than one crime at a time, usually part of a team of officers who share both the work and the credit. The best known are Ed McBain's 96th-precinct novels.

Bridging the space between the psychological and procedural novels are the official investigators who are treated as though they operated with individual license. The novels often contrast the limited position of the police with widespread social and even governmental corruption. Certainly, Nicholas Freeling's Inspector Van der Valk and Lillian O'Donnell's Nora Mulcahaney illustrate this development. Despite their positions, they are less involved with routine police work than with the implications of crime in an increasingly divided society.

Nonetheless, not all postwar fiction follows these forms. Instead, Mickey Spillane's Mike Hammer novels dominate the best-seller lists (Hackett, *Eighty Years* 50) and his imitators fill bookstore shelves. Noting Hammer's status as a fifties cultural hero, Kay Weibel writes, "Spillane's treatment of women is particularly significant . . . since the hard-boiled detective formula, of which Spillane is the master seller, is the first fictional formula for men to focus explicitly on sexual relationships between men and women" ("Mickey Spillane" 114). Mike Hammer adheres firmly to a double standard which conveniently dichotomizes all female characters. Conventionally good women are domestically used while being idealized; bad, i.e., sexual, women are brutally used and killed.

But what of real women? There's no doubt that women's increasing rejection of the postwar propaganda which encouraged their devotion to domestic responsibilites provoked a backlash of interest in the easy answers offered by Hammer and his cohorts. The *Playboy* philosophy provided one view of women through redefining the conventional male role. From the magazine's first issue in 1953, it has offered a coherent program for male rebellion in its critique of marriage, strategy for rebellion, and utopian vision. Certainly it helped promote the sexual revolution of the 1960s (Ehrenreich 50).

In Britain, this revolution led to revisions in laws affecting individuals' sexual behavior: in 1967 private expressions of homosexuality were decriminalized; the Abortion and Family Planning Acts were passed. In 1969 the Divorce Reform Act succeeded; by 1970, contraceptive advice was officially available to women over sixteen (Bouchier 27). Similar legal changes affected women in the United States: the combined effect of the birth-control pill, the Civil Rights movement (begun in the 1950s but coming into its own in the early sixties), and the demonstrations against the Vietnam War all highlighted new attitudes about public and private responsibilities.

The rise of a new women's movement in both countries following the publication of Betty Friedan's *The Feminine Mystique* in 1963 signaled a potential change for women's self-image and societal position. Just a year after its founding in 1966 the National Organization for Women drafted a Bill of Rights for Women which demanded: 1. An equal rights constitutional amendment; 2. The enforcement of the law banning sex discrimination in employment; 3. Maternity leave rights in employment and social security benefits; 4. Tax deduction for home and child-care expenses for working parents; 5. Child care centers; 6. Equal and non-segregated education; 7. Equal job training opportunities and allowances for women in poverty; 8. The right of women to control their reproductive lives (Oakley, *Subject* 28). British women's demands at the Ruskin College (Oxford) conference in 1970 were similar: 1. Equal pay; 2. Equal education and opportunity; 3. Twenty-four-hour nurseries; 4. Free contraception and abortion on demand. Their manifesto read, in part, "women in our society are oppressed. We are economically oppressed: in jobs we do full work for half pay, in the home we do unpaid work fulltime. We are commercially exploited by advertisements, television and press, legally we often have only the status of children. We are brought up to feel inadequate, educated to narrower horizons than men. This is our specific oppression as women" (*Shrew* 3.6 [July 1971] cited in Oakley, *Subject* 30). Most of these critiques and demands remain unmet.

Among the most potent conservative forces defining and reflecting society's view of women are the mass media. In prime-time television programming only situation comedies balance the numbers of female and male characters or show a female character equal with the males. By contrast, adventure and dramatic shows repeat old stereotypes about heroic men and passive women (Weibel, *Mirror* 59). Stereotyping in advertising can almost be taken for granted. A 1971 study reported in the *Journal of Marketing Research* saw passivity in only two of the following typical images of women in ads: women don't do important things; women don't make important decisions; woman's place is in the home; and men regard women primarily as sexual objects, not as people (Weibel, *Mirror* 167). It is difficult to understand how the study's author calls any of these images non-passive.

If society has been loathe to grant women equal rights and opportunities and the detective formula has retained its earlier modes while gradually developing commercially viable new ones, it should be no surprise that women detectives are not at the forefront of social emancipation or fictional innovation. Many of the novels I discuss in chapters 7, 8, and 10 reflect attitudes current in the 1950s and 1960s although written from the mid–1970s through 1985. As a variation on the original rather than the primary model herself, the woman detective trails several steps behind her male counterpart. Novels featuring women as detectives in the various sub-genres appear on the market only after the new fictional model with male protagonists has proved successful.

This fact merely reinforces the point that feminist scholars have made about both human enterprise and the academic fields which study that activity. As it is commonly assumed that male behavior and experience are the norm for the entire human race, readers find in fiction and criticism "a truncated and distorted picture of women, which reflects and justifies our society's oppressive stereotypes of what it is to be female" (DuBois et al. 36). To be female is to be not-male; female and male authors I have considered throughout this book have known that society cannot accept women's functioning like men while retaining the attributes of women. But these authors have not simply written women's traditional stories; instead, they have apparently challenged the men's stories with women heroes. In showing the efforts and some successes of women detectives, authors offer readers an excitement unmatched by staying with the old formula. By undercutting those successes to reveal a stereotyped picture of women inevitably limited by their gender, authors reinforce the conservative attitudes of the genre, going even beyond its traditional support for power and property. Although their treatment of women protagonists conflicts with generic demands, authors seem unaware of their dual sabotage. Upholding patriarchal values at the expense of formulaic integrity again attests to the strength and importance of gender bias. Sex-role stereotyping is so automatic, readers and writers alike perceive it as natural and logical even when it undercuts the novels they produce or consume.

The different attitudes and expectations authors and readers have of professional women and men become clear in comparing female and male characters created by a single writer. The author of six novels about Chief Superintendent Adam Dalgleish, P. D. James has also created Cordelia Gray, an independent investigator. Dalgleish is an admirable and interesting detective and hero of the novels; he is neither infallible nor inept. As a poet, he displays talents beyond routine investigative work; as a person, he is charming, articulate, intelligent, and occasionally moody. In short, Adam Dalgleish is a plausible human being. However, he is also a very successful detective, having worked his way up in the hierarchy to an important position which the novels clearly demonstrate he deserves. Working to his advantage are the stature of his official position, his age, his experience and success, and his gender as well as his structural position as the hero of the novels. Cordelia Gray shares only the position as nominal hero of her two novels; this is not enough to compensate for her limited experience, youth, and particularly her gender.

Cordelia Gray is undoubtedly one of the better known female detectives of the seventies; the title of her first appearance seems to summarize social opinion of her and her sister professionals—*An Unsuitable Job for a Woman*. In Cordelia's case, the accusation initially seems more than slightly justified. In her early twenties, she has neither the qualifications nor experience appropriate to investigative work unless one were to count a brief time spent carrying messages between her revolutionary father and his comrades. However, she considers herself more his opposite, having been raised in foster homes and a convent school with no real memory of her mother who died at her birth and only fragmented images of the father who ignored her until she could be useful in the movement. He had forestalled her scholarship examination for Cambridge and set her to domestic tasks for the comrades who, although they believed in sexual equality, could not be bothered to practice it. So, always Cordelia turns in her mind to her mother for affection and reassurance: "Gradually out of a childhood of deprivation she had evolved a philosophy of compensation. In her imagination she had enjoyed a lifetime of love in one hour with no disappointments and no regrets. . . . This belief in her mother's love was the one fantasy which she could still not entirely risk losing. . . . Now, in imagination, she consulted her mother. It was just as she expected: her mother thought it an entirely suitable job for a woman" (*Unsuitable Job* 21–22). This reassurance is, of course, emotional and not based strictly on an assessment of Gray's own suitability. She has become a detective quite by accident, having been taught the craft and invited to join the agency by its owner; but she originally was hired as a temporary typist. What Cordelia Gray learns comes secondhand through Bernie Pryde from Chief Superintendent Dalgleish; the value of Bernie as an instructor/interpreter can be ascertained from the fact that he was fired from the CID for general incompetence. Cordelia even wonders whether she accepted the offer of partnership in a fit of depression or perverse masochism, so sadly unprofitable and unsuccessful is the agency. When Bernie commits suicide, leaving her the business, Cordelia can barely imagine how to go on except that she is determined to honor her friend's memory by trying.

Despite similarities in Gray's style of investigation and threats to her safety, the two cases presented in *An Unsuitable Job for a Woman* and *The Skull Beneath the Skin* are widely divergent. In the first, her ostensible instructions to discover why Mark Callender committed suicide mask the murderer's desire to learn who interfered with his carefully staged crime. She penetrates the false directions, identifies both the motive and the murderer, and brings the case to a morally satisfying if legally horrendous conclusion. She relies less on the skills Bernie taught her than on her native intelligence and sympathy; she makes a difficult ethical decision at the conclusion and has the moral strength to maintain it. The case and its solution, at least, are appropriately scaled for a young, inexperienced detective. Although the second novel was published ten years later, Cordelia Gray is only slightly older and, in the brief interim, her agency has developed a reputation for finding lost pets. It is surprising then to find her being hired to safeguard a famous actress from threatening letters or possible harm. Given the genre's demands, it is not surprising that she fails and the actress, Clarissa Lisle, is brutally murdered. In a closed world (on an island) with an abundance of plausible suspects, she assuages her guilt over the murder by searching for the criminal. Nevertheless, there is another death. Her own murder is attempted, and a callous rational explanation is offered by the criminal. The criminal's disavowal of his supposed actions, the confusion surrounding a second suspect, and Cordelia's own ambivalence make for a much less satisfying conclusion. Finally, she decides only this: "Suddenly she felt inviolate. . . . She would tell the truth, and she would survive. Nothing could touch her" (*Skull* 416).

Cordelia Gray's character and personality are developed slowly throughout the two novels, with changes and growth apparent from the first to the second. Whereas she was initially satisfied with a bedsitting room in Bernie's house or a sleeping bag in an abandoned cabin while out on a case, later she is pleased to be able to buy her own flat with an unanticipated inheritance from her father. Her "obsessive need to be able to pack the whole of her wardrobe into one medium sized suitcase like a refugee perpetually ready for flight" gives way to three drawers and a cupboard full of the clothes in which she takes an intense but spasmodic interest (*Unsuitable Job* 54). She looks considerably younger than her age and often worries that her appearance and behavior mark her as unprofessional. The fact that no one suspects she is a detective without her telling them reinforces this assumption. Her frequent moves from one foster home to another in childhood and the demands of those families that she be always happy have left her slow to confide in people or reveal her emotions; self-control is vitally important to her sense of self. Still, her feelings run deep; she has a fairly demanding moral and emotional code.

In view of Gray's obvious intelligence, powers of observation, and deductive sense, it is difficult to understand why she never really seems like a modern detective. Insofar as the usual detective script is concerned, she is too young, too sweet and sincere, too unsure of her ability. On the one hand, she seems to lack the cynicism or experience which seems necessary to understand crime and evil; yet she lies directly and knowingly to the police in both novels to defend her ethical code. She seems a combination of experienced naiveté and innocent worldliness. The police assistant in *The Skull Beneath the Skin* speaks of her "gentle, uplifted face, the immense and resolute eyes, the delicate hands folded like a child's in her lap" (233). Adam Dalgleish complains bitterly of feeling as though he has corrupted a child in *An Unsuitable Job for a Woman*. Warring throughout the novels are images of Cordelia as a solemn, wise child and a decent adult; it is not that the solemnity and decency cannot coexist within her, but that the tension established between the child and the adult is unresolved. Something of this dichotomy is revealed in the description of her sexual life. Seeing virginity as an inconvenient state which emphasizes the vulnerability of the young, she deliberately chose experience. She concludes that lovemaking is overrated; she was not less lonely afterwards, only a little less inexperienced.

Occasionally Gray's self-doubt reinforces the societal criticism she both anticipates and receives. She is reminded that hers is an unsuitable job for a woman frequently enough for her to assume that all clients believe this; that some do not is a pleasant surprise to her. In fact, criminals in both novels count on the prevailing opinion, claiming that they will charge her with being an emotional, hysterical young woman if she accuses them; the threat would have been laughable if the detective were male. Likewise, she finds herself uncomfortable as an employer, not knowing all the rules. When Bernie was alive, although they were supposed to be partners, she fixed tea and washed up after; when she has her own typists, Cordelia alternates doing the task with them. More important, despite encouragement of clients and friends plus a qualified endorsement from the police, she is pensive about her professional decisions: "Wasn't it one of the commonest of human vanities, this preoccupation with the motives, the compulsions, the fascinating inconsistencies of another personality? Perhaps, she thought, we all enjoy acting the detective, even with those we love; with them most of all. But she had accepted it as her job; she did it for money. She had never denied its fascination but now, for the first time, it occurred to her that it might be presumptuous. And never before had she felt so inadequate for the task, pitting her youth, her inexperience, her meager store of received wisdom against the immense mysteriousness of the human heart" (*Skull* 349).

It is reasonable to say that like Harriet Vane in *Gaudy Night*, Cordelia Gray is in search of her full identity in *An Unsuitable Job for a Woman.*[2] Her education journey takes her to Cambridge—indeed, where else should a quest for education, even self-knowledge, take one? By definition, the colleges of this great university are a place of and for the young, where apprenticeship to life is the main business of life. Those who grow into the maturity which the world recognizes as sufficient "come down"; those who cannot are "sent down." For most, it is a place for learning and then leaving; Cordelia uses it in exactly that way although for her it is not really "coming up" at all. She does not find the ivory-tower refuge she had expected; instead murder and malevolence mark these streets. In her investigation, she suspects not only individual members of the college but also the university itself. Cordelia's indictment of Cambridge sees the system, which she had once dreamed of being a part, fail Mark Callender. This, inevitably, becomes more important than the possibility that Hugo or Sophie Tilling might have participated in his murder. Finally, the actual criminal is of and not of the university; Ronald Callender is a graduate, an employer of former students, and a visitor to the High Table, but a scientist outside the academy. However, in clearing the university of direct complicity and responsibility in the crimes, Cordelia indicts them indirectly. Jane Bakerman describes the university as "a key symbol of western civilization, supposedly the sum of the best humankind has yet achieved. . . . [yet] one of its great covenants, the system of justice, is sometimes inadequate" (106–

7). In solving the mystery, Gray surpasses institutionalized, codified knowledge and judgment to apply her own. The end result is that Cordelia learns she can leave Cambridge, never having possessed it herself; in so doing, she learns that she need not compromise with society outside this institution or with the university itself. But James does not follow through on Gray's rite of passage; the second novel shows only a superficially changed woman.

The ways in which Cordelia's position is undermined differ drastically in the two novels. In the final chapter of *An Unsuitable Job for a Woman*, James unnecessarily and intrusively includes her series character Adam Dalgleish as Gray's interrogator. He admits to respecting, possibly even admiring, her determination and guiltless insistence on her version of the case. As the text makes clear, however, Cordelia's and Adam's impressions of the interview are in direct contrast. While she believes that he is treating her as an adult, crediting her with the same intelligence and deductive abilities he himself possesses, he is uncomfortably viewing her as a child. " 'I took to her,' he tells his superior, 'but I'm glad I shan't be encountering her again. I dislike being made to feel during a perfectly ordinary interrogation that I'm corrupting the young' " (286). She, despite her feeling of equality, is convinced that he knows she is lying. Not only that, but the advice which shapes her responses is Bernie Pryde's version of Adam Dalgleish's official wisdom about witnesses. That she officially outwits Dalgleish by his own advice is an ironic point in her favor; that he knows what she is doing seems to negate the advantage. This still leaves him in the better position by virtue of age, power, experience, and gender. The second novel's revelation of Cordelia's limitations is far less subtle. Framing the Clarissa Lisle story are the agency's other cases—lost pets. After escaping and facing down Ambrose Gorrige, Cordelia Gray returns willingly to search for a child's cat and a persistently lost Pekingese: ". . . she had a job waiting for her. It was a job that needed doing, one that she was good at. She knew that it couldn't satisfy her forever, but she didn't despise its simplicities; almost she welcomed them" (*Skull* 415). Readers who would not consider pet-finding an appropriate occupation for Sam Spade or Spenser are not likely to see Cordelia Gray and Maggie McGuane, who accept such cases, as detectives worthy of the tradition. Although the agency survives under Cordelia's management, her professional career seems to have taken a distinctly downward turn.[3]

Structurally, both novels emphasize Cordelia's youth, inexperience, and tentativeness at the beginning and the end. It is as though she is solving her first case twice; what is plausible, if not well-meshed with the demands of the formula, in the first novel is inappropriate in the second. This is particularly true because only the reader, not the detective herself, knows how Dalgleish felt about their interview. Her successful uncovering of the Mark Callender murder and subsequent cover-up of the murderer's death should have provided Gray with confidence and impetus; instead, she seems to move backward into less important and less challenging cases than her first. The important cases she solves would challenge Dalgleish but the narrative frames in which they are set are not worthy of even Gray. Not content to identify her detective hero with lost pets at the opening and conclusion of *The Skull Beneath the Skin*, James also puts her on a level with her two temporary typists as employer, tea maker, and finder of lost animals. Finally, many readers have noticed that although Gray's second murder case is much like her first, she makes the same serious mistakes in confronting Ambrose Gorrige as she had in challenging Sir Ronald Callender's thug, apparently not having learned from experience. James is clearly telling two stories; her success with the Adam Dalgleish series makes it clear how well she writes the modern detective novel. Her decision to cast Cordelia Gray's story in that genre (unlike her so-called serious novel *Innocent Blood* which also uses a young female protagonist) marks a different impulse: the double-voiced discourse between the detective novel as it ordinarily is and the cases of Cordelia Gray which only borrow elements of that format for their central tale but not the full narrative, provides a sharp contrast between the presentation of a women detective and the male model.

The only other modern British female private investigator, Anna Lee, leads a professional life which diverges considerably from that of her American counterparts.[4] By comparison, it is boring, circumscribed, and controlled, but it is also likely to be much more realistic. Her cases begin as small-scale investigations—an auto accident, child custody suit, business fraud, a missing person, and bodyguard duty; only two eventually involve murder. Even when her cases lead to death, Anna's kidnapping, or other physical danger, they never match the punch delivered by the typical hard-boiled detective novel. She is the most junior, least respected, and only female investigator working for Brierly Security where she resents the pomposity of her employer and the power-enhancing moves of the office secretary. Liza Cody portrays Lee as part of the business machinery, not a knight-errant righting ancient wrongs. Anna recognizes ". . . that was the nature of her job: to paddle on the edge of other people's dramas, usually long after they had lost significance to the major participants" (*Stalker* 161).

Throughout her five cases, Anna is as resourceful and independent as her position allows her to be. In several instances which are not presented, she is removed from cases because the clients refuse to work with a woman. Other times her ability is challenged by prospective clients. Her colleagues have mixed reactions to her talents; her employer, she is convinced, only defends her for the sake of the agency's reputation while agreeing privately with the criticism. When Brierly "lends" her, in *Under Contract,* to a larger security firm which does not have its own female employees, the arrogance and sexism of the men in charge makes them ignore her observations and warnings. But with suspects and informants, the unexpectedness of a female investigator provides her a built-in disguise, although she does worry about taking advantage of decent people who are willing to trust and help her. Still she encourages them: "Anna's favorite device for drawing people out was one that Selwyn [Price] had once called Narcissus Ploy. Quietly responsive, she would become a mirror to the person she was talking to, who gained confidence in the presence of someone so like himself and often revealed more than was wise. It demanded time and patience, though" (*Dupe* 90). Although she insists that she is as ethical as she can be, given the constraints of her boss, the problems of the client, and the need to complete an investigation, that is not quite good enough for her. Rejecting the pressure of others, she relies on her own judgment and experience. In each of the novels, this attitude leads her to share confidential information despite Lee's awareness that her behavior would be labeled unprofessional. Only occasionally does she indulge her impatient side: as a result, she gets beaten up less frequently than many fictional detectives.

Her kidnapping in *Bad Company* is the best example of how Anna Lee functions when limited, although this time the restrictions cannot be blamed on her boss or his secretary. She battles against her captors, fully investigates the room where she and a teen-aged girl are being held, withholds her identity, and comforts the frightened and whiny teen. Plotting their escape, she straightens a coiled bedspring and manages to unlock the door which is, unfortunately, also bolted. In the end, she is forced to wait for her captors to make a mistake; but, when they do, her companion is too frightened to help Anna. Working to keep up her spirits, she also berates herself: ". . . she felt profound humiliation at her circumstances. She had been hijacked by a bunch of half-wits who thought with the seat of their pants if they thought at all. And she, the "superior cow," hadn't been able to do a thing about it. Now here she was, shoeless, witless, and lost. You should've joined the Girl Guides when you had the chance, she thought, it's about all you're fit for" (*Bad Company* 255). She is, of course, too hard on herself; even working on the outside, the police, her colleagues at Brierly Security, and the organized criminals for whom her captors thought they were working cannot trace her whereabouts; they may act, but like her they accomplish little.

In choosing plausible behavior for her protagonist over more typical genre heroics, Liza Cody challenges the formula of detective novels. But, because that character is one of a long line of women detectives who have been portrayed as less able or less complete than their male counterparts, Cody also undercuts her own efforts to revise the genre. The cumulative effect suggests that Anna Lee's gender rather than Liza Cody's composition is responsible for the novels' difference.[5]

These British novels differ from their American counterparts of the 1970s in a number of ways. There is a tonal difference in which the violence, although it exists, is more muted and less frequent. Cordelia Gray's investigative style has more in common with the classical detective whereas Anna Lee's work is similar to the plodding, unspectacular efforts of the police. Neither is modeled on Sam Spade; rather than hard-boiled, they are—in a phrase of the eighties—soft-boiled. They are joined in this mode by one distinctive American.

Even the dust jacket copy of *Discretion*, David Linzee's first book featuring Sarah Saber, categorizes her as soft-boiled; she certainly conforms to none of the stereotypes established by Hammett and Chandler or imitated by their successors. Rather than walking independently down mean streets, she is sent by her conglomorate employer, Inquiries, Inc., to investigate corporate crime and security. Although most of her cases are undoubtedly mundane, the two featured in *Discretion* and *Belgravia* are special assignments which take her out of the United States to spectacular settings and even more extravagant crimes. Though she is separated from her usual working partner and lover, Chris Rockwell, their cases overlap in both novels so they wind up unexpectedly collaborating. Both of Sarah's cases follow a similar pattern of independent investigation with an ensuing joint chase that ends in Chris's solo capture of the criminal.[6]

Because their company has changed ownership and management, it has a rather schizophrenic image; nowhere is that reflected better than in Sarah Saber and Chris Rockwell—she the newly hired female and he unwillingly carried over from the old staff. Whereas he is outspoken, generally cynical, inclined to reading rather than action, and highly critical of the new style of operations, she fits right in. The boss ". . . had once told her that she 'embodied the new corporate image I'm trying to project—you're the kind of person a top executive can *relate* to' " (*Discretion* 29). But she was scarcely hired on the strength of that image; instead, she used family connections.

Saber's reasons for joining an investigations firm seem to be a lack of other interests and an urgent need for enough money to support her elegant style. She doesn't go beyond that: " 'All right. The fact is I think we've got pretty good jobs. Most of the time we're together, and we just sit around in our company car and play gin rummy. I don't see there's anything so dangerous about that. O.K., so the jobs are distasteful, and it gets to you once in a while, but hell, we're well paid—incredibly well paid. I really don't know what you think is so wrong with Inkwink—' " (*Discretion* 42). For the sake of a fashionable Central Park South address, she lives in a tiny studio apartment; rent, BMW and garage charges, tennis club payments, and her Saks bill keep Saber bound to the job. So, she invests in soybean futures and hopes to make a killing on the market which will allow her to retire. Chris, on the other hand, wants marriage and threatens to join his family's aluminum siding company in Connecticut where business is bad enough to allow him plenty of time to read.

Clearly, Linzee is not writing only about a woman private detective but also—or even primarily—about corporate management of an investigations agency, lovers as colleagues, and the interactive contrast of male and female detectives. If Chris Rockwell is typical of the old style detective, the loner or the knight-errant, then Sarah is typical of the new model of investigator—sleek, blonde, and "dressed for success." At the end of the second, messy and corrupt case, Chris resigns and Sarah remains, barely escaping being fired. The indictment of the conglomerate model of doing business, both the agency and the client company, is savage and pointed. Sarah's complacent acceptance of its morals, her own aims and way of living, and her identification with the corporate image serve to condemn her also.

As lovers, Chris and Sarah seem evenly matched despite their disparate lifestyles and tentative accommodation of the other's inclinations; but, as detectives, their equal position is sharply negated at both the beginning and the end of the novels. Sarah was originally assigned as Chris's assistant to learn the business from him. This immediately puts her at a disadvantage in their professional relationship; at best she is the eager learner while he is the bored instructor. The only two solo cases she investigates become joint ventures in which Chris captures the criminals and, thereby, saves the day. Linzee's replacement of the woman detective with a team and then only the man at the conclusion parallels Harlan Halsey's treatment of Cad Metti and Mlle. Lucie more than eighty years ago in the dimes. The apparently dominant plot recedes to allow readers a more familiar story of male principals and secondary females.

Unlike Sarah Saber and her British counterparts, the dominant American mode in the 1970s and 1980s is the hard-boiled detective, here in female dress. When transferred straight from the male private eye to the female, the role fits poorly. The characteristics of the formula identified so closely with the male hero, including violence, sexual activity, and the arrogance which allows him to assume a judge-and-jury role, have not been historically associated with women or with the few women detectives in the genre. Modeling the female protagonist on a male prototype establishes the conditions for her failure as either an investigator or a woman—or both. In the false belief that the liberated woman of the 1960s was a "female man,"[7] authors carelessly reproduced the formula without rethinking the stereotypes of either the genre or the historical picture of women.

The limitations of this forced marriage are clear in Fran Huston's *The Rich Get It All*, which is blatantly modeled on Ross Macdonald's private-eye fiction. Set in Southern California, the novel calls for the investigation of a decades-old family secret which eventually results in five murders before the combination of unethical business dealings, wealth, and incest are revealed. The only difference from Macdonald's well-known formula is the detective, ex-cop Nicole Sweet. From the novel's opening she is in love with a possible suspect, Kerr Donahue. Emphasizing her "liberation," Sweet describes the freedom she seems all too willing to abandon for Donahue: "Men on whom I refuse to depend accuse me of excess independence, of being too self-sufficient, too—in the current jargon—liberated, as though there is only one kind of enslavement for a woman: enslavement to the male. They are arrogant damn fools, men who think that" (174). Yet this pandering to current feminist attitudes is merely an opportunity to demonstrate what a woman will give up for her man: "I wanted the chains of my work off me; I wanted the freedom to stop here, stop now, stop the forces I had given inertia to, to terminate my involvement and responsibilities and commitment, to not care, not give one damn" (174).

Having unravelled a tangled, complicated story, Nikki takes charge, providing the necessary information to the police who arrive too late to save her lover from being shot by his mother. Her response is threefold: she envies family members who can embrace and cry; she smokes again after stopping for five months; and she acknowledges—in the last lines of the novel—her love for the "beautiful" Kerr Donahue. In the end, her human reactions, which she would have called her woman's reactions, overcome her professional detachment; the novel's straightforward acknowledgment of that emotion suggests that in this time and place, she was right to do so. But who ever sees Lew Archer cry? So, while her behavior as a feeling, emotional woman is validated, what is left unmentioned is her status as a detective. The omission suggests that inasmuch as Nikki Sweet has proved her womanliness, the narrator finds all other categorization irrelevant. In this con/text, she is a good woman, therefore she need not be a good detective.

As with Nikki Sweet's sloganeering, something about the portrait of the liberated woman of the seventies simply does not click in Arthur Kaplan's *A Killing for Charity*. Both the narration and the character's behavior alternate between the new mode and the old, caught in contradictions which are apparently unrecognized by the author. As a hard-boiled detective with a heart, an adult who refuses to be called a girl, a career woman whose recipes for pasta sauce are included in the book, Charity Bay initially offers an interesting mix of interests and attitudes. But this is frequently contradicted by her unpredictable, implausible reactions. Similarly, it is clear through the narrative, plot, and character development that Kaplan has unsuccessfully grafted an emerging stereotype of the liberated woman onto an old formula of patronizing sexist fiction.

The reader's first view of Charity Bay exemplifies the dichotomies: she is comfortably in bed with a Swiss businessman she just met, and is making plans to visit him ten days hence. The episode suggests the casual, wealthy, sexually free lifestyle publicized by *Playboy* or *Penthouse*. When she joins the police outside the hotel room, her sexual encounter is revealed as an undercover operation to regain a client's stolen securities. Initially, the reader is as deceived as her partner; but an image of her emerges as sexually emancipated, devious, calculating, dedicated to her work, cool, and unemotional. Reinforcing the reader's impression that sex is a casual matter for Charity is her invitation to police Lieutenant Dunn for dinner and bed—despite his earlier near-rape of her—because he has a nice face, likes her spaghetti sauce, and can recognize her exhaustion. She assures him that "[m]aking love is the ultimate friendship" (163).

If Kaplan intends Charity's decision to be sexually active and her ability to choose her own partners to symbolize the new egalitarian relationship between women and men, little else in his novel reinforces it. Dunn's attempt to force himself on her is revealed as the inevitable result of a woman's life in male society. Bay's first job as secretary to a one-man security agency left her vulnerable to sexual harassment which she tolerated in order to learn the business. Cabbies, an airline check-in clerk, a customs official, and coffeeshop counterman all assume their right to harass her verbally while several informants imply that sex is the price of their assistance. Throughout the novel, police teams casually and repeatedly tell gender-related, sexually explicit jokes which demean women; her introduction as a private investigator at a murder scene is the impetus for a widely repeated *bon mot:* "Me dick. You clit" (83). The atmosphere which the novel projects is not one of an outspoken woman making her way in a sexist society despite these obstacles but one of tacit complicity with harassers; their behavior is explained, excused, tolerated. Bay is even considered responsible for one informant's murder because she wouldn't sleep with him: " 'You could have caused him to drop his guard, become less cautious. You got him all hot and bothered, any woman would have, and he probably went out to find someone. Someone who was looking for him spotted him, and that was it' " (157). Throughout the novel, there is an unresolved narrative tension between the development of a strong, competent protagonist and an underlying message that she is too strong and too competent for her gender.

Earlier clients preferred Charity Bay over a male investigator for her competence, refusal to intimidate, and rejection of sexual harassment. Like them, two other women—widely separated by occupation as though to emphasize the universality of this experience— explicitly describe their impressions of female-male relationships. The mother of an emergency room physician, as a nineteen year old in occupied Budapest, avenged the concentration camp deaths of her entire family by killing German soldiers, enticing them through sex; at least ten times she was able to deceive these young men with an invitation they felt entitled to. This same awareness that men see women primarily in terms of their sexuality is articulated by the mother of the kidnapped child Charity hopes to rescue. Aware that she has never put these ideas into words before, she confides: " 'Men always want a tactile relationship with you. Am I right? Regardless of who they are, how old they are, they are always looking at the soft parts of you, the touch parts. . . . You can never really talk to them, not one hundred percent kind of conversation, always twenty to forty percent is feel on their part' " (205). However, the message which this awareness might convey is undercut by narrative patterns and an essentially irrelevant plot episode. Bay's body receives as much attention from the narrator as from the more obvious harassers she encounters: her bathing, showering, and habit of exercising nude are repeatedly noted; all her clothing is described and evaluated. Improbably, Charity is left hanging by her fingertips to the outside of a building with her clothes almost completely ripped away as she chases what turns out to be an uninvolved petty thief. Her rescue by an Hasidic Jew who can initially only stare at her naked body conveys an authoritative put-down of women's physical being. God, her rescuer informs Charity, does not permit him to touch women. It does not seem here that the proscription is to protect women from men but vice versa.

The novel's final two chapters reiterate the contradictions in Charity Bay's introduction. Using all the resources available to her—

police reports, her informants, intelligent observation, and sympathetic listening—Bay discovers the hiding place of the diamond thieves and kidnappers of Joel Koenig and his young daughter. Working her way inside the house, she memorizes the floor plan, identifies a way to capture the criminals, and then decides that the risk to the child is too great. She alerts the police, shares all her information, and repeatedly reminds them of the danger to the little girl. Her methods and decisions are sound; her manner is professional and competent. Despite their explicit joking, the police are similarly restrained. However, when the child is killed in front of them, the police remain collected while she does not. Angrily and tearfully in front of television cameras and reporters, she accuses Lieutenant Dunn, his men, and—by extension—society: " 'You've got to stop liking this horror, these books, those movies, that television!' She was screaming at the top of her lungs now, twirling the canvas bag furiously over her head, the diamonds spilling out in every direction and becoming part of the rubble around her" (264). Dunn's controlled but angry reaction is the book's last line: " 'I'll have your ass for this' " (264). In view of the novel's earlier emphasis on women's body parts, this threat carries overtones beyond its usual metaphorical implications. Even more telling, however, is the way in which Bay's emotional outburst is treated narratively. It should be an indictment of anyone who can see a child killed and remain unmoved. Instead, her reaction is treated as all-encompassing, unprofessional, and probably unwarranted hysteria; her strength is redefined as weakness worthy of censure. More explicitly than Nikki Sweet, Charity Bay is divided into two apparently irreconcilable parts, detective and woman; unlike Nikki, she is condemned in both roles.

Although the portrait of the female hard-boiled detective in Charity Bay has changed considerably from the caricatured sex objects and teases seen in Honey West and Marla Trent, it still reflects basic and traditional assumptions about female and male behavior. This is clear in the automatic validation given to male behavior and the persistent questioning of female reactions and concerns. Anthropologists Shirley Ardner and Edwin Ardner use the terms "dominant" and "muted" groups to distinguish between men's power to define culture and reality versus women's position on the boundaries of men's world (Showalter, "Feminist Criticism" 261). Kaplan and other creators of the female hard-boiled detective unconsciously accept these definitions of society's operational process. Although the protagonist expresses both rage and frustration with her treatment by male characters, and other female characters share this outrage, the narrator firmly supports the established, dominant point of view. The novels come to uphold dominant and muted positions even when the choice to identify the protagonist with an unpowerful position violates the conventions of the genre.

Chicago ex-cop Madge Hatchett has even less success in avoiding role stereotyping than Bay; Lee McGraw seems determined to join the standard descriptions of the hard-boiled private eye with that of a so-called liberated woman. The two images rest uneasily side by side. Hatchett's toughness dominates the book: she kills unhesitatingly; she punches, chops, or kicks petty crooks and recalcitrant informers; she often aims her blows directly at men's genitals. When not physically attacking, she talks tough, trading insults and threats with mobsters and muggers. In a tour de force scene, she escapes a soundproof room where she has been held by an organized crime leader and his attack dog and guarded by half a dozen thugs; she burns down the building while they are trapped inside.

Despite her performance, it becomes clear that Madge is being used in both of the apparently unrelated crimes she is investigating. Her self-confidence makes her slow to see through their tricks and games. She responds angrily when her former mentor on the police force warns her against grandstand plays and hotshot moves: " 'Why are you handing me all this stuff? If I were a man, they'd be calling me a goddam hero' " (84). She's right, of course; no matter how capable she shows herself, the men she encounters (whether apparent ally or unknown enemy) assume that somehow "something" will make her fail, fall into their hands, or just get in the way; that undefined something is her gender.

Neither Hatchett nor the reader is allowed to forget that women are defined differently in this world than men: she is mistaken for M. L. Hatchett's secretary; a pair of hubcap thieves see her as an easy mark; conventioneers on the street verbally harass her. Men talk of women in this novel as sexually available objects whom they can use and demean. Here, the explicit language and descriptions plus the pleasure men take in humiliating and using women are not intended to illustrate the conditions of women; nor do they offer Hatchett clues to solving the crimes or motives for killing the criminals. They are intended to titillate the reader. They are offered in compensation for making the protagonist a strong, competent woman who does not allow men to tell her how to act, rescue her from danger, or make a fool of her. By contrast, they emphasize what femininity ought to be. Women who choose to be detectives should expect to be harassed; they are not the "good" women who deserve society's respect and protection but are competitors in the male dominated, male controlled public arena.

Shifting the focus of the argument away from legitimate and plausible investigation and slightly toward the exploration of women's feelings, Phyllis Swan devotes three novels to the life and young career of Anna Jugedinski. Very little about her professional or personal behavior makes much sense. The tangled complications of her cases have less to do with detection than improbable plot lines which consistently mock her professional endeavors and her personal trauma.

In two ways, Anna's gender is consistently used against her as an investigator. Police chief Mike Roark—not only her former boss but also her natural father and, before this revelation, her fantasy lover—attacks and threatens her: " 'You girls with this lib idea gotta face the facts of life. A woman just doesn't have the muscle or the guts to do a man's job' " (*Find Sherri!* 46). He urges her to quit work, marry, and have children. When that tack fails, he forces her to apply for a vacant desk job in the police department, haranguing her until she agrees. His possessive protectiveness is echoed by her younger brother who favors the same plan; the two disagree only on the man with whom she will settle down. The second abuse of Anna's gender is more obvious and frequent: because she is female and attractive, virtually every man she encounters assumes that she is sexually available. The novels abound with propositions, attempted rape, partial seductions, partial and complete undressing. Inasmuch as Jugedinski rejects both the men who appeal to her and those who coerce her, each scene of sexual activity titillates both readers and characters while making little distinction between the two kinds of approaches. Bridging the gap between those who force and those who seduce is Anna's childhood friend and rescuer (from an attempted rape) Chino Parini. Knowing the reason for her rejection of men yet not wanting this withdrawal to apply to him, Chino is seductively persuasive and Anna reluctantly responsive. Just short of forcing her, he continually pressures Anna; whether he would like marriage or merely sexual intimacy is unclear. Each of the three novels ends with Anna alone, confused and longing for a sexual or romantic liaison.

Jugedinski's image as a detective is equally confused. Although she can shoot with accuracy, she usually refuses to carry a gun. Sometimes she is able to free herself from the traps she foolishly walks into; other times she needs Chino, his gangster boss, or her cop father and his men to save her; occasionally, a deus ex machina allows her escape. She gets shot, beat up, stripped, or threatened regularly; the persistence of these episodes suggests that she is either incompetent, extraordinarily vulnerable, or stupid. The combined impact of her personal and professional behavior makes it impossible for readers—and to some extent other characters—to take her seriously.

The typical antagonism between private investigators and the police carries a different message when the investigator is female and the cop male. In Phyllis Swan's novels, all the permutations come together skewed in the relationship between Anna Jugedinski and Mike Roark, her father, mentor, "lover." In over half the hard-boiled novels, the female-male relationship includes at least one of these alternatives without sacrificing the long-established hostility between private eyes and police. The power balance of father and daughter or mentor and pupil invariably rests with the man who uses it to criticize, mock, or threaten the woman. Despite the hypothetical possibility for equality between lovers, the same dominant and subordinant pattern occurs in these pairs. As a result, the women suffer on both professional and personal levels from the recriminations of an official who has power over their careers and from manipulation by someone they love. In every case, the men confuse their roles to take advantage of the power they hold through their positions, the relationships, and their gender.[8]

If being a female and a detective was a contradiction during the late nineteenth century, it is no less so a hundred years later. Only the external manifestations of the two scripts have changed. More than half of these modern women detectives are visibly caught in the contemporary quarrel between the *Playboy* philosophy of sexual emancipation without commitment and the women's movement manifestos of equality. The others are also affected by this conflict. As though they are being taught a morality lesson, most of the sexually active detectives are punished by men who betray, rape, or reject them. And, if their private lives are failures in both traditional and modern terms, their professional lives do not offer compensatory success and fulfillment. All are reduced by fictional structures which persistently undermine them in the areas being claimed by the women's movement. Attempting to meet society's ill-defined and fluctuating expectations of women, these characters are judged and found wanting. For readers equally confused by society's changing views of women, the message of these novels seems remarkably clear: when women try to share men's freedom of choice in public and private lives, women lose.

Catherine Belsey addresses the role which fiction (in addition to education, convention, and culture) plays in the creation of a subjectivity which may explain why women have not overthrown the patriarchy: ". . . if we accept Lacan's analysis of the importance of language in the construction of the subject it becomes apparent that literature as one of the most persuasive uses of language may have an important influence on the ways in which people grasp themselves and their relation to the real relations in which they live" (51). For the reader of detective fiction, which is admitedly not realistic despite a superficially plausible plot line, the protagonist is normally the point of identification. Historically, women have identified against themselves with male heroes, but given men's reluctance to read women's stories it is unlikely that men are willing to identify with female protagonists; this holds as true in detective and crime fiction as in mimetic novels, romances, or postmodernist fiction. To satisfy female and male readers, authors construct novels in which the fantasies of both have a position. For women, there is the dream of an independent, public life with the freedom to act separate from the dominant culture's directives; this is counteracted by their awareness of "the real relations in which they live." Men's fear of a reality in which women can become the dominant group is assuaged by the persistent fantasy of women who fail; these women may be inadequate detectives, bested by the criminals they seek, or inadequate women, rejected by the men they seek. The female and male readers locate alternating fields of narrative with subjectively different scripts oscillating forward and back. Reading the same novels, they can read altogether different stories.

Notes

1. John Cawelti concludes that "the classical formula is related to a dis-

tinct historical period" and that stories of adventure or melodrama have overtaken it in popularity (80).

2. Jane Bakerman persuasively describes *An Unsuitable Job for a Woman* as offering a new pattern of *Bildungsroman*. The protagonist undergoes severe trials, is chastened by the world, and understands that the way to survive comfortably is to compromise. But she does not; instead she defeats the system, although paying a price. Like her model Persephone, she emerges from a long, difficult journey in a dark underworld and, like her she walks now, if she survives her triumphs, in a world where winter comes and temporarily drives away fertility. But also like her, she has been reborn (or has remade herself) and she has achieved her goals. Cordelia Gray's trip to Cambridge is a symbol of her search for self. The pattern of male and female mentors from whom she learns and whom she finally rejects is negative. Women unconsciously teach her important, negative lessons, confirming her desire for a profession and an identity of her own and cautioning her that traditional female roles may bar her from achieving power and worth in society. Male mentors also teach her what not to be, for none is a whole person, although they do teach her skills.

3. Many critics have commented on James's tough-minded character. Among the more egregiously patronizing is Bruce Harkness; he insists that Cordelia has been found "most fetching by all readers" who must agree with him that "this gamin is delightful." He believes that a "women's magazine interest" has developed among readers wondering if Cordelia will succeed in marrying Adam Dalgleish (123).

4. Briton Kiss Darling, discussed in the next chapter, is more a spy than a private investigator and shows no similarity to Cordelia Gray or Anna Lee.

5. Liza Cody believes that her character is a better detective than society will allow her to be. There is no authorial complicity with society's devaluation of a woman detective.

6. Sarah Saber is discussed here rather than in the chapter on partnerships because the assignments she is given are designed for independent investigation; Chris Rockwell's participation then becomes a way of undercutting her, suggesting that she can't handle these cases successfully alone.

7. The term is, of course, Joanna Russ's.

8. Although many modern women private eyes have had experience as police officers, only Janice Law's Anna Peters brings her criminal experience directly to bear on her new employment. In a sequence of five novels, Peters begins as a research assistant at a large oil company and later she blackmails her way into a position as head of the department and finally establishes her own investigations business.

Undoubtedly, Anna's background as a blackmailer and her ability to know people as well as they know themselves lead to one of the more prevalent elements of her style as an investigator: she is a con artist. Frequently, the con includes a feminist trick as one of its elements; she uses men's stereotyped expectations of women's behavior against them; men are, she knows, vulnerable to "a woman who conforms to their expectations" (*Par* 182). However, it is difficult to reconcile Anna Peters's apparent independence with the nature of her last two cases and the fact that they are her *last* two. As soon as she sets up as an independent professional, her only "case" is undertaken as an amateur. Also challenging the image of Anna Peters as a successful, independent, professional private investigator is the fact that her honeymoon case is her last; the novel itself ends in a conversation with her new husband about a prospective client, but there are no more novels. Throughout the earlier novels, Anna had resisted marriage as a bourgeois institution; her marriage in the fifth novel has the effect of proving her correct. Her career, if not deliberately stopped because of the marriage, is left unimaginable in that context by the author. So, like her counterparts caught in the marriage plot at the end of the nineteenth century, Anna does not combine marriage and a career; it is not, a reader senses, that she could not, that her husband or society or stereotyping would deter her—it is just that she does not. The effect on the reader, when there is no sixth novel, must be to locate the only unique factor in the fifth novel—marriage—and draw, with no way of knowing how accurately, a negative conclusion about the possibility of integrating the two.

8

The Moderns Continue:
Variations on a Theme

When John Cawelti describes variations on the stories of adventure which have achieved postwar popularity, his list includes "the hard-boiled detective story, the spy story, the police procedural tale, the gangster saga, and the Enforcer's caper" (80). Clearly, not all of these feature a professional detective or even any detective at all. That the hard-boiled private eye is only one in a list of five (which might have been longer) demonstrates a resurgence of the energies which molded detective fiction in the nineteenth century before the dominance of Sherlock Holmes. Some of these modes have been incorporated into the detective novel, giving it a new look; even the female private eye is not always a predictable figure in this period.

A fictional form so well defined and predictably structured as the detective novel lends itself easily to parody. And, like the romance, gothic, or western, it contains all the elements of potential self-parody even when the author does not directly or consciously express that impulse. In particular, authors looking to vary the format without abandoning the formula often unconsciously create exaggerated versions of the standard model; imitation without reconsideration leads them to it. In a general way, all novels featuring women private eyes could be described as parodies; their authors adopt a fixed formula while making one significant change. Yet the authors do not take that change seriously; given societal biases about women's roles—which writers and readers must share to some extent—replacing a male detective with a female one is not a simple substitution. By not reevaluating the parameters of a particular detection formula, these authors bring their novels to the edge of parody: they undercut their protagonists to reinforce a social standard of female inequality and, in so doing, undermine the genre in which they write.

Through exaggerated characterization and plot, some authors carry their parody beyond the general tendancy. They involve improbable protagonists in unlikely investigations with implausible conclusions. Some divert the formula into stories of caricature, espionage, and sexual exploitation. Yet, metaphorically the woman detective has always been spy and sexual object even when her explicit makeup as a classical or hard-boiled investigator seemed to suggest otherwise. Like a spy, she is an intruder into the public realm controlled by masculinist, patriarchal power. She attempts to infiltrate another culture, to learn its secrets, and to either make a place for herself there or remake that world to suit her values. Her deviance in abandoning, however temporarily, her proper domestic sphere is usually rectified by demonstrating her failures in the larger world or by returning her rapidly to the home via marriage. And her sex is a persistent, inescapable fact; it "may carry with it an aroma . . . the swish of petticoats" as Virginia Woolf recognized (*Room* 50). But whether the detective is multi-petticoated in the nineteenth century or stripped naked in the twentieth, the men around her reinforce her primary definition—"woman." These men—allies and opponents alike—might romance and marry or rape and abuse her; she might acquiesce or fight, respond or reject. But she cannot escape. However, the eight characters in this chapter are not metaphoric representations of the woman detective. More than most, they are parodies, exaggerations, and commercialized responses to the fantasies of a mass audience.

Dashiell Hammett is supposed to have introduced novelist Ellery Queen to a lecture audience by asking, "Mr. Queen, will you be good enough to explain your famous character's sex life, if any?" (Hoffman 99). In the classical tradition, the detective didn't need one. However, the hard-boiled hero, expecially since the 1950s, could hardly survive without one: Travis McGee is a sexual healer and Mike Hammer a sexual killer with their male colleagues filling in all the spaces on the spectrum between the two. Most women detectives after the fifties also have a sex life, frequently more limited and usually less consistently described than the men's; for example, Marla Trent, Charity Bay, and Nikki Sweet share the *Playboy* ethos. In these novels, however, detection still dominates; when that balance shifts, investigation and the woman private eye are merely excuses for stories of sexual exploitation and adventurism.[1]

Found on the racks in an "adult" bookstore, Jim Conaway's *Deadlier than the Male* loses its balance between crime-solving and sexual exploitation.[2] The difference in tone between the chapters featuring detective Jana Blake and those describing the motivations and murders of Sunny Surgeant sets up the friction and awkwardness in this alternately superficial and serious novel. The murderer is a childhood victim of parental abuse, incest, neglect, and abandonment, as well as teenaged gang-rape condoned by her mother.

In explaining her motives for choosing this profession to the police lieutenant with whom she is now sleeping, Blake shows how ill-prepared she is to undertake a case of this dimension. Her childhood fantasies of crime-solving contrast too sharply with the victim/murderer's childhood nightmares: " 'I like helping people. I love solving problems. I know you'll think I'm foolish, but I've been an Agatha Christie fan ever since I was a little girl. I always pictured myself as a young Jane Marple, who had all the answers. But I'm afraid it isn't like that. . . . For one thing, you have to get hired first' " (89). Like the lieutenant, her sympathy is more with the original victim than her subsequent ones. But whereas he maintains emotional distance, she proposes to abandon her career. His response, despite talking, going to bed, and investigating with her, is a lukewarm one: " 'You're just talking. And you know something? You're a damn good one [detective], too!' " (188). Blake makes no direct response to either of these statements; instead she responds to his kiss and invites him home with her. Her talk of not being a detective is both a response to the abusive motivation of these gruesome crimes and a request for reassurance. She trades a sexual invitation to find this approval; but the lieutenant does not need her reassurance or approval for his professionalism. The direct contrast between female and male needs for professional validation follows a pattern established in the nineteenth century: the norm of male behavior is taken for granted but the deviance of women's activity is suspect. Here, even the protagonist has internalized her abnormal status.

The novel is filled with sexual episodes and double entendres. Jana has a leering landlord and several lovers; her sexual activities are described in detail. The victim/murderer's childhood abuse and later gang rape are fully and graphically described, as are her successful seductions of several victims before their deaths. The image of the detective's free, open lifestyle and liberated, consentual sexual activity clashes abruptly with the picture of a defenseless girl permanently scarred by men's casual and proprietary use of her body. A similar tension exists between Jana Blake's attributed feminism and her quest for male approval. Here, the titillating elements seem to be provided as a payoff for less palatable details of reality; or conversely, the horrors could be the price exacted for the pleasures of the titillation. Either way, it is a cheap trick. The novel reifies conventional criticism of women who are sexually active while simultaneously stressing all women's position as sex objects.

A more extreme example of this "soft pornography" are James D. Lawrence's four novels featuring Angela Harpe, the Dark Angel—all published in 1975. The only black protagonist among the women detectives, Harpe demonstrates the quintessential success story. But, the narrative subordinates all her talent and training to her appearance: "An incredibly sexy-looking black fox with lustrous hair piled high on her head. Apricot stretch pants that seemed sprayed on, and a low-cut well-filled peekaboo top. . . . Tony Troy could see how her taut bikini panties creased her flesh under the velvety apricot stretch fabric. He sensed that she was wearing them deliberately to guide his eyes" (*Dream Girl* 6). Written in the era of *Superfly*, the novels' cases and their solutions are straight out of the movies. As Harpe is more of an adventurer than a detective, she is usually shooting, kicking, or escaping rather than checking out facts, interviewing suspects, or locating clues.

There are no more than three intersecting cases in each novel but at least twenty episodes of sexual activity; so the novels' focus rapidly becomes clear. Particularly important are the forcible rapes which actually or almost occur; when she can, Dark Angel avoids the violence of rape by quoting the popular cliché about enjoying what cannot be avoided. Other times, she turns this seeming acquiescence against the criminals, arousing them through an artful striptease and her apparent sexual expertise only to physically overpower them and escape—usually nude—into the streets. She understands that "sex was her easiest weapon" (*Godmother* 23). In addition to intercourse and rape, the novels include a wide range of frequently described sexual groping and fondling as well as explicitly sexual conversations. Nothing in these novels—sexism, pornography, racism—is subtle. The claim that Angela Harpe is "lust personified, the wet dream made real" is far more important to this series than any claims about her talents, abilities, or expertise as an investigator (*Godmother* 24). Her qualifications are merely incidental. The novels even go beyond the explicit promises of the cover pictures and comments as they reduce the protagonist to a sexual machine who cooperates in her own objectification. Although she escapes some rapes and evades some harassment, neither Angel nor the narrative even questions the assumption that she is, and should be, sexually available.

The link between espionage and investigation has traditionally been a tenuous one in fiction, with each contained by its own genre, although there has been some interweaving in novels set during war years. Three modern novelists—Walter Wager, James Yardley, and Amelia Walden—use international intrigue to provide adventure for their series. Despite Walter Wager's designation of his character as a Beverly Hills private investigator, ex-CIA agent Alison B. Gordon is more an international agent like James Bond or Modesty Blaise than a typical hard-boiled detective. Her three adventures begin with conventional detecting but end in international activism. The CIA's willingness to provide massive covert assistance upon her request is a far more valuable asset than her sleuthing. The exploits she organizes have more in common with elaborate comic books than with traditional or contemporary novels of detective action.

Inevitably, some men in the novels underestimate her—a macho cop, an aging general, a Japanese bomber pilot, a Mafia client. But, she has her own share of macho accomplishments: " 'Seven years with The Company. The Agency. The CIA—the professionals. Not pushing memos in Virginia, general, but in the field. Two years in Africa, three in Vietnam and two in Thailand' " (*Leader* 74). Other men seem to accept her leadership and authority without details or demonstrations, but this appearance is misleading. Her closest associates are ex-CIA agents who have known her work in the field and who, despite their knowledge of her apparent abilities, protect her in ways they do not safeguard even each other. When a mission requires additional manpower (and it is always male power) her credibility is often enhanced by the men with whom she is affiliated. As there are no other women on her operating teams and almost none elsewhere in the novels, Alison is constantly in the company of male cohorts. Wager clearly defines her as a "man's woman." In fact, the novels seem to be written for men interested in adventure and sexual action (despite Alison's occasional feminist remarks or description of herself as a new "new woman"). Not only are Gordon's three affairs related in some detail, but her narcissistic attention to her own body is also fully described in each book.

Alison Gordon is triply sabotaged by her author in these caricatured tales of high adventure. She is a cartoon figure engaged in exploits which are difficult to take seriously. She relies on others to execute her plans without any means of assuring their success. Finally, she is denied continuing love and affection; her ties are only with men involved in dangerous business who are invariably killed. Through the fictional structure, she is shortchanged on every side.

By contrast, it is difficult to know exactly how to place Britain's Kiss Darling whose adventures are also more espionage than detection; even more than Alison Gordon, she belongs in an illustrated comic book. Her character in the novels is shaped around two factors: computerized intelligence therapy, which means that her brain has been conditioned to assimilate information directly and rapidly; and, despite the explicit enticement of the book covers, her virginity.

Generally, James Yardley's novels are as much interested in her lecherous boss's sex life and Darling's absence of one as in the improbable villains they face. Interviewing her, Angus Fane is already making plans to bed Kiss; she, planning the "delicate job" of "dispos[ing] of woman's greatest gift," is waiting for "finely tuned delight" when she is "finally overwhelmed and possessed by the male animal" (*Boys* 13). Her rejection of her boss, Fane, doesn't faze him, nor does it make him turn celibate as he continues to pursue Kiss. His many women and details of their activities together provide regular counterpoint to the investigation. Eventually, Kiss begins to reevaluate her decision. "There was a limit to feeling apart from other women, unable to join in the fun and games; isolated by her own bloody brain. Why couldn't she be amoral and uninhibited? She really didn't want to join 'Virgins Anonymous.' She knew she was jealous of Lucky [Fane's newest companion]. But if that wasn't bad enough, worse still, she was just plain *envious*" (*Corpse* 125). Like Honey West who is also forever advancing and retreating in the sexual game, the equally improbably named Kiss Darling is designed to tease the male reader as much as the male characters. Her unwelcomed naiveté matches her professional inexperience; she is merely a plot device to generate two exotic and erotic cartoon-like adventures of sex and espionage.[3]

These two series parody both spy and hard-boiled detective novels, albeit unconsciously, although the Kiss Darling novels occasionally seem to be authored tongue-in-cheek. Conscious and humorous examples of parody are rare in this book but excess which mocks the genre is more easily found.

Deliberate parody is successfully handled in David Galloway's humorous, clever, and well-written 1979 novel. Although set in California during World War II, *Lamaar Ransom* might never have been published then as it features a white, lesbian detective as the protagonist, and a gay, black, cross-dressing male as her secretary and assistant; rounding out the racial balance is Lamaar Ransom's not-so-bright Chicana lover. With relish, Galloway parodies the genre, its new directions in the 1970s, and 1940s society. The major clue to the novel's modernity is the complete absence of homophobic comments or attacks; clients, suspects, and police are all silent despite their obvious knowledge of the sexual preference of the detective and her cohorts. And the narrative contrasts the wholesomeness of homosexual behavior with the perverted desire of a male industrial tycoon who prefers bondage and has a high-heel-shoe fetish.

On the other hand, if her sexual preference is not the subject of comment, Ransom's combination of gender and profession is. Two of her three official clients are surprised or uncomfortable hiring a private eye and doubly so when the investigator is a woman. The neighborhood coffee-shop owner's attitude is typical—she should remarry. Her negative retort is equally direct and deliberately vulgar: "And wash pee stains out of some guy's boxer shorts for the rest of my life? Sorry, Nick, but that's not my poison anyhow" (26). Still, just as Lew Archer would have done in her place, she talks tough and works hard. Like his cases, hers depend on long-hidden secrets, dead bodies, threats against her lover, and an ambiguous relationship with the police. Her office, with "just enough dust to make it look lived in," and her ethical refusal to investigate slimy divorce cases also tally with the model established by Archer (10). And although her client eventually wins the argument about fees, she prefers her integrity to payment: " 'In the end, I was only working for Conchita, and for myself. It wouldn't be right to get paid for that. Every time I turned a corner in this case, somebody else was being bought or sold. It's kind of nice to have a different set of motives' " (245). Industrial espionage, radio transmission inventions, and pornographic film-making complete the parallel with the Archer model.

It is difficult to convey the humor of this novel briefly. Lamaar's conversation and narration are carefully molded and stylized to be just enough of an exaggeration of the real tough-guy private eye novels of the forties. She explains her bad mood with a female metaphor, then continues in the jargon of the period: " 'I'm on the rag—spiritually speaking. Somebody's playing me for a patsy, and I want to know why, and I don't know whether people want me to find the vanishing bust [woman] or don't want me to find it' " (50). Lightheartedly and affectionately, she characterizes her secretary-assistant Lavendar Trevelyan playing "Nick of the Woods" on one investigation and describes his departure for another assignment: "He was off and away with a couple of pirouettes in the doorway, spun back to snatch the photograph off the desk, and disappeared like Tinker Bell" (23). These descriptions are amusing rather than offensive for three reasons: they are typical of her style of observation and conversation, applied equally to straight and gay; they are as frequently turned on herself as anyone else; and, they are part of the bantering style in which employer and employee relate to each other without being the sole motif in their relationship.

In the final chapter, after a recapitulation of the investigation and its conclusion, the novel ends on a domestic/sexual note. Lavendar wants Lamaar to return his borrowed earrings for an important date at the U.S.O.; Conchita wants her to bring home a dozen eggs; and Ransom, with her feet propped up on her desk, falls quickly asleep. If Lew Archer could only see her now!

In an inadvertent parody, Eve Zaremba sets up her hard-boiled detective to play Sam Spade but fails to provide a workable script. In *A Reason to Kill,* Helen Keremos quickly realizes that the missing Martin Millwell must be dead and her case turns into a search for his killer. She bullies suspects and informants, expecting them to go along with plans that jeopardize their safety as well as hers: " 'Call it dumb. Call it what you like. That's how I play my hands. To the end' " (102). And *it* is dumb; she guarantees that her most likely

suspect will attack when she is more vulnerable than he. She un-
flinchingly beats up Martin's gay lover to force information from him,
knowing he is accustomed to responding to his father's dominating
behavior. Even though she follows her hunches, accepts uncertainty,
and takes risks as part of the job, she also trusts a sleazy music
promoter with whom she plays an "exhilarating" game of "get[ting]
to know each other"; and, what is more crucial, she dismisses the
murderer casually as someone too weak to kill (56).

It is difficult to know what to make of Keremos or the case in
this poorly written novel; as the first-person narrator, she filters information through improbable jargon. She is enough of a contemporary woman to refuse sexist labels: " 'No "broads," "chicks," or
"little ladies." You know better. I'm doing a job' " (57). She doesn't
take being called a lesbian as an insult.[4] But, ordinarily, her tough
talk is more a parody of Mike Hammer or Sam Spade: " 'Hey, turkey!
Get it through your head that your bribery-and-farewell story just
doesn't scan. Nobody believes it. Get it? I'm giving you a chance to
prove to me that it really happened. So persuade me. I'm doing you
a favor' " (104). The case also parodies well-known fictional formulas. The conclusion is straight out of Christie's *Murder on the Orient Express*. Throughout, the case and the character are equally unbelievable; so much near-caricature comes from poor writing rather
than from deliberate choice that it is impossible to judge either Helen
Keremos or her investigation independently. She makes an unbelievable hard-boiled detective not because the role is unassumable but
because it is only a role; there's no person underneath the Sam Spade
costume.

In a parody of the *Playboy* ethos superimposed on the detective
novel, Victor B. Miller introduces "the famous rape-lady," a beautiful
private detective who specializes in women's cases. However, from
the opening of *Fernanda* where she looks at her "massy" breasts in
the bathtub to the closing where she returns to bed with the police
captain investigating her case, Fernanda's own sexual behavior is
much in evidence (16). Contradictions abound; but her behavior is
neither explained nor explicable. The two rape cases which overlap
in this novel carry a similar message.

The first case involves a murdering rapist who kills one of Fernanda's assistants; later he threatens Fernanda herself. But she reads
this case wrongly: the suspect Dunlop has committed only half of the

rapes and murders attributed to him before he commits suicide. The others have been committed by Fernanda's assistant, who " 'wanted to experience the violent part of me' " (146). He has been motivated by envy of the dead man's amorality and by sexual jealousy; an intermittent lover of Fernanda, he resents her recent rejection of his overtures and her resumed affair with Police Captain Bonaventura. Becoming like Dunlop, he wants her naked and acquiescent; when she refuses to make love, he is willing to rape.

The distinction between love making and rape is one which Fernanda claims to understand well. In the second case of the novel, she is hired by a woman who has been raped but refuses to report it to the police. Because of the way the victim dresses, Fernanda announces judgmentally, " 'You weren't raped; you were taken up on your word' " (11); and she continues to insist on this conclusion throughout her investigation of the case. " 'A singles-bar neurotic and a pathetic tease' " is how she describes rapist and victim (13). Insisting that Liz Conlon see a therapist for her problem, Fernanda then moralizes: " 'You're one of the reasons people rape people. . . . I'm sorry . . . but making love is a good thing. I'm sorry you don't like it' " (12). Despite her claims to understand and investigate sex crimes, Fernanda does not admit that "people" are not rapists and victims; men rape women. The novel tries to suggest that as a woman Fernanda solves crimes against women better than a male investigator might, and, especially, that she understands gender-related crimes like rape or sexual harassment. Instead, she mouths the jargon of sexual liberation and plays "blame the victim." She trades on a climate of fear and shame by seeming to offer a woman's insight but then betrays that promise.

Nonetheless, any woman who participates in the oppression of other women is herself victimized by a society which has rewarded her for identifying against her own interests. In a gender-determined society, the impact of parody, exaggeration, or caricature in these detective novels is limited because any degree of deviation from prescribed roles is demonstrably inappropriate. When a modest variation on the traditional gender roles assumes as much importance as a total rejection, parody—itself minor or magnified—becomes lost.

What these eight characters clearly demonstrate is that breaking out of the formula of either the classical or hard-boiled detective novel cannot offer a female protagonist the chance to emerge unstereo-typed. These improbable spies and sexual adventurers offer little scope for analysis; they range from stereotype to caricature. However, like their counterparts throughout this book, they too are shown up as frauds. Their authors do not even sustain the fictions they establish. This is not where readers will find competent, confident, complete pictures of professional women; the scripts, once again, interfere. Indeed, here they virtually cancel each other out.

Notes

1. I've chosen not to discuss the pornographic novels in which detection is merely a convenient introduction to exclusively sexual narration; these cannot really be called detective novels.
2. There is a second novel featuring Jana Blake, *They Do It with Mirrors,* which I have been unable to obtain.
3. Also virginal but untroubled by the fact, Amelia Walden's Lisa Clark is what Ellery Queen once labeled another of her type, a "detectivette." *Where Was Everyone When Sabrina Screamed?* is negligible as a detec-tive novel; instead it is a romance using spy-like detective action as the basis for bringing a couple together and creating tension between them. Compounding the insidiousness of the message is the fact that the publisher, Scholastic Book Service, serves the junior and senior high school student market. In promoting the dichotomy between profes-sionalism and love for young female and male readers, Walden em-phasizes all the tired old stereotypes about female-male relationships. Gary Mitchell accuses Lisa of being a "little girl" when she refuses to submit to his various demands, all couched in terms of love, that she return home to safety (93); however, he acknowledges her as a "woman" when she flirtatiously responds to his proposal and abandons her profes-sional competitiveness (204). The book's underlying propaganda is worst in showing that Clark's confident and capable beginning is false, her independence is undermined by romance, and her submissiveness leads to happiness. The initial descriptions of the character and action are appealing enough to correspond with many girls' fantasies; in showing her strengths abandoned for the approval and subsequent love of the tough-but-tender Gary, the book validates a purportedly desirable real-ity. As is true in other mystery novels, detection is a cover for preaching social standards; here, it is done more blatantly and with a more vul-nerable audience.

4. In a newspaper interview with Chris Bearchell, Zaremba indicates that Keremos is a lesbian; but a reader must either accept blatant stereotyping or recognize subtle references to the Toronto gay scene to ascertain this from the text.

9

Female-Male Partnerships: 1924–78

The fictional male detective is a superior, solitary figure. Although he may require assistants, clerks, secretaries, and other forces to supplement his activities, these figures are subordinate in every way. Often others may gather information and tail suspects, but their knowledge is fragmented and their participation limited. The detective is the novel's hero not only in structural terms but also in the content, tone, and impact of the story. His deduction, ratiocination, intuition, charm, class, and talent (choose several) are not shared by his associates; he is the superstar while they are the supporting cast. Only the modern police-procedural novel attempts to establish a team approach to detection; even here, there are varying degrees of participation and certain characters clearly lack star status.

In the paradigmatic detective stories identified in this book's introduction, the limitations of the detective's "partner" are most evident in Conan Doyle's development of Dr. Watson. Although he can follow Holmes's orders, Watson seldom knows why he acts and usually needs to have the outcome explained. There is a greater sense of equality and shared responsibility between Spenser and Hawk; still the principal detective's identity is clearly established by Parker who frequently makes Hawk a paid employee rather than a fee-splitting colleague. Clients, conditioned by a racially conscious society, often relegate Hawk to an even more inferior position. The only actual partnership—legal and public—among the models is between Sam

Spade and Miles Archer; but Miles is dead. And, Spade seeks Archer's killer more to uphold his own reputation than to avenge his partner.

Among the women detectives discussed in this book, just seven of the seventy-one have female associates; only two are actually women partners. Three pairings are based explicitly on the Holmes-Watson model: Madelyn Mack and Nora Noraker, Rosika Storey and Bella Brickley, Flora Hogg and Milly Brown. Implicitly based on the same pattern are Olga Knaresbrook and Molly Kingsley plus Balmy Rymal and Toosey Attrell. The promising financial partnership of Dol Bonner and Sylvia Raffray exists only briefly at the opening and close of *The Hand in the Glove*. This collapse leaves Lutie and Amanda Beagle, who also have both a female Watson and a constant male assistant, as the only partnership consisting of two professional women detectives. However, this arrangement occurs merely by chance as they have not decided to be detectives but have inherited the agency from their brother. Few authors seem drawn to explore same-sex, egalitarian detective partnerships.

A detective "partnership" connotes shared responsibilities; it implies equivalent if not equal participation; it presupposes mutual respect and trust; it suggests an equality between partners. Inasmuch as this presumed equality is not a feature of female-male relationships in society, it might not be expected in detective fiction. However, the deliberate creation of an economic, contractual, legal, or quasi-legal partnership by detectives seems to imply a different authorial attitude—even if the partners are female and male. Nine legitimate, professional, or contractual partnerships in detective fiction covering the fifty-some years between the early twenties and late seventies demonstrate the differences and the essential similarity of the female-male alliance. Although six of the partnerships are initiated by women, their control, participation, and status are defined differently from the men's because of their sex.[1]

In constructing these novels with their apparent fidelity to the genre and simultaneous adherence to traditional attitudes about women, the authors have written what Gilbert and Gubar call "palimpsests." Both to express and to camouflage, the authors create surface designs which conceal or obscure deeper levels of meaning (73). In these novels, the detective partnership story with its implied parity and cooperation has been overwritten by the more familiar tale of female-male inequality and of male privilege and power contrasted with female limitations. Although the stories meet the ordinary demands of the genre for crime solved by a detective hero, they abandon the promised variation on the standard for yet another opportunity to undercut the woman detective. In these novels, the orthodox plot advances and then recedes, revealing the muted plot of restrictive gender roles.

Three male American authors take advantage of narrative techniques as well as plot line to undermine the female half of the team. Rejecting an objective narrative stance which could treat their characters similarly, they opt for a first-person narration by the male partner. This focused attention is intensified by the plot and structure which treat the man as the sole hero and protagonist, reducing the woman to a secondary position. With the gender contrast made explicit by these partnership novels, she is presented as no more than an encumbrance to his investigation or a sub-plot of obstructions he is forced to overcome. In this double-voiced discourse, in this conversation between the authors' expressed fictions and the narrators' contradictory expositions, the two voices, two meanings, and two expressions which Bakhtin believes emerge from such a dialogue conflate to offer a single message encapsulating a nostalgic view of female-male interaction (324).[2]

Because Brad Solomon establishes a male, first-person narrator in his 1979 female-male partnership novel, *The Open Shadow*, Fritz Thieringer dominates both its action and its mode of thought; as a result, he also seems to dominate the McGuane and Thieringer agency. The novel's opening conversation between the partners is deliberately constructed to exclude personal pronouns and any sex/gender referents to leave the unexpected introduction of Maggie McGuane at the end of chapter 3 a surprise to both the client and any reader who has not read the misleading cover blurb. The subject of their opening conversation also sets the tone for their supposedly professional relationship. Maggie has independently hired a new employee whom Fritz immediately distrusts. Rather than accept his partner's judgment, he argues with her, criticizes Paul Brade, and frequently refuses to use him although this results in overtime work or hiring additional help they cannot afford. Although regularly making mistakes in judgment and observation himself, Thieringer continually retests the new employee's skills, occasionally in confusing or insignificant episodes. However, when the case breaks open with a fight where all three are seriously threatened, McGuane's judgment in favor of Brade is confirmed as he outsmarts the killer. Neither then nor later does Fritz acknowledge Brade's competence or Maggie's in hiring him; in fact, he continues to withhold essential information about the case and becomes angry with Brade's subsequent behavior. At one point he lumps Brade and Maggie together as difficult problems he is forced to cope with: " 'They're driving me goddamn crazy! I got a kid who's scared of guns! I got a woman who can't take a goddamn trip to Vegas without taking a goddamn gun with her! I'm going out of my goddamn mind around here!' " (218). Although there is acknowledged tension which provokes this outburst and a sense of tolerant, even affectionate, backchat between Fritz and Maggie, he regularly assumes an authority and a superiority to which he is not entitled, forcing his own way on Maggie and the partnership. He treats her as an emotional female, allowing her to cry, sulk, or rage rather than seeing her as a fully competent, thinking professional.

Like Bertha Cool and Charity Tucker in earlier novels, Maggie McGuane seems to have the organizational skill and business drive in the partnership. She arranges to lease a better office, hires an assistant operative, and keeps track of their finances—a difficult job in view of Fritz's unanticipated expenditures. She is twenty-six, has a master's degree in theater arts, writes movie reviews, and likes to drink and drive fast. With a wealthy client, in a moment of anger she explodes: " 'I don't like people telling me how to do my job. I don't care who they are, I don't care how much they're paying, if they don't like what I'm doing they can go elsewhere. If they don't want to do that, they can just be patient and wait for me to do what I'm going to do. One thing they can't do is come into my office and tell me what to do. I don't accept that' " (245). Thieringer and McGuane make an unlikely team. Although Fritz insists that " 'having a partner ain't the sweetest thing in the world,' " he turns down a counteroffer from a male operative (52). He is a petty thief (pencils, stationery, books, etc.) and chisler who carries a cooler of Cokes and a large selection of disguise hats in his car. He is a former delinquent who stayed just within legal bounds. He lies as a way of thinking and, in a small-time way, grabs for what he wants—food, sleep, "anything when you can get it" (59).

Although Fritz agrees to a casual affair with a receptionist—in what he calls "women's lib" style, she propositions him—he is emotionally interested in Maggie, who refuses to trust anyone's affection (19). Having been divorced, she is devastated by an intense feeling of rejection, her inferred inadequacy, and the fear of being hurt again. She reminds Fritz: " 'People let you down. The only thing you can count on is that they're going to let you down' " (231). He is philosophical, understanding, supportive, and interested. Unfortunately, his admiration sounds patronizing; the novel's last paragraph idealizes Maggie: "The sun hit her from behind and combed it's [*sic*] rays through her hair. Whenever it does it that way there's nothing quite like it in the world. There are plenty of things more perfect, even more beautiful, but nothing quite like it. It's a good face, too. Strong. Healthy. Sometimes it gets bruised up, but somehow the bruises always go away. She's good at that" (359). His sensitivity and concern seem to be plot devices more than character descriptions, as though Solomon needed to produce the obligatory romance.

McGuane is a shadowy figure throughout the first two-thirds of the novel with Thieringer dominating action, dialogue, and narration. Although her participation in the typical hard-boiled action increases as the case comes to a climax, she never becomes an equal partner in either fighting or sleuthing. In fact, while Fritz is initially investigating the Isenbart-Morrison case, she undertakes separate cases which are not played out in the novel but only related by Maggie in monotonous chapter-long reportage. Her work is not shown in action but only described in narration which is at odds with the rest of the novel's form and content. Two episodes she reports correlate to the Isenbart investigation which Fritz dominates; her two independent cases involve snaring a blackmailing, pornographic-photo peddler and finding a very large, very impressive lost cat. She concludes the former case in a burst of self-righteous violence and the latter by imagining the tom's sexual frustration. Neither case strongly establishes her credentials nor reinforces her professional status.

The novel poses an interesting set of contradictions with its four important women characters. Annie Deveraux, the sexually emancipated receptionist, persists until she finally establishes an affair with Fritz then decides she should "try not coming on so strong" (234). Their secondary client, Mrs. Morrison, is the wealthy owner of a string of San Francisco restaurants whose initial financing was based on blackmail which led to her only child's death twenty years later. Mrs. Isenbart, a former dress model whose husband insisted she quit work when they married and who can't even spend money without his approval, regains her confidence under Fritz's encouragement and advice to begin running her dead husband's dress company. Maggie McGuane, whom a competitor describes as "the skirt" with whom Fritz hung out his shingle, is alternately emotional and bloodied, searching for cats and killers. The novel's mixed messages about aggressive, competent, self-confident women are all reflected through Fritz Thieringer's perception of them and their appropriate strengths; none is objectively presented by an unbiased narrator. In filtering the novel through Thieringer's consciousness, Solomon chooses a male model of thought and judgment; he directs and restricts the reader's identification and participation in a gender-specific way despite the apparent choice of a female detective as co-protagonist.

Like *The Open Shadow*, the four novels of Patrick Buchanan are narrated in the first person by the male half of the team. Ben Shock and Charity Tucker are "[n]ot 'Private Investigators,' who have to carry a license." According to Shock, "What we do is private and probably a shade illegal" (*Swine* 3). Their casually defined arrangement also begins at the woman's instigation; Ben notes that they formed a "sort of" partnership partially as therapy Charity designed for him but also as a reason to be together doing something they both liked (*Swine* 6). The technical device of Shock's first-person narration emphasizes the inequality between them. Not only his words and actions but also his thoughts dominate the novels. Attention is focused on Ben Shock; events are narrated by him; interpretations, valid or invalid, are controlled by him.

The disparity between the partners goes beyond the narrative form to the behavior they exhibit with each other. They met when Shock, a New York cop, shot Tucker's rapist during the rape. Just before being fired from the police for using excessive force, he resigns. When he is plagued by doubts, Charity not only reassures him but also promotes his emotional rehabilitation by creating a vehicle for maintaining his professional activity. Her traumas are the fear of sexual intimacy after being raped and bitter self-accusation about enjoying rape. Ben sees affection and sex as his contribution to her recovery. Although both of them claim to like investigating and copulating, he can function and even heal his anxieties through the work she offers him; she finds only rejection and pain in the sex he offers her. Her solution provides him the professional work he does so well;

his solution ignores her real problem to concentrate on his own version of her needs. Frustrated by being stripped of his profession, Ben takes it out on Charity: "Look, this is my *business* . . . I'm a professional at it. You're just a lucky amateur. You hit a couple of good ones, but you can't be right all the time" (*Owls* 148). Not only does he avenge his hurt professional feelings by belittling her, he eventually severs the partnership when the sexual therapy he has prescribed for her does not produce a quick cure.

Throughout the novels, Shock is the only active detective despite Tucker's ability to locate clients and her access to information through her former news-reporting job. As he goes after the murderers, drug smugglers, thieves, and kidnappers, Charity only gets herself in trouble. Twice she is caught, forced to strip, and barely gets away; one escape is attributed to her "instinctive" defense against rape and the other to her captor's stupidity (*Swine* 99). Charity's subordinate position in the partnership is emphasized by Ben's persistent efforts to leave her behind when danger threatens, to protect his "turf," and to keep her uninformed at his discretion (*Owls* 54). No wonder the publishers label a paperback reprint of *A Parliament of Owls* as "Another Ben Shock Mystery" (front cover); whatever roles she plays in the novels, Charity Tucker is not the real detective.

Using a first-person male narrator for the novels of a female-male partnership was introduced by A. A. Fair in the earliest example of such a pair. In twenty-nine novels from 1939 to 1970, the Mutt-and-Jeff team of Bertha Cool and Donald Lam develops from employer and employee to a legal, contractual detecting partnership. Like Maggie McGuane and Charity Tucker, Bertha Cool is the instigator of this partnership, having hired Lam for her own agency; however, the narrative structure joins with characterization and plot to undermine Cool's role as an effective detective.

In all but two of the novels, Donald Lam narrates; he also solves all the cases himself. His ability to maneuver is established in the first novel, *The Biggger They Come*, as he proves it is possible to get away with murder. In all the subsequent cases, he evades the criminals, the police, and the well-meaning but misdirected Bertha to increase his successes. In the two novels where Donald is absent, serving in the Navy in World War II, Fair does not continue the established pattern of detective-storyteller by now using Bertha Cool to narrate; instead he turns to a third-person narrator, indicating clearly how devalued the female point of view is in this series. The plots further this conclusion; in both instances (*Bats Fly at Dusk* and *Cats Prowl at Night*), Bertha bungles the cases by trying to think like Donald because she has come to mistrust her own instincts and value his. Naturally, she has to be rescued; once, she is saved by Donald who has figured out the problem from censored letters and solved the case in a thirty-six-hour emergency leave. Even when Fair does not make Lam his principal detective and narrator, he persists in using the male partner as the exclusive crime solver. Cool becomes merely a humorous adjunct or a troublesome sidekick.

Their contrasting abilities are paralleled in Fair's persistent references to their appearance and attributes. Almost every novel opens with Cool's physical description and emphatic references to her size: "Bertha Cool is middle-aged, weighs a hundred and sixty-five pounds, has a broad beam, a bulldog look, little glittering green eyes, and is just as hard and tough and difficult to handle as a roll of barbed wire" (*Bedrooms* 11). Little changes, in either Fair's style or Cool's size, in fifteen years. Both Bertha Cool and Donald Lam reassure clients worried about Lam's slight build by insisting that "brains count in this organization" (*Double* 9). Donald does not need brawn: " 'I figure things out. I always have. If a man starts pushing me around, I find a way to make him stop, and before I'm through he's sorry he ever started pushing. I don't mind hitting below the belt if I have to. I guess I even get a kick out of it. That's because of the way I'm made. A runt is apt to be mean' " (*Bigger* 6). Since Bertha's description contrasts her size with Donald Lam's, she must be the brawn to match his brains. This implication minimizes her role since brains are ordinarily valued over mere brute force no matter how strong. However, the novels go further in undercutting Cool, since, with one or two exceptions when she sits on female suspects to prevent their escape, she doesn't use brawn successfully either.

Like narration and characterization, Fair's plots demonstrate the clear-cut superiority of the male partner. Donald's instincts, skills, and judgment are so complete that he has no need for a colleague; the female—"bulldog" Bertha—is a plot device used to intensify the impact of his success (*Grabs* 1). Although "B. Cool—Investigations" had successfully concentrated on small cases before Donald Lam's employment, Bertha is portrayed as incapable of even accepting a client much less solving a case after Lam's arrival. She admits this when he returns from wartime duty: " 'When you went away,' Bertha said, 'you'd got us into the big-time stuff. Damned if I know how you did it. You could take even the most insignificant little case, and before you got done it developed into big business and big money. Then after you left, I could take what seemed to be the biggest case and it would peter out into little business and little money. I did all right for a while. Two or three cases went just as though you'd been here. And then the bottom dropped out and it's been a whole procession of little stuff like this' " (*Ax* 18). With Donald's efforts, this "little stuff" also turns into a major case with a sizeable fee. Although greed and financial management are supposed to be her specialties, Donald invariably has to unravel cases Cool has taken on too quickly and thoughtlessly just for the fee. On other occasions accepting a case despite her criticism and carping, Donald brings the agency a huge fee or bonus. Invariably, Big Bertha makes erroneous decisions and has to accede to lamb-like Donald.[3]

The apparent humor of Fair's novels disguises a misogynistic sub-text. More explicitly than *Open Shadow* where Maggie McGuane is a secondary character or Buchanan's novels where Charity Tucker is primarily a sex object, these works disparage women through the persistent mockery of Bertha Cool whom the genre would designate the co-hero. Caricatured as the leading male characters are not, she shares none of their redeeming talents. Unlike many examples in this study, Fair's submerged text shows that as both a married woman and a detective, Cool is a failure: both her husband and her partner outsmart her. Her only revenge is eating; the results—her weight, diets, appearance, meals—only elicit further mockery from Fair and his narrator, Lam. Nothing she is or does can be right; she is always ludicrous.

The ways in which these authors use male narrators to enhance the gender restrictions in the novels become even more apparent when they are contrasted with two series which the female partners narrate. The male pattern of narrator as singular protagonist-hero-detective is broken; but even her status as narrator is not sufficient to redeem either Petunia Best or Mavis Seidlitz from silliness and sheer stupidity.

The superficial humor suggested by Fair's mismatched team is extended beyond plausible limits in Brigit Chetwynd's two novels. No one could be more ridiculous than British Private Enquiry Agents

Petunia Best and Max Freund. They long, somewhat breathlessly, for serious cases: " 'Murder? . . . How much of *that* do we get? I'm beginning to fear we shall never get beyond keyholes in divorce cases, or shady dowagers who want to put something across insurance companies' " (*Death* 7). Eventually they achieve their goal: " 'a beautiful murder and us right on the spot for it,' " although they are inept and unconvincing in their investigations (*Death* 30). Little sensible thought or analysis of their qualifications and abilities has influenced their decision to try detecting; instead "[we] wanted to start something that would be interesting and perhaps even exciting, as well as keep us going" (*Death* 7). Their success is paradoxical. What success Best and Freund do have is coincidental or accidental; little in their backgrounds or behavior convinces the reader otherwise. Their questioning is amateurish; their deduction or ratiocination limited and weak; and their charm insufficient. The partnership is based on his tempering her silliness and her limiting his sensibleness.

Petunia, who daydreams of Wimsey, Poirot, and Marlowe, could easily be an amateur of the golden age variety. When challenged by a Scotland Yard detective, her only professional talent is defended: " 'I have trained myself always to observe as accurately as I can. . . . noting times in my mind helps me do that.' [Smilingly he responds] 'That would be part of your profession, wouldn't it?' " (*Death* 43). Romantically interested in Max, Petunia uses detection and investigation to further their relationship. And, at the conclusion of each case, she regrets her independent behavior:

> How I wished it were Max, not I, who had made this discovery! I felt very flimsy and feminine, not wanting responsibility and full of quite irrational bias. Hell, hell, hell, *what* to do? I wanted advice, but not Max's, because I knew in advance what his attitude would be. (*Death* 185)

> Any moment now, I thought, and what a fool I was to come! Why hadn't Max slapped me? Why should he, though? He knew I wouldn't like it. Independence: that was my great line. But what about danger? (*Rubies* 201)

Petunia is quite right to worry about danger except that her concern comes too late. At the conclusion of *Death Has Ten Thousand Doors*, she goes alone to a suspect's home, announces her conclusions about his participation to him and his partner, and is drugged and left unconscious while the murderers escape. Not having learned her lesson, she repeats this behavior at the end of *Rubies, Emeralds and Diamonds* where she is attacked by the criminal, left unconscious and locked in the drawing room by the murderer who almost escapes before the police arrive. In both events, she is finally as literally unconscious as she has been figuratively unconscious of what she is doing.

Chetwynd's use of a female narrator intensifies the tone of foolishness which dominates these novels. What little investigation is carried out seems to be the man's province; Petunia spends as much time visiting, partying, and worrying about clothes as she does solving a case. She persistently signals her lack of foresight with "had-I-but-known" announcements. Although her role as narrator in the novels' construction is central, she is peripheral otherwise. This contrast, directly opposite that of the male narrator-detectives, transforms the novels from conventional detective stories to entertainments with an investigative motif.

The American version of a foolish, unaware female private eye comes, naturally enough, from Hollywood. The paperback covers of Carter Brown's twelve Mavis Seidlitz novels, whether original or reissued, make as clear a statement about the role of the female half of the Rio Investigations agency as any of the novels themselves. Each shows a fully or partially naked woman provocatively posed, with copy announcing "the dizzy darling of the detective set," the "torrid blonde private eye," and the "curvy blonde bombshell." A typical cover blurb describes her for the perusing reader: "Mavis Seidlitz is the grooviest private eye in the business. A decided asset to the squad of LA's Rio Investigations. Topnotch in the numbers game (38-23-37). Hotshot in the dope racket. Sexpert in the art of self-defense. A kitteny man-killer who learns the hard way that it's what's up front that counts" (*Seidlitz and the Super-Spy*, back cover). Mavis's physical aspect attracts most of the novels' attention. At least once in each book she inhales too deeply and breaks a bra strap with predictable results; several times in each novel she "loses" her clothes. Her body and her tight clothes, peekaboo blouses, or see-through nighties fill her narration and the men's imaginations.

Although her body is perfect, Mavis's mind is a muddle. She can't tell a story straightforwardly, her "jokes" are senseless circumlocutions, and her understanding of others' points is confused and misleading. Her malapropisms rival Sheridan's originals. Her logic is of the same order: ". . . what was the use of being a confidential consultant if people wouldn't confide in me? I mean how would a burlesque queen feel if her audience all went home when she started to unzip?" (*Tomorrow* 16).

In the partnership of Mavis and Johnny Rio, she begins as a stenographer, not having won a hoped-for star's contract in Hollywood. Their subsequent partnership brings her only a salary cut. Twice she demonstrates some business acumen, announcing that she'll begin her assignment after signing a legal contract assigning her full partnership and half the profits. When Johnny attempts to terminate the partnership, she sets him up: " 'You agreed to settle on my terms— I want everything. The business, the bank account, the office—everything. You're trespassing, Mr. Rio. Get out of here before I call a cop and have you thrown out!' " (*Lethal Heart* 99). Of course, Mavis is being momentarily difficult. She is really romantically interested in Johnny to the point where she coos over his masterful behavior when he spanks her. Occasionally, Mavis is accidentally successful: she gets in the way of the criminal who cannot then escape or she blunders into the middle of a shootout on a movie set and unwittingly follows the movie's scenario.

As a first-person narrator, Seidlitz cooperates in her own minimization. Like Honey West and Angela Harpe, she is a sex object; like Miriam Birdseye and Flora Hogg, she is a foolish incompetent; like Petunia Best, she tells her own story with neither insight nor self-awareness.[4] Mavis's male author matches Petunia's female author in using narration against the model which male writers establish for their male narrator-detective-heroes. The use of male and female narrators reinforces the authors' evaluations; the narrative stance implies the complicity of individual women and men with society's disparate evaluation of them. And, unlike male readers who find themselves positively reflected in both narration and plot, female readers must continually resist identification with both male and female narrator-protagonists.

Obviously, the male-female detective partnership is a fallacy; there is no partnership. The Random House Dictionary offers "a sharer or partaker; associate" as the primary meaning of "partner." But it suggests additional definitions as well; the fourth is "a husband or a wife; spouse." These investigative marriages are organized like other marriages in a patriarchal society; except for Cool and Lam, even the sexual components are explicit.[5] No matter who proposes, the male partner decides. Like unlucky spouses, these women devote themselves to associations where they are protected against their wishes, managed, and used. Although publicly claimed as partners, they are undermined and discredited by their colleagues, the events of the novel, or the narrative structure. As in conventional marriages, either through the form of the institution or the choice of an individual male partner, the women relinquish their right to function separately and independently but receive little of value in return.

Notes

1. Two arrangements which might be called partnerships consist of one woman leading several men in vigilante-style actions. In fifty novels written by Mark Cross between 1924 and 1961, Daphne Wrayne and the Four Adjustors "adjust the inequalities that at present exist between the criminal and the victim" through what Scotland Yard initially calls "another private detective agency with a fantastic name and a high falutin' slogan" (*Perilous Hazard* 9). Like most of these formal or understood arrangements, the Adjustors are the direct result of a woman's initiative and planning; and, like the other female members of partnerships, Wrayne believes that the men are necessary to her organization's success.

   The position of Daphne Wrayne with the four adjustors is somewhat paradoxical: although the most visible member of the group, she is often treated as merely a conduit to the more important male figures; she is not herself "one of the four." This calculated division between the sexes and their appropriate roles effectively eliminates Daphne Wrayne's options. Her partners also recognize this restriction, admitting that if she marries, they'll have to shut down their operation; however, none of them sees himself denied marriage if he wants to remain an adjustor. In fact, the men have the freedom of four roles: husband, father, public figure, and private crime-fighter. For their female partner there are choices—wife/mother or crime-fighter. Unlike them, she cannot have it all.

   Despite a manifest range of differences between the creations of Mark Cross and Graham Montrose, Angel Brown and her Band of Angels can be compared with Daphne Wrayne and the Four Adjustors. Both groups investigate crime more from the women's need for vengeance and the men's inclination to antisocial, dangerous behavior than a strict passion for justice. In twelve novels, the Band's regular target is organized crime.

For all her assertive acumen, Angel regularly gets kidnapped just like others in her Band and the criminals they capture. Violence and torture are the hallmarks of these episodes on both sides. The criminals seldom escape; Angel rescues her men and is, in turn, rescued by them. What is different for her, however, than for all the others is that her captors take special delight in torturing her both as they would a man and as they think will hurt a woman. In almost every novel she is stripped naked, ostensibly to incapacitate her and make escape more difficult because of the humiliation this treatment brings. Neither the same treatment nor the same argument is applied to any of the captured men, either Angels or criminals. She is singled out for this treatment because as a woman she has had the temerity to challenge and beat men; to assuage their humiliation at being bested by a woman, they must humiliate her in return.

2. In Reed Stephens's two novels, *The Man Who Killed His Brother* (1980) and *The Man Who Risked His Partner* (1984), the pattern of a male narrator undercutting his female coworker is even more emphatic. In both novels, the woman who owns the agency, holds the license, investigates the case, and helps her drunken colleague is a secondary character; the drunken, demoralized, ex-private eye Mick Axbrewder is the protagonist and hero of his own narration. Despite the second title, these are not partnership novels; their working relationship is employer and temporary employee with a strong emotional tie.

3. Frank Robbins's article on the pair follows the series in devoting primary attention to Donald Lam.

4. These conclusions are based on eight of the twelve known titles, although Hubin acknowledges that there might be as few as eight actual books.

5. A more conventional male-female arrangement narrated in the third person operates for J. T. McIntosh's "working partners" in the only arrangement based on marriage. Dominique Brienne Frayne joins her husband Ambrose in one of his established firms as a detective and investigator as well as a secretary-typist (*Private Eyes* 49). Her participation is neither legal nor contractual, made barely explicit by her husband, "agreed [upon] without any need for discussion," and dependent on his continued willingness to allow her activities (*Private Eyes* 110). Dominique's contributions to the physical and intellectual solutions of the crimes are limited. The ideas with which she is credited actually turn out to be random remarks whose significance and usefulness are recognized by either her husband or her father-in-law. De-

spite one or two hints that their partnership might be egalitarian, the Fraynes are part of an unspoken but admitted hierarchical relationship. Upon their marriage, Dominique adopts her husband's name, nationality, profession, values, and judgment. However unconventional their union may seem, it is a traditional pairing where the man's vision dominates. In that, these novels are no different from any others which use the implied collaboration of partnership as a device rather than an integral aspect of the plot and structure.

Like the Fraynes, Agatha Christie's Tommy and Tuppence Beresford base their partnership on marriage (although this does not occur until the end of the first book), but are not legitimate private eyes. In four novels they either act for the British government secret service or investigate cases as amateurs who stumble upon suspicious events; ordinarily Tommy initiates the former and Tuppence the latter. Although both frequently get into trouble, she needs to be rescued more often than he. In a series of short stories, *Partners in Crime,* they are established by the government in the International Detective Agency for espionage; simultaneously, they investigate the legitimate cases which come to the agency. Christie's humor parodies her writing colleagues as the Beresfords mimic famous fictional detectives practicing their craft. Tommy is more prone to adopting roles than his wife, but while she can take on both male and female guise, he limits himself to imitating only male detectives. Christie does not sustain the parallels for long; most cases are solved in her typical style rather than Conan Doyle's or Chesterton's. The Beresfords' private joking and investigating are at odds with their public image of detective-agency owner and his secretary-assistant in which traditional sex roles are maintained.

10

An Unsuitable Job for a Feminist?

Whereas radical or socialist feminism demands sweeping social re-creation, liberal and revisionist feminism suggest that although the current, patriarchal organization of society is flawed, women should work through existing systems to effect change and to expand women's opportunities. The literary canon and publishing industry are among such systems which have responded to pressure from the women's movement—the former because of academic feminists and the latter for commercial gain.

The benefits of reclaiming popular literature for women as authors, readers, and characters seem considerable. One recent example of these efforts is the introduction of the self-aware feminists who appear as protagonists of private-eye novels.[1] These characters are important for being not only women in a male-identified profession and popular genre but also feminists. At first, this appropriation of traditionally male space for women appears to favor feminist goals; coincidentally, it might even help modify the attitudes of readers of a reactionary literary mode. But, the task is more complex than simply replacing a male protagonist with a female one.

Emphasizing how completely the formula of detective fiction rejects feminist change, Dennis Porter notes that the role of detective celebrates traditional heroic virtues and validates hero worship. These stances are rejected by such ideological adversaries of heroic male action as radical feminists whose aim is to forge new attitudes and forms of human interaction (126). Furthermore, the feminist detective who restores order to a disordered world by investigating murder may be serving justice, but although the justice *may* be personal, it is also public.[2] Consequently, the feminist detective winds up supporting the existing system which oppresses women when she reestablishes the ordered status quo. This contradiction between feminist ideals and detectives' behavior is more apparent when the private eyes turn their criminals over to the law; however, no woman detective escapes the prospect of assisting in her own or other women's oppression whether women characters are the criminals, victims, or merely bystanders. Adopting the formula traps their authors.

The formula of the hard-boiled sub-genre in which all these detectives act has widely accepted characteristics. Crime is committed in the public sphere; it is urban, often is based on corruption, frequently involves institutions as well as individuals. The crimes are complex, making neat, complete solutions difficult; even though the detectives frequently act as judges themselves rather than trust the system's handling of the criminals, they are bound to that system which they may despise but cannot escape. Thus, the detective is a loner, increasingly isolated and cynical, forced into compromise, and limited in maintaining satisfying friendships or love affairs; the most interesting are psychologically complex but many are only a collection of identifying traits. Repeated episodes of physical violence and frequent sexual activity—both committed and casual—are standard plot features. The detectives are ordinarily male. Feminism, on the other hand, is more subjectively defined. Marty S. Knepper offers the following criteria: feminist writing shows "as a norm and not as freaks, women capable of intelligence, moral responsibility, competence, and independent action; . . . reveals the economic, social, political and psychological problems women face as part of a patriarchal society; . . . explores female consciousness and female perceptions of the world; . . . creates women who have psychological complexity and rejects sexist stereotypes" ("Agatha Christie" 399). Additionally, feminism rejects the glorification of violence, the objectification of sex, and the patronization of the oppressed. It values female bonding, awareness of women without continual reference to or affiliation with men, and the self-knowledge which prompts women to independent judgment on both public and personal issues.

What finally keeps feminism and the detection formula from meshing is the subsequent necessity of creating a female private eye who refuses to play games within a system which seems to exist to support male hegemony. A feminist private eye who is both aware and committed could not be shown subscribing to any social paradigm which dishonestly pretends to uphold a system of values based on a disinterested ethic but actually is grounded in interested power structures, especially as those structures and systems deliberately exclude women. The private motivations of the investigator do not lessen the impact of her bolstering a system which exists, at least in part, to uphold male privilege. Traditional hard-boiled fiction with male heroes and male values is limited by a socially validated, gender bias which it does not recognize; feminist fiction must be more aware.[3] Inasmuch as such mass-mediated culture, like detective fiction, primarily serves the interests of the relatively small political-economic power elite which sits atop the social pyramid (as Michael Real notes of non-print media), authors trying to create a feminist detective face their own set of necessary compromises. Either feminism or the formula is at risk.

A few detective novelists have attempted to resist this contradiction between the character's ideological position and her behavior. Other novelists have been caught between making a feminist statement and participating in the commercially successful production of widely read formula fiction. The genre's emphasis on power and the defense of private property is not easily replaced or blended with feminists' awareness of gender as a major organizing principle of society. Such a shift requires authors to re-vision both the purpose and the formula of detective fiction. These five novelists—Sue Grafton, Marcia Muller, Susan Steiner, Sara Paretsky, and M. F. Beal—attempt to integrate gender awareness into the most resistant form, the hard-boiled novel. Their characters are more than emancipated or liberated women like their predecessors; they are conscious of gender as a way in which the social system categorizes, judges, and responds to people. All their behavior reflects this recognition, but several are more aware than others. The characters Kinsey Milhone and Sharon McCone might best be described as having feminist inclinations without explicitly defining themselves that way. Alex Winter, V. I. Warshawski and Kat Guerrera are self-defined feminists for whom this identification is both a conscious act and an apparently consistent feature of their behavior. Nonetheless, all of them are forced to compromise between their ideological position and their official professional careers.

Born during the Korean War, Kinsey Milhone is naturally a product of both the new feminist movement and the traditional view of women's lives. She is often caught between the two. Author Sue Grafton also invests Kinsey with most of the typical detective's trappings, accommodating her gender and potential self-awareness in only minor ways. Neither too young nor too innocent of the world to be a plausible detective, Milhone is a thirty-two-year-old, twice-divorced woman without children, plants, or housepets; she is a loner whose friendships do not seem to pass beyond a carefully modulated phase. She comes closest to establishing ties with just two women and two men—her eighty-one-year-old landlord, the black female owner of her favorite bar, an arthritic retiree who jokes about becoming her partner, and a recently divorced cop who is willing to help her. Her attitude about intimate relationships is equally self-protective: "Whatever the surface appearances, most human beings come equipped with convoluted emotional machinery. With intimacy, the wreckage starts to show, damage rendered in the course of passions colliding like freight trains on the same track. I'd had enough of that over the years" ("*D*" 29–31). Ironically, her professional life contradicts the isolation of her personal one. Naive, frustrated, and idealistic, she left the police force because "back then, policewomen were viewed with a mixture of curiosity and scorn. I didn't want to spend my days defending myself against 'good-natured' insults, or having to prove how tough I was again and again" ("*B*" 1). She did not go immediately into independent private detective work but held several non-investigative jobs before apprenticing two years with a small detective firm. With five years of being in business for herself, she is well established even to the point of having a connection with California Fidelity Insurance Company which trades her a two-room office in exchange for investigative work. Although three of her clients are vastly different women, she tends to overgeneralize: "I like older women as a rule. I like almost all women, as a matter of fact. I find them open and confiding by nature, amusingly candid when it comes to talk of men" ("*C*" 15). And despite this avowal, she can be snide about other women she meets in her investigations; despite some feminist inclinations, she is not uniformly sympathetic to women.

Kinsey's style of operation is a two-fold blend of traditional women's and men's work. She notes that most of her job consists of tedious, monotonous, boring checking and cross-checking—plodding and patient routine. Wryly she acknowledges in both books that society has inadvertently been preparing women for these roles for years, turning on its head the stereotype of the macho detective, knight-errant, man in a man's world of mean streets. In defining her performance, Kinsey continually tests herself; more than just being a detective, she is fitting herself into an external model she has seen. Methodically, she runs daily "for the same reasons I learned to drive a car with a stick shift and drink my coffee black, imagining that a day might come when some amazing emergency would require such a test" (*"A"* 80). When she is wrong, she criticizes herself and then more fairly reconsiders, recognizing that she had made only the same mistakes as everyone else. Even so, she admits that feeling good about her professional behavior is as important as the money she earns for solving a case.

The novels' conflicts are more the result of Milhone's errors than either the criminals' cleverness or the pace of the investigation; this device makes it difficult for Grafton to recover her protagonist's stature. In all three of the cases described, Kinsey significantly misjudges the situations with client, criminals, or friend. Most important, she trusts and sleeps with a murderer who is trying to keep her from the truth. Her attraction to Charlie Scorsoni is immediate and powerful. Their relationship is marked by her self-consciousness at being so vulnerable to his sexual charm and, eventually, a nagging recognition that mixing business and lovemaking is both unprofessional and dangerous. A sharp irony arises: early in their affair, he makes her feel comfortable and safe; at the end of the case, she is forced to kill him when he hunts her down with a butcher knife. Before she calls a temporary break from seeing him, he forces an argument about how she is using him, pumping him for information. At first, she is angry—"I've never been good at taking shit, especially from men"—and labels his offer of compromise as giving away half of what is rightfully hers (*"A"* 155). But later she apologizes, wonders if she has misjudged him, and hops back into bed from which she emerges feeling smug about their sexual compatibility. Until almost the end of the case, she is ambivalent about her decision not to continue seeing him, worrying that she is using her job and her claims of integrity to avoid commitment. Grafton uses this concern, expressed only for an intimate heterosexual relationship, to reassure readers of this strong woman's traditional femininity rather than to develop her character or personality.

Grafton has created a thoughtful, self-aware if sometimes self-deluded woman who is also a detective; her work gives Milhone both reasons and opportunity to consider her own life: "I tried to imagine myself dead, someone sorting carelessly through my belongings. What was there really of my life? Cancelled checks. Reports all typewritten and filed. Everything of value reduced to terse prose. I didn't keep much myself, didn't hoard or save. Two divorce decrees. That was about the sum of it for me. I collected more information about other people's lives than I did about my own, as though, perhaps, in poring over the facts about other people, I could discover something about myself. My own mystery, unplumbed, undetected, was sorted into files that were neatly labeled but really didn't say much" ("*A*" 119–20). With this attitude, she has stripped down her life; when in doubt she falls back on routine. Even on a case, she wants to cut through the surrounding game-playing, hoping for straight answers without conniving and manipulating. Although she saves herself from Scorsoni and later from the Grices and Dr. Fraker, Kinsey questions her own professional judgment. Killing Charlie Scorsoni leads her to reconsider how she can be a good person if she has killed; attacking and shooting Leonard and Marty Grice causes her to wonder "how many times I'll dance with death" ("*B*" 229). Guilty at not being able to forestall Tony Gahan's suicide, she muses, "Perhaps in this case, all of the accounts are now paid in full . . . except mine" ("*D*" 229). She worries that she has made peace with corruption—or been a detective too long.

Her relationship with authority is contradictory. Milhone recognizes that her sense of self in the power structure is based on being sent to the principal's office when a schoolgirl. As a result she alternates between trying to inform the police about her case, promising Jonah Robb not to "be stupid" ("*C*" 230), being nervous when a cop offers to pass along privileged information, and refusing to report a break-in at her apartment because she feels harassed by the cops. This ambivalence traps her between being independent and unconsciously expecting to be protected by the system. Even when she seems to take reasonable precautions for her own safety independent of police protection, it is just barely enough. So, she must bail herself out of trouble. Later, her victorious feelings of escape and self-preservation vie with others of guilt and regret.

What eventually emerges about Milhone's relationship with the patriarchal system is conventional, even traditional. Her personal ties with police officers may be both hostile and congenial but they signal her acceptance of the system despite her personal inability to fit into it. When she kills Scorsoni, she reports the shooting to both the police and the Bureau of Collection and Investigative Services; when she captures Leonard and Marty Grice and Dr. Fraker, she turns them over to the police. Even though Milhone is cautious about assuming that the courts will punish them, she takes her use of the legal system for granted. Her professional behavior is at odds with her awareness, but she still does not see herself challenging the process. The closest she comes to challenging the prevailing attitude is to acknowledge how simplistic (at least in the John Daggett case) her conventional view of morality is. Her latent feminism is individual rather than communal; she sees both problems and solutions in personal rather than systemic change.

Milhone is not unlike Sharon McCone in adopting individual solutions for societal problems. One of the most promising women detectives of this period, Marcia Muller's McCone has become conventional by her seventh appearance. McCone, just under thirty when introduced, is staff investigator for the All Souls Cooperative, a legal and residental commune in San Francisco working with middle-class clients. This alternative to the corporate model of litigation parallels Sharon's apparent disdain for rigid, official systems. Intensely interested, she is willing to risk her license by investigating two cases without having a client, continuing a third when the client ends the case, and talking a fourth prospective client into joining the cooperative to legitimate her already initiated investigation. With a background that includes department store security, night security while working on a sociology degree at Berkeley, and being fired from a large detective agency for not following orders, she is well satisfied with the casual independence allowed by All Souls.

McCone is a fairly traditional investigator, using some logic, some intuition, and plenty of legwork to solve the thirteen murders which seem to dog her personally and professionally. She considers her strongest point to be her ability to ask the right question without also answering it herself; responses come because she looks like a person in whom others can safely confide. Quick thinking in a tight spot, hard working enough to stay up all night or drive monotonously long distances several times, and determined to continue despite opposition, Sharon has come to terms with both the demands and the ethics of her profession. She can rationalize breaking-and-entering or entrapment in her own cause. Luckily, she has both friends and supporters who help her by supplying information, offering cautionary warnings, or hiding her from police scrutiny. She carries false identification, uses judo on thugs, or cuts a deal with the police to solve her cases. But, too often she takes unreasonable risks. Traps she has set lead to suicide or shooting, leaving her to wonder: "But there were more deaths, and the older I got and the more violence I saw, the more I wondered if I could go on like this indefinitely. And when I wondered that, I also wondered what I would do if I couldn't go on. What on earth *could* a former private eye with a useless sociology degree do for a living?" (*Games* 49). When Sharon considers her choices, the direction is unclear; she knows only that she loves her work, feels she's "a person who lives it every hour, every day" (*Double* 153). She sees the difference between herself and high school friends with striking clarity on a visit home; she recognizes both vicarious excitement and distance in their eyes. But her older brother also reinforces this divided reaction: he admires her drive and success but insists that she's played safe by never allowing herself to be in a position where she could lose too much.

McCone runs into the usual array of reactions to the combination of her gender and profession. She is surprised when Lt. Marcus doesn't pull the standard "what's-a-nice-girl-like-you" routine on her and only slightly amazed when a woman-hating inspector uses her supposed reputation as a troublemaker to make a pass. With her lovers, Sharon encounters vastly different responses: the cop is so persistently hostile to private investigators that her gender is negligible. Her second lover is taken aback by the gun in her glove compartment: " 'You're for real, aren't you? . . . It's one thing hearing you talk about an investigation, but seeing that . . . ' " (*Games* 86). Her mother wants her to settle down, marry, have kids. Other professional women note, without comment, her choice of profession. The real hostility is voiced by an angry bail-bondsman/suspect/thief; he hopes to insult her— " 'little girls playing detective' "—then threaten, then frighten her off the case (*Edwin* 90). But, Sharon McCone also aligns herself with this last attitude; when she succeeds in standing up to a tough ghetto lawyer, her self-congratulations are for the ex-cheerleader and homecoming princess that she was, not the competent investigator she is. She is surprised to discover her own strength.

In her first cases, McCone investigates amidst sharp conflict with an alternately hostile and patronizing homicide lieutenant, Greg Marcus; although the tension between them never fully abates, it does relax long enough for them to have a two-year affair. Sharon McCone sees their similarly volatile personalities and the traditional rivalry between police and private eye as the reasons for their breakup despite Marcus's sensitivity to art, parallel obsession about chocolate, and lovemaking style. Her second lover is more easygoing and accommodating; Don del Boccio tends either to let her set the tone of their relationship or to be comfortable with his own life and activities. Of course, it may also help that he is a radio disk jockey and so not professionally competitive with McCone. In Sharon's relationships with these two men and the admittedly more parent-child one with her temporary partner, Wolf, she more often re-acts than acts. Of course, as the novels are told in the first person, it is impossible to know how the men think or behave except through Sharon's perceptions. However, she describes them as thinking about themselves and then acting, which is not to say that they are selfish or insensitive but only that they initiate action based on their lives. Even though Don waits until Sharon is out of town to hire a house cleaner (she has insisted that he should be self-sufficient), he does hire someone. Sharon is first jealous, assuming the woman in Don's apartment when she phones is a rival. Later, she laughs at her misperception and Don's secret maneuvering, but she also agrees to find and share a new cleaner, completely contradicting her earlier attitude about self-sufficiency. More seriously, she is competitive with Greg Marcus to the point of endangering her life and her license in order to be first to find the killer in cases they both investigate. In their personal relationship, she alternately loathes and tolerates his racist, sexist, and ageist nickname for her—"papoose"—without ever insisting firmly that he abandon it. Only in their breakup does she come close to the active role; but she halfheartedly regrets the results: "I was glad the relationship was over; it was a relief to be without the constant, energy-sapping conflict. But still, you get used to that daily phone call after all that time. You get used to shared laughter and loving and nice moments. Not finding a message left me with a mild sense of depression. I needed to do something. I needed to get out of here. Now" (*Games* 18).

Midway through the first McCone novel, Muller suggests her character's feminist inclinations: "She [informant/murderer] was my kind of woman, one who made her own way on her own steam and refused to be held back. That was what I had always done . . ." (*Edwin* 106). However, this motif fades away in subsequent novels. Sharon is specific about her relationships with men, wanting equality but not marriage. However, she has little to say about her consciousness of women's position in society except as men exasperate her with patronizing remarks. Through her affair with a cop and her employment by a legal cooperative, she, like Milhone, is tied to the police and legal systems. Occasionally, these two institutions are at war with each other, but Sharon has no sense that both are part of a larger, flawed system needing to be changed.

However, Milhone and McCone are not alone in tolerating a system which their ideological orientation would suggest they should reject. Even the self-identified feminists are able to split themselves between awareness and behavior. For Alex Winter, feminism is inextricably bound up with her own experiences of marriage. She tends to divide men into two camps—those who remind her of the charming but unfaithful ex-husband whom she put through Harvard Law School and those who don't. Assistant Detective Alexandra Winter of the Abromowitz and Bailey Investigation Agency is introduced by Susan Steiner via a journal entry which makes her appear a mixture of innocence and cynicism, a combination seldom found in the masculine hard-boiled hero. Although she is free to fantasize great success as an investigator leading to book, movie, and television contracts, she is also cynical enough to know that truth is only a luxury she indulges in "whenever possible" (*Murder on Her Mind* 1).

Unfortunately, Alex is too easily used professionally and personally; her inexperience as a detective and her incompletely resolved post-divorce problems leave her vulnerable on both fronts. Having escaped the worst of her orgy of alcohol and depression, she still lacks the kind of confidence which would allow her to meet men as themselves, not as shadows of her ex-husband. As a result, she can be used by reporter Paul Moreley whom she thinks is a lucky contact while he is actually feeding her misleading or false information. Similarly, as she is falling for client Jay Southwood's charm, she first doubts him and then her doubts of him. Thinking he'll be able to manipulate her, Southwood insists that she be the primary investigator—his excuse is that meetings with an attractive woman will be less noticeable. Because she immediately and continually compares his behavior, style, and attractiveness with that of her ex-husband, she is slow to see his manipulation of her as a professional issue rather than a sexual one.

Although Winter complains that her looks mislead people into speaking of her as merely pretty or sweet, missing her "natural shrewdness . . . [and] determination" (2), she too mistakes surface for depth. Comparing herself adversely with other fictional detectives, she stresses both her differences and her inadequacy. She lacks self-confidence, mistrusts her better instincts and gives way to the negative ones. She is the kind of woman who compliments herself for thinking like a detective and immediately recognizes that socialized feminine behavior still keeps her from questioning a suspect. "You're a coward," she accuses herself, only to recognize quickly that she also is "a victim of cultural myths" (96). Cleverly, Steiner plays Alex Winter against herself in the contest between old and new woman.

Alex describes herself in feminist terms; her bosses and assistant have no doubts that she thinks and acts accordingly. This feminism worries George Bailey, the business-oriented agency owner who sets a spy on her: " 'Alex is such a fucking feminist that she's bound to cry over Coral [woman who was raped] and wind up shafting our client [Southwood]. So keep track of whatever she finds out' " (91–92). The masculinist implications of his language notwithstanding, he's very nearly right. But even Alex abuses Coral, pumping her for information while claiming to be a battered wife who needs help. She is a mixture of awareness and unanalytical naiveté. Southwood's compliments on her brains flatter her more than ones on her looks might have; she's aware that he has figured her out. Paul Moreley, George Bailey, and Jay Southwood all goad her inadvertently or deliberately by sexist remarks which provoke her anger and, consequently, strengthen her self-confidence.

The case, as well as the players, has a feminist message: years before, a young woman from a prominent family was raped by Southwood's half-Mexican half brother who used her in retaliation for her father's racist, capitalist tyranny. Now that the rapist is running for political office, he is being blackmailed by the woman's ex-husband, despite the woman's desire to dissociate herself from both men and their actions. The candidate's lies and Southwood's evasions lead to the woman's discovery by Winter and eventual murder by an opposition candidate. Both women—the seeker and the sought—are at the mercy of these men who see women only as objects or tools to achieve their own ends. The women share the same background of pain and battering at the hands of men, either charming or unscrupulous, who felt themselves entitled.

Not even Alex's inexperience makes it possible for Steiner to reconcile her behavior and her acknowledged feminism. Alex uses another woman, and it is her feminism which gives her the tools. That woman is then killed because Alex can be used by men. The fact that other men then catch the killer does not minimize Alex's responsibility; instead, their success may compound her fault because again they limit her ability to act according to her announced principles. She too chooses the established norms of her profession over her personal ideology.

The conclusion of the novel returns to what seems to be the more important issue throughout: Winter's responses to men. First, she successfully rejects her ex-husband's demands for accommodations and assistance when he arrives in town; she also is able to resist his no longer charming overtures. Second, she acknowledges that she is falling in love with Jay Southwood, but accepts his selfishly described departure: he insists that she would have had to fit in with his life and acknowledges that would never work. She agrees, still harping on her ex-husband: " 'No . . . And I was hurt so badly before. I just don't want pain like that again' " (241). Nevertheless, in the final paragraph, she is rethinking her decision. Given the circumstances of the novel and the history of her marriage, this plan is mere daydreaming; nothing in Southwood's behavior or her own experiences should lead Alex to accept his terms. Her uncertainty can only be seen as a sentimental, romantic response which negates all that she might have been assumed to have learned in the course of this investigation. More than the cuts and bruises from her physical attacks, she has emotional scars which, until this conclusion, her own behavior suggests she fully recognizes and respects. Instead, she is responding to the nostalgic appeal of the marriage plot with its myth of the self-sacrificing woman. Steiner's rejection of Alex's hard-won knowledge manipulates and trivializes her in the same way that men treat women throughout the novel.

Her refusal to compromise her feminism is only the first of V. I. Warshawski's differences from Alex Winter. Known as Vic only to her friends, Victoria Iphigenia Warshawski uses her initials otherwise because patronizing her is more difficult when men don't know her first name.[4] Appearing in four novels to date, she is one of the best developed and most convincing female private eyes in contemporary fiction. Virtually every aspect of Sara Paretsky's novels relates to gender. The reader is always made aware of Vic as both a woman and a feminist, both in her positively attributed independent stance and in defensive responses appearing in dialogue, descriptions, and thoughts. As a first-person narrator, Vic reveals a great deal about her life; as a feminist she devotes considerable thought to women's roles and their treatment in explicit gender-role terms. She clearly recognizes oppression, paternalism, and patriarchalism in the behavior of others around her and reinforced by society at large.

Paretsky provides the background details which make these concerns plausible; Vic is no newcomer to either detection or political awareness. After her graduation from the University of Chicago Law School, Warshawski entered the public defender's office, a starry-eyed rookie whose experience in an underground abortion referral service and in Louisiana freedom marches had previously put her on the other side of the law. Although her father had been a cop, clearly her mother's drive was the more important influence in Vic's life; but, she believes, neither parent would have approved of her decision to become a detective. After their deaths, this attitude is echoed resoundingly by family friend Lt. Bobby Mallory who criticizes her decision, subverts her investigations, threatens her license, and urges her to marry so she can bear children. Divorced after just fourteen months from a man who could only admire independent women from a distance, she is wary of commitments. Her mother's advice is more to her liking: " 'Any girl can be pretty—but to take care of yourself you must have brains. And you must have a job, a profession. You must work' " (*Indemnity* 10). And work is what V. I. Warshawski does best.

V.I. has become a private investigator not only to be her own boss but also—"a la Doña Quixote perhaps"—to redress the imbalances between guilty and innocent she'd seen in the public defenders office (*Deadlock* 38). As a detective, she contrasts herself unfavorably with Lord Peter Wimsey, who would have charmed rather than bullied; favorably with Mike Hammer, who could barely think; and grudgingly with the host of hard-boileds: "Of course, a hard-boiled detective is never scared. So what I was feeling couldn't be fear. Perhaps nervous excitement at the treats in store for me" (*Orders* 226). Law school colleagues remind her of maverick approaches and bullying in moot court; her closest friend, Dr. Lotty Herschel, calls her a pit dog and Jill-the-giant-killer. Vic's own description of her methods is more benign: "My theory of detection resembles Julia Child's approach to cooking: Grab a lot of ingredients from the shelves, put them in a pot and stir, and see what happens" (*Orders* 58). Her action is rarely so mellow.

All four of her cases involve fraud and multiple murders; two of them involve members of her family—a favorite cousin is not a suicide but a murder victim in *Deadlock* and a distinctly unfavorite aunt fears being framed in *Killing Orders*. Even her earlier client, union boss Andrew McGrath, has a connection through her father, although it is slight enough for him to be looking for a son rather than a daughter in the investigations business. His reservations about hiring "a girl" provoke a calmer response from her than most other gender-related remarks: " 'I'm a woman . . . and I can look out for myself. If I couldn't, I wouldn't be in this kind of business. If things get heavy, I'll figure out a way to handle them—or go down trying. That's my problem, not yours' " (*Indemnity* 7).

Her detective style is active and involved. Searching for her cousin's killer, she jokingly wishes to disguise herself as a load of wheat on the shipping line where he worked to learn the truth of his death. And she does stow away, braving the captain's anger and a deadly explosion. She faces her share of threats and fist fights, usually acquitting herself well, sometimes leaving her opponents humiliated as well as hurt: "It's not very nice for two men to go after one woman and only get her after losing a rib and a kidney, and then to have her vomit down your jacket front and not be able to move or clean it off . . ." (*Indemnity* 51). This humor is a defense against both pain and vulnerability; her bruises don't heal quickly or easily and she feels forced to buy a gun. She admits to fear without panic, to paranoia and to caution. She is willing to force people to provide information even though she is occasionally disgusted with her tactics; she will inflict and accept pain as a means to her ends. In the early novels, her relationship with the authorities is the typically hostile one between police and private eyes strained further by gender conflicts between women and men. But, in *Bitter Medicine*, Paretsky explores the possibilities of cooperation without cooptation; Vic knows that "it's not good for a PI to get too sociable with the police" even as she sometimes includes Detective Rawlings in her investigation (320).

Warshawski's independence and her profession contribute to conflicted relationships with her lovers in each of the novels. When Ralph Devereux compares the likelihood of her being a detective with his being a ballet dancer, she verbally dresses him in tights and a tutu. Unfortunately, his disbelief is almost fatal. Unwilling to trust Vic's assessment of his boss, he is almost killed: " 'I couldn't believe you knew what you were talking about. I guess deep down I didn't take your detecting seriously. I thought it was a hobby, like Dorothy's [his ex-wife] painting' " (*Indemnity* 208). Although her language varies, her statements all repeat the same message: "[I]t would piss me off in a major way to have you butting into my business" (*Bitter Medicine* 120–21). But, the protectiveness of men simply because they are men draws Vic's greatest anger. She reminds a lover/informant/client that her autonomy is as important as his; he should not interfere in her more dangerous activities. "I was clenching and unclenching my fists, trying to keep rage under control. Protection. The middle-class dream. My father protecting Gabriella [her mother] in a Milwaukee Avenue bar. My mother giving him loyalty and channeling her fierce creative passions into a South Chicago tenement in gratitude" (*Orders* 188). She is afraid of reliving her mother's past while simultaneously cherishing her mother's strengths.

Throughout the novels, and especially in their conclusions, Warshawski's special links with women become more apparent. Because she relies unfailingly on Lotty Herschel for assistance, advice, and affection, their brief estrangement in *Killing Orders* is extraordinarily painful for both. Their reunion establishes clearly how they view each other. Lotty admits, " 'You have been the daughter I never had, V.I. As well as one of the best friends a woman could ever desire. And I abused you. I want your forgiveness. I want to—not to go back to where we were. We can't. I want to continue our friendship from here . . .' " (286–87). And, it is Lotty who comforts V.I. when the image of her mother is threatened; she forces Vic to set aside the frightening story of Iphigenia destroyed by her parent (seen here as Gabriella) for the powerful image of Iphigenia as Artemis the hunter. This concluding affirmation of a pair of women speaking with truth and caring is echoed in the earlier novels as well. When Vic is able to tell Anita McGrath of her father's unknowing role in her lover's death, she protects the younger woman without offering her false comfort or dishonest evasions. She can do the same for the discarded wife of shipping giant Niels Grafalk as together they illuminate the character and the activities of a man driven by power and his mistress propelled by greed. Without Warshawski's admittedly unprofessional behavior in these cases, she would have been deliberately leaving women ignorant, ostensibly for their own good, for their mental ease, or for their protection. With them, and the husband of a sick woman indirectly responsible for her daughter's death, she reveals the secrets which the system would keep hidden, shares the truth with those who have a real right and need to know, and defines her professional responsibilities for herself. Her independence is uncompromised by demands made from outside herself; Bobby Mallory, the authorities, and society all come second to her own mind.

Sara Paretsky comes closer than any other novelist to writing a feminist private-eye novel; although her success certainly involves the intersection of historical time, a moment in the genre, and a feminist author, it requires more. What has worked for Paretsky is the simultaneous rejection or minimization of typical features of the formula and the explicit introduction of some essential elements of feminism. These changes are apparent in characterization, plot development, and ambiance. Unlike the preferred male hero, V. I. Warshawski is neither a loner nor a cynic. She forms strong emotional bonds, makes friends, worries about people toward whom she has no professional obligations. In her sexual relationships, she persistently treats men as individuals even when they display sexually stereotypical behavior, not demeaning them as either romantic ideals or available sex objects. Finally, she displays a wide range of emotional behavior: notably, introspection, guilt, self-awareness, and uncertainty. In plotting, Paretsky chooses her crimes and villains carefully: all are associated with corruptible institutions or systems which have traditionally excluded or oppressed women. The criminal underworld and organized labor in *Indemnity Only*, a capitalistic empire in *Dead-*

lock, the Roman Catholic Church in *Killing Orders,* and the medical establishment in *Bitter Medicine* stand behind the individual killers, offering not only motives and rewards but also fostering arrogance which grows from the long-time assumption of undeserved superiority. Concluding the plots, Paretsky downplays the protagonist's role as judge of the criminals;[5] instead, Warshawski's important task is to share information with those who have been kept systematically uninformed. In this, Paretsky shows her detective breaking down the system; however, this attack is not undertaken in a heroic manner which elevates the protagonist individually (as is true when he bases his judgment of criminals on a private and personal code of morality). Instead, Paretsky's detective expands the collective base of power; her style is inclusive rather than exclusive. Certainly, in this so-called age of information, nothing could be more valuable to the powerless, the unwillingly ignorant, or the disadvantaged than knowledge.[6] Further, the atmosphere of these novels explicitly rejects the masculinist glorification of violence. Certainly, violence itself cannot be avoided in novels centered around murder; however, Paretsky limits the violence initiated or inflicted by her detective, making Warshawski react in these episodes. Finally, Paretsky's novels provide an explicit and persuasive awareness of the gender inequality which pervades American life, persisting despite the hopeful promise of a competent woman doing what is still often called men's work. The tensions between the demands of the detective novel and the feminist ideology require a careful balancing act; Paretsky's is not the only way, but it is virtually the only example.

A very different choice is made by M. F. Beal in her explicitly feminist novel. Although *Angel Dance* is described by its publisher as "a thriller" and its protagonist as a Chicana detective, both are far from typical of the formulaic plots and characters in the other novels discussed throughout this book. And yet, it is difficult to say whether the differences or similarities with the established form are superficial; is this a feminist, political, revolutionary novel which organizes itself around the familiar story of mystery or is it a mystery novel which adopts the look of the times for its authenticity and immediacy? Published in 1977, it is among the earliest of what has become a subgenre of the eighties—the explicitly feminist detective novel usually published by a women's press. Ordinarily about amateurs, these other novels also tend to raise the same kinds of questions about the foreground versus background emphasis of feminism or detection.

The first-person narrator, Maria Katerina Lorca Guerrera Alcazar, is the daughter of refugee parents, but her own childhood and youth in New York carry some marks of privilege. A National Endowment grant to a street theater group after her graduation was the unlikely sponsor of Kat's first overt revolutionary engagement, carrying on the tradition of "fifty years of Guerrera Alcazar commitments" (9). Arrested several times and still wanted on an outstanding warrant in the Midwest, Kat recognizes that the underground network with whom she operated often did not know what they were doing or why they did it; "but you found something and did it; that was the price of survival" (8). Like other women in the sixties, she abandoned the male-dominated left movement for feminism and, at the novel's opening, is part of a collective which publishes a women's newspaper.

A combination of the women's movement and the revolutionary left is responsible for Guerrera's being hired as a detective both to guard feminist writer Angel Stone and to investigate her grandmother Rachel Stone for radical filmmaker Michael Tarleton, who is also Angel's husband and unacknowledged brother. The plot is a complicated one with overlays similar to Ross Macdonald's—a California setting, a decades-old family secret, money and power in jeopardy, and murder. Eventually, Kat discovers that Michael has been murdered by Andrew Stone, Michael and Angel's CIA-fronting father, because Tarleton had filmed U.S. soldiers and civilians packing heroin in the Far East. Inasmuch as Angel could name the faces on Michael's film, she was being hunted by the well-connected and powerful organization which wanted to prevent a government scandal and to reopen the drug pipeline to the States. Tarleton's life, Angel Stone's mental and emotional peace, their racially mixed, incestuous marriage, and Kat Guerrera's innocence are all casualties of the governmental and nonofficial forces whose own secrets they deem worth the cost.

The feminist network connects Kat with Angel. These ties, however, are only their first link; both also see themselves as fugitives from the system, which they can identify, and its enforcers, whom they cannot always recognize. Finally, there is sexual attraction: a bisexual who prefers female partners, Kat is attracted to Angel. From the beginning, an odd sort of trust permeates their relationship. Angel keeps valuable information about the murder and the agents who are searching for her from Kat and instead goes into hiding in various feminist underground safe houses. Nonetheless, she subtly encourages Kat to learn the truth about Michael's discoveries so that his murderer can be identified. Guerrera is not initially aware that this, in addition to protecting Angel, is to be her task. As other women in the network make the choice to protect Angel, they jeopardize Kat; searching for her supposed client, Kat also jeopardizes Angel by leading their adversaries to her hiding places. In an attempt to discredit Angel, agents produce photographs of her with a number of black men in sexually explicit poses; as much as anything else, this governmental behavior convinces Kat of the seriousness of the attack against them and the value of the information which Angel must have. But, herself the victim of governmental hassling about fugitives she is believed to know, Kat never abandons her faith in Angel.

Guerrera is not, of course, a licensed private detective; she is not even a detective-for-hire although she is hired and paid by Michael Tarleton. More as a result of her revolutionary activities, her networks of radicals and feminists, and her own status as a fugitive, she understands how to investigate the criminals and the crime, to protect and secure Angel and the information which Tarleton provided. Many of her activities fit the typical pattern of the private detective: she checks out people and their stories, uses informants to gather information on suspects, tracks her disappearing client, fights, is harassed by the police, and—like few of her counterparts—is raped. However, the tone of *Angel Dance* is such that her safety is never as easily or naturally taken for granted by the reader as it would be with the protagonists of other hard-boiled detective novels. The threat of arrest is a serious one: the charges are clearly and admittedly trumped up to force her to exchange information about her friends and clients for her own freedom. The feeling it generates is unsettling: "... it's twice as weird to be busted for something you didn't do because if you didn't do it by definition you don't know what it was you didn't do. And if you don't know what it was you didn't do then how can you know you didn't do it?" (87). Her being raped becomes doubly serious in this context. Unlike Angela Harpe who, among the other detectives in this study, is threatened with this explicitly gendered violence from which she escapes easily while wreaking vengeance on her potential assailants, Kat Guerrera is not so fortunate. She is raped genitally and orally, her face scraped and bruised, her ribs cracked; she is handcuffed and threatened with a gun. She does not heal quickly, immediately ready to do battle with the world. Although she has been severely injured before in other kinds of fights and riots, this time her body warns her, *"you quit or I split"* (127). But, instead of quitting, she buys a gun.

The growing complexity of the situation forces Kat into some painful comparisons between herself and the wealthy, privileged Angel Stone. Her sympathy comes, she says, "from deep inside the languorous freedom of my own family, in which so much of the time Ideals were maintained even though the shape of the Structure was somehow always taken for granted. Working people can't afford not to be Marxians . . ." (76). Nonetheless, moving further out than ever before, she becomes paranoid, a feeling which is fed by her having lost all sense of the search being an exercise, trip, or job. For action, she relies on male help, whereas for information and other assistance she usually calls on women. Her willingness to use men's assistance may stem from her beginnings in the left movement or her distinction between white men who are able to be invisible and minority men who, like women, are always on the line. Kat's male allies are black and Chicano; their help is tentatively given and seems to be on the men's terms. In the physical fight she shares with Tarleton's brother, he acknowledges her ability as the leader, but their alliance is as shaky as the one called off earlier by her distant cousin. Contrasted with this is the aggressive retribution exacted by the women of the commune where Angel Stone is hiding: stapling a rapist to a tree by his testicles, they offer him the choice of freezing to death or cutting himself free only to bleed to death. Perhaps it is their extremism which makes Kat suggest that Angel might need help from her Chicano cousin. Her motivation for this extraordinary suggestion is never discussed. But Angel declines, not because she needs no help, or at least no male help, but because she sees her fate deterministically: " 'There is a curse on my house. . . . I know they are always out there. I understand that I will die' " (258).

Both her own frustrated sense of helplessness growing from having information which she cannot use and Angel's fatalism lead to Kat's separation from the case. Although she completely avoids any involvement with government, law, or the system, she is also unable to complete her job. She has discovered for herself what a

number of others seem to have already known: she has exposed Angel
to more rather than less danger; no accusations which she can make
against the government or Andrew Stone and his foundation will be
believed or acted upon. The novel suggests that the only action anyone
can take is guerilla warfare against individuals who represent the
attitudes of the patriarchal system. Knowing the truth does not lead
to justice or action; and radical feminism cannot work within the
system.

Similarly, radical feminism cannot work within even the broadest boundaries of the detective genre. The private eye who is licensed
by the state has made an official and a silent contract with the system;
she or he is a part of the power structure. If they undermine it at all,
they work from the inside; then, progress is slow and the reformers
(for that is all they can be) are subject to temptation and corruption.
To avoid being co-opted, revolutionaries must operate outside the
system like guerillas. In *Angel Dance*, Beal has chosen this mission
for her protagonist and so cannot simultaneously choose the detective
novel for her form. Instead, she produces a thriller—not as the term
is used generically in Britain to cover all categories of crime fiction—
but specifically as suspenseful or sensational fiction with its hunt-and-
chase motif, lacking any promise of a safe world restored at the conclusion.

Readers are certainly justified in assuming that if any examples
of the integration of the woman's script and the detective's script are
to be found, consciously feminist detective fiction would provide the
models. Feminist ideology rejects sexually differentiated spheres for
women's and men's work, assumes women's competence and independent judgment, and encourages the transformation of existing
societal values and systems. The difficulty which earlier creators of
female detectives had with revising the genre should fall before a
deliberate intention to change the formula. However, except for Kat
Guerrera, these feminist detectives are more inclined to participate
in the system than to destroy it. Perhaps they hope to subvert it from
within but the strength of established institutions, especially the law
which grows out of and then systematically supports gender-based
oppression, easily outweighs the efforts of single individuals; even V
I. Warshawski's efforts are limited and indirect. Authors have difficulty in showing their characters breaking free from traditional as-
criptions of value and legitimacy to the social structure which they

deliberately and unconsciously validate. This demonstrates the primacy of the conventional private-eye fictional formula over the feminist ideology which falsely seems to signal a change in the genre. Ironically, Grafton, McCone, and Steiner's novels demonstrate a triumph of the genre over feminist ideology in much the same way that patriarchal/sexist ideology triumphs over the genre in most of the preceding novels. Standing alone on a bridge between what has been typical for over a century and what might be possible eventually, Sara Paretsky demonstrates how much more is required of feminist detective fiction than the substitution of a feminist for a male private eye. The genre must be completely remade, stripped of some of its most characteristic elements and reinforced by a new ideology and awareness. But will the result be either detective fiction or feminist? Or will it simply be an unsatisfactory, watered-down version of both which has compromised all of their greatest attractions?

Notes

1. There are also feminists among amateurs and police officials, especially a large contingent of lesbian-feminist amateur detectives; however, their responsibilities and investigative process require a separate analysis.

2. John Cawelti notes the typical hard-boiled novel ends in a confrontation between detective and criminal because of the former's involvement and emotional or moral commitment to the people involved or "because the crime poses some basic crisis in his image of himself." As a result, the detective frequently defines morality and judgment, often in conflict with the social authority of the police (143). Women in these novels seem far less confident about setting themselves up as judge and jury. At most, they achieve some compromise between private and public versions of justice. Only the feminist guerrillas in Beal's *Angel Dance* act independently of social expectations.

3. This argument was worked out in extended conversations with Ray Keller.

4. Paretsky's choice of names establishes the contradictions of strength and underlying vulnerability in her character; the triumph of Victory is set against the parental betrayal suffered by Iphigenia and her need for rescue by Artemis, the virgin hunter (herself a divided symbol).

5. In fact, Paretsky shows Warshawski disposing of criminals in various ways: in *Indemnity Only* she turns them over to the police, specifically to Lt. Bobby Mallory; in *Deadlock* the criminals are killed in a boat explosion; in *Killing Orders* she is ignored by the police, FBI, and SEC

when she tries to give them information but she also sets in motion retribution through a local underworld leader; and, in *Bitter Medicine* she works with the police, both deliberately and accidentally, at the conclusion.

6. This pattern of information sharing is reversed in *Bitter Medicine:* fraud, medical negligence, murder, and suicide result from deliberately withheld information; Warshawski overrides self-serving, arrogant doctor-patient and attorney-client confidentiality in solving the case.

Afterword to the First Edition

Q: Has there been any change?
A: Not much.
Q: Should readers have expected any change?
A: Not really.
Q: Why not?

In view of the changes in women's economic and political conditions since the mid-nineteenth century, readers of both detective novels and this book are not unreasonable in expecting some changes in the portraits of fictional women detectives. And these readers are not entirely wrong: developments in the genre have been accommodated; variations in style, dress, and custom have found their place; and contemporary issues (like political conflict or the sexual revolution) have been acknowledged. Yet, the laconic answers in my imaginary dialogue more accurately describe the degree of change than any recital of superficial innovations might. The contemporary authorial stance toward the women characters who are the ostensible heroes of the fiction remains more like than unlike the position taken in 1864. With noticeably few exceptions, the authors maintain and reinforce a conservative political ideology toward sex/gender roles which accords with the conservative implications of the genre.

The relationship between detective fiction's conservative position and the persistent undermining of the woman detective's credibility is located in three competing and cooperative arenas: the literary, economic, and political. Because of the strength of this triad, detective fiction with a professional woman protagonist is almost always a kind of parody, for even while it reproduces the form of the original, this new version deliberately alters the essential element—the detective hero himself. As the protagonist is not simply a man but the glorification of masculine traits, the substitution of a woman with her own feminine virtues or incompletely assumed masculine ones leaves the novel without its center. But, it is not the decentered genre which is mocked. Rather, it is the deficient hero/ine. A conflation of literary, economic, and political motives have led authors to reduce her to less heroic, more manageable and familiar terms.

The literary conservatism of detective fiction is well established. Although its formula has several variations, the conventions are consistent and recognizable; many of the rules have not changed in almost a hundred and fifty years. The reassuring effect on readers of this generic familiarity is matched by the formal predictability readers encounter. Despite some examples of complexity, the overwhelming majority of published detective novels provide the safe view of a world in which a single hero can both know and correct an important problem, usually one as serious as deliberately caused death. Yet, the world the reader inhabits (and may be trying to escape through reading) is real whereas the genre's world, like the genre itself, is artificial.[1] Despite the illusion of plausibility which authors strive to create, mimetic reality is neither their intention nor their effect. And, like the image of order restored, the justice they choose, create, or produce is also illusory. Rather than propose a vision of achievable justice and the means to reach it, detective novels instead offer a denouement which is like Virginia Woolf's "nugget of pure truth to wrap up between the pages of your notebook and keep on the mantlepiece forever"—a chimera (*Room* 3–4).

The formulaic illusion is perpetuated in the generic differences (in the classical and the hard-boiled detective novels) between heroes, order restored, and justice. The pattern of the classical novels is *socially* conservative: the protagonist distinguishes between good and evil, applies approved punishment, and returns to the world the feeling of security it had before the outbreak of evil. On the other hand, the style of the hard-boiled novel is *individually* conservative: the protagonist also distinguishes between good and evil, but in the absence of widely approved standards devises his own punishment; the order he restores is internal as he feels satisfied with his actions. Yet neither matches reality where the questions of morality, ethics, and justice are too complicated for easy resolution. In real life, social justice may be unachievable.

The predictable formula of detective fiction is based on a world whose sex/gender valuations reinforce male hegemony. Taking male behavior as the norm, the genre defines its parameters to exclude female characters, confidently rejecting them as inadequate women or inadequate detectives. A detective novel with a professional woman detective is, then, a contradiction in terms. The existence of the one effectively eliminates the other.

The economic consequences of a conservative posture are equally clear. The enormous and ever-increasing popularity of the genre as registered by published titles, sales figures, best-seller lists, and library circulation numbers could not have occurred unless detective fiction were successfully meeting a wide variety of social needs and expectations. Authors and publishers might rightly conclude that there would be no advantage in tampering with a proven success. Additionally, as socialist or Marxist ideology would note, these texts are primarily produced for consumption rather than created for reading; the producers, like all entrepeneurs, have a vested interest in certain arrangements of the status quo which they are unwilling to see challenged in the materials they finance. Their business interests are served directly and indirectly by the reinforcement of conventional and legalistic attitudes about property values and political realities. Economics influences the publication of radical or revolutionary feminist detective fiction even more directly since the feminist presses which might be expected to support such novels are themselves without substantial financial backing.

The political conservatism of the genre most directly affects the minimal changes in the treatment of women detectives between 1864 and now. The widespread popularity of detective fiction whose readers cross economic, social, educational, and gender lines suggests that it makes an important political statement about how the culture works; when women are involved, that statement is traditional, stereotyped, and restrictive. When detectives are amateurs, they can be ignored and their behavior seen as a momentary intrusion into public life. And, the changes in social organization which would arise from women's active participation in public life, disruption of economic activity, and involvement in the political process could be dismissed as short-lived and inconsequential. But because the women detectives described in this book are professionals, they are threatening; readers must acknowledge their career decisions as deliberate and long-term. To evade this recognition, authors (who share the socialization patterns of their readers) prefer to reject both plausibility and generic demands. They do not model their characters on contemporary women, at least some of whom have been able to combine a non-traditional career and more conventional women's activities; nor do they endow their protagonists with the heroic abilities to do their jobs properly. Instead, authors undermine their characters as either women or detectives, succumbing to an ideology based on nostalgia for a world which never was. When the woman detective is also a feminist, authors allow the genre to triumph over feminism as they had earlier arranged for a sexist ideology to supersede the genre.

Beyond the reasons encoded in the genre itself, there are additional responses to the question, why has there been so little change? First, it is important not to confuse change with progress, as Virginia Woolf reminds her readers: "Almost the same daughters ask almost the same brothers for almost the same privileges. Almost the same gentlemen intone almost the same refusals for almost the same reasons. It seems as if there were no progress in the human race, but only repetition" (*Three Guineas* 66). Hers is a sharp analysis of the difficulty of achieving change: those outside the power structure lack the capacity; those inside lack the inclination. The outsiders, whom Woolf cherished and encouraged, can neither force nor sponsor change because they lack the mechanisms by which the power structure recognizes its proper business. Then, the insiders find themselves conforming to masculine norms in order to remain part of the group. While sabotaging their individual development, they also distance themselves from causes they might otherwise be expected to support. The difficulty which authors have in affecting the conventions is paralleled by the problems of their characters, caught also between inside and outside in adopting a traditionally male profession.

A final pair of questions remains: What can be done? Should anything be done? Already sub-genres have made distinctions between kinds of women detectives: the classical novel has become the refuge of the amateur detective while the professional is to be found almost exclusively in the hard-hitting, hard-boiled novels. But, this division is not a satisfactory answer. It limits authors and readers, needlessly re-stereotyping female characters in ways that male heroes (private eyes, deductive sleuths, and official cops) are not stereotyped.

To take on the genre; to rethink it, reformulate it, re-vision it: this is the challenge to contemporary authors. But the change must be radical and complete. The difficulties inherent in anything less are articulated by Gilbert and Gubar: "[E]ven when male mimicry does not entail moral or aesthetic compromises . . . the use of male devised plots, genres, and conventions may involve a female writer in uncomfortable contradictions and tensions" (70). The truth of their argument is clearly illuminated by the problematic examples of feminist detective novels where the imperatives of the genre overwhelm the political implications of the novel. But, it is not necessary to abandon detective fiction in order to write valid women's stories.[2] Indeed, the advantages of converting rather than rejecting a popular, economically viable product are numerous. Writers need to take up Linda Yeager's challenge: "[W]omen artists not only *can* borrow from male-authored fictions to create feminocentric plots: they must. A reinscription of phallocentrism may be a sign not of weakness or plagiarism but of woman's own ability to signify, that is, her ability to play with, to control, and to restructure patriarchal traditions. If a dominant discourse not only defines woman as 'other' but becomes the source of her self-alienation, it is only in the act of appropriation that her own heteroglossia may be freed, that she may, in other words, be freed to speak" (959).

To reimagine the genre, an author will want to consider both content and structure; as this book demonstrates, reclaiming detective fiction requires changes in both. A feminocentric novel does not necessarily need a feminist detective but it cannot evade questions of gender—intertwined with those of class, race, sexual preference, and social attitudes—if it is to succeed; it must, in Carolyn Heilbrun's words, "deconstruct . . . the structures of the patriarchy" ("Science Fiction" 119). Foregrounding gender leads to questioning patriarchist assumptions through creating an interrogative text which urges readers to solve not only the problem of the crime but also the problems of the social system.

To begin, writers can abandon the Detection Club dictum which considers only murder an important enough crime to warrant attention. They can instead borrow the nineteenth century's fascination with all varieties of deception, mix it with the hard-boiled interest in corruption, and add the procedurals' awareness of the apparently mundane. In short, writers can redefine the genre's boundaries, opening them up to legitimate a wider focus in which a variety of social issues can be explored. The body in the library or the back alley need not be the only generating force; social injustice, industrial corruption, rape and battery are serious crimes which also ask the readers to rethink their expectations of fiction and life.[3]

In the cast of characters, representations of women should be replaced with a wide range of plausible women. The excuse of familiar stereotypes for formula fiction does not serve the needs of feminocentric detective novels. The partial, narrow, and restricted view of "woman" drawn from nostalgic myths and sentimental images which have influenced the genre's creation of murderers, victims, and detectives is not sufficient; real women portraying authentic, lived experience are necessary.

But the writer's imagination will need to go further to evade the trap of a formula which inscribes masculinist values and norms on the text; structural reconsideration is crucial. In particular, if the traditional closure of detective fiction were abandoned for more open-ended uncertainty, then the status quo would not be reestablished as though all social problems had been solved.[4] The identification of criminals and their motives would no longer be paramount. This attitude about conclusions might then suggest how fluid and political any society's definitions of justice can be, how false the characters' apparent relief from disruption might be, or how temporary and limited the feeling of progress usually is. By contrast with the cathartic satisfaction readers feel at the conclusion of a traditional detective novel, both anticipation and a felt need for action would grow from open-ended conclusions, as Brecht suggested they would result from his epic theater. This dramatic shift in the ultimate moment of linear, sequential detective fiction could provoke change, or an awareness of the need for change, in the patriarchal social system of the novels' and the readers' worlds.

In addition, if women's stories are to be authentically told, they must be spoken in women's voices. It is obvious that the male first-person narrator cannot truthfully tell a woman's story, but neither can an implicitly phallocentric third-person narrative voice which cleaves to the generic formula. Although the first-person woman narrator provides one alternative, even more productive is what Joanne Frye calls "community" (3).[5] When not only the single voice of the narrator but also the single image of the heroic detective are diffused, the many voices of women in the novels—their heteroglossia, if you will—can emerge. In rejecting the monolithic world view of patriarchy and the narrative imperatives of the genre, this feminocentric detective fiction would replace received attitudes with open-ended diversity.

Such approaches to re-visioning the genre are suggestive rather than conclusive. Adopting any one of them will require an author's deliberate effort and self-conscious choice. And, although neither these ideas nor other changes which are implied in this text are offered prescriptively, the fact that they come from a critic's perspective rather than a novelist's imagination might make them seem so. Nonetheless, a reinterpretation of detective fiction is crucial; abandoning the formula as an unprofitable site for women's stories merely leaves the old imperatives in place. Women-centered, gender-aware detective fiction can and must reinvent the genre; its beneficiaries will be writers and readers alike.

Notes

1. For a further discussion of the genre's artificiality, see Keller and Klein, "Deductive Detective Fiction: The Self-Destructive Genre."
2. A small number of novels featuring amateur women detectives by Amanda Cross (*Death in a Tenured Position* and *No Word From Winifred*), Barbara Wilson (*Murder in the Collective* and *Sisters of the Road*), Valerie Miner (*Murder in the English Department*), and Barbara Paul (*The Renewable Virgin*) consciously and carefully tell women's stories through feminocentric plots and structures which challenge the generic restrictions.
3. Maureen Reddy argues that "[f]requently . . . the answer [to the mystery] lies in character with its revelations depending on the investigation of personality and on the conjunction of the personal and the social," not on physical clues which point to a murderer (7).
4. Sharon Russell introduces this issue to suggest why Chelsea Quinn Yarbro found the fantastic genre more appropriate for her feminist views than detective fiction.
5. Frye speaks of community providing narrative authority for the writer; plausibly, then, it would also provide similar authority for readers.

Afterword to the Second Edition

Between 1987—when the first edition of this book went to press—and 1994, women private eyes have flourished in detective fiction; some might say they have taken over. By contrast with the seventy-one characters appearing in the first 120-odd years of this literary genre, sixty-seven have been created in just the past seven years.[1] Most are Americans; only ten Brits, three Canadians, two Australians, one Panamanian living in the U.S., and one Catalan have joined the ranks. Two characters were created by men, the others by women writers. These two imbalances reflect a significant shift from the production of novels before 1987, in which the Anglo-American proportions among detectives and the female-male division among writers were fairly equal. But the recent novels are not, as readers might expect, in the true hard-boiled mode; few writers follow Sue Grafton down the mean streets without softening both their characters and their settings considerably.[2] The greatest proportion of the novels meet what might be called liberal feminist criteria: women doing the same job as men and nobody making too much of a fuss about it.[3] References to "an unsuitable job for a woman" or "lady dick" have declined notably as the p.i. role has gradually been reconfigured to accommodate women (or, as I will argue later, women writers and characters have forced a change in the role).

As a marketing device, the presence of women in an historically male heroic role may have become less useful with the rapid proliferation of female private eyes. This may partially account for the more unusual characters among the new sixty-seven: an Aleut, a nun, and a woman in partnership with a 400-year-old vampire. More conventionally, authors have created protagonists who are former cops, district attorneys, schoolteachers, reporters, and housewives. But, even if readers in a changing culture have been willing to accept increasing numbers of paid women detectives, their interest may not be enough. At a recent mystery convention, a large publishing house's editor announced "no more women private eyes"; it is almost impossible to imagine any editor deciding that there had been enough male private eyes. And certainly, the latter outnumber the former exponentially.

It is not easy to determine what led to this mini-explosion of women detectives. Certainly any universal theories should be automatically suspect as there is too much diversity among the writers and characters to warrant reductionist analysis. But if motive is almost impenetrable, opportunity is only ambiguous. Readers have clearly been willing to accept women characters in this generally male domain; but, how authors have moved their female private eyes from curiosity pieces to a critical mass during the late 1980s and early 1990s is open to at least two interpretations. Both explanations depend upon a changing cultural climate for women; it would seem that detective fiction has finally caught up with the feminist reexamination of women's roles during the 1970s and early 1980s. However, this new facet of the genre may also soon suffer the subsequent antifeminist backlash, if the editor quoted above is typical. Unlike the amateur detective whose legitimacy seems unassailable, the female private eye occupies a hard-won and easily destabilized position within the genre.[4]

There was no sea change in 1987; instead, there were hardcover sales, paperback rights, and three powerful names: Sara Paretsky, Sue Grafton, and Marcia Muller. These three women proved to a doubting marketplace that the woman p.i. was plausible and saleable. V. I. Warshawski, Kinsey Milhone, and Sharon McCone put women detectives on the map in ways that begged for other characters who also challenged the familiar fiction. Had the genre changed in recent years to accommodate women protagonists or had the presence of best-selling women detectives forced a crack in the hard-boiled walls? The frequency with which authors of the women p.i. novels have challenged the conventions of the hard-boiled mode suggests that they exerted pressure on the genre, insisting on change, convincing through numbers. The fact that writers of male-hero private-eye novels have appropriated some of these changes only confirms their marketability.

Half a dozen challenges to the old model are easily noticeable; these newest women detectives are not wearing borrowed trenchcoats. First, their authors do not define these women as loners without family or friends; even Kinsey Milhone discovers previously unknown cousins in *J is for Judgment*. Kate Shugak, who lives twenty-five miles from her nearest neighbor in the frozen wilds of Alaska, has sufficient family and friends to embroil her in their problems and then to help her resolve them. Laura Flynn is a former member of a women's communal household with which she stays in contact; Hannah Wolfe's parents, and her sister Kate with her obnoxious husband, Colin, and two children, provide Sara Dunant's character a sympathetic grounding. Taking a more unusual tack, Winona Sullivan gives Sister Cecile Buddenbrooks an entire religious "family." And Kat Colorado determinedly adopts a grandmother and a younger sister to replace her alcoholic, neglectful mother and dead sister. Although only five detectives are married–Quin St. James and Anna Peters have conventional, heterosexual marriages while Lauren Laurano, Eliza Pirex, and Helen Black have lesbian ones—and a few have children, most have close relationships and intimate partners. Their range of connection with families of origin and families created out of shared feelings and concerns keep them woven into the fabric of society.

The characters' integration into the larger society, to some extent, affects their tolerance for corruption. The only "crime" routinely engaged in by these detectives is breaking and entering; this seems to have become a prerequisite for passing the p.i. exam. In the more typical hard-boiled novel, the detective positioned himself between society and the evil represented by the criminal, usually favoring the latter end of the societal spectrum. In short, to catch the criminal and neutralize the evil, the detective had to become much like his prey. But—their second difference—women detectives generally stay closer to the opposite end of the continuum, often identifying more with the victims of crime or with the social disruption caused by murder. Catherine Sayler puts the distinction succinctly in Linda Grant's fourth novel, about sexual harassment and snuff photos: "A lot of this job is understanding your quarry, getting inside his head. But I didn't want to be anyplace near this guy. Managing my emotions could be as tough as catching the prankster" (*A Woman's Place* 53).

For Elisabeth Bowers's Meg Lacey, a raped, divorced, single mother who investigates teen pornography and spouse abuse in two novels, her identification with her clients—and thus her commitment to them—far outweighs any pleasure she finds in outwitting the criminals. Similarly, Lena Padgett in *Satan's Lambs* specializes in cases involving battered wives and children unprotected by conventional measures. And, although Phoebe Siegel is often aggravated by her client's drugged and abused daughter, she continues her investigation to clear her brother, a police officer who committed suicide after being accused of sexual misconduct. Rather than catching a killer by becoming like a killer, many of these characters choose instead to avenge a victim by caring about the victim.

Resisting the impulse to identify with the criminal may also explain why a greater proportion of women private eyes than men prefer not to carry a gun—even when they do. Nell Fury is not alone in explaining her refusal in terms of fighting the likelihood of using it. Others argue, like Lane Montana, that they've never needed a gun and so never got one. And, with an intertextual swipe at the competition, Helen Black rejects owning a gun because she wants to break the stereotype of the hard-boiled male private eye. Even when it's not always wise—as when Ronnie Ventana comes up against a criminal armed with an Uzi—many women p.i.'s persist in refusing guns. But even many who have them leave their guns in closets, bedside table drawers, glove compartments, abandoned purses.

Most critics of the genre have noticed that the female-centered novels also eschew excessive violence. Their approach to solving crime and apprehending the criminal does not depend on gun battles or fistfights. Christine Green's nurse detective, Karin McQuillan's safari-guide-turned-detective, Gillian Farrell's moonlighting-actress detective, K. K. Beck's Jane da Silva at the Foundation for Righting Wrongs, and Carol Higgins Clark's globetrotting Regan Reilly are almost like amateurs in their general avoidance of hard-boiled violence. Authors have explained the reduced violence by having their woman detectives willing, in recent novels, to bring the police onto the scene—a fourth difference. Gwen Ramadge works easily with Lieutenant Sackler in *Bride;* although he thinks of her—with Lillian O'Donnell's approval—as an amateur, he lets her help execute a search warrant. The subtext of both of Kay Hooper's novels is p.i. Lane Montana's decision to cooperate with the local police officer—

eventually her lover—who is willing to use her semi-psychic powers and insider knowledge to solve three murders. Jazz Jasper works side by side with a local police official in Kenya; Devon MacDonald notes in *A Slash of Scarlet* that Lieutenant Douglas Winthrop not only likes her but doesn't try to keep her out of the case in a typical p.i.-cop conflict. In the most interesting change, Blaine Stewart, Claudia Valentine, Laura Principal, Barrett Lake, and Lil Ritchie interact with a female police officer as friend or source of information. As more of the women private eyes are former police officers it is natural that they should maintain friends or, at least, contacts among their former coworkers. The female p.i.–female cop connection in these novels may be a signpost for a different kind of interaction between the two groups in the future.

The appropriate and necessary violence of an arrest is thus displaced onto the police where it is more plausible, and the cooperation involved—difference number five—reduces opportunities for the gender hostility that intensified the traditional cop-p.i. exchanges. In *The Hour of the Knife* and *By Evil Means,* the hostility masks police corruption; for Jeri Howard and Catherine Sayler it is the mark of an overprotective ex-husband still on the force. The best demonstration of the change is the widespread absence of such abusive relationships and the rare presence of one example: Michael Hendricks's two novels. In these, Rita Noonan's ex-husband, a cop, tries to rape her, and one of his colleagues uses dirty sex talk to push her around. But Hendricks also shows Noonan getting information by using another cop's fantasies about her, letting him see her in bed or walking around braless in a t-shirt. However, this sort of reader titillation has generally disappeared. More typical is Kate Kinsella's experience; a British R.N. who takes on medical cases, she encounters a police officer who is not unfriendly but didn't expect a woman detective: "I don't approve of women private detectives." What is unclear in this context is whether he disapproves of private detectives or women; and the ambiguity is something new for women p.i.'s. Although few novels include all differences and some include none, the overall picture of a genre in transition is clear.

The final distinction between the earlier male-centered p.i. novels and the recent crop of female-oriented ones circles around the detectives' often-cited "knight errantry." Critics and reviewers alike have been fond of seeing the male detective as the lone righteous hero in a sea of corruption: a good guy, the white hat, Sir Galahad in modern dress. This appealing image suggests a hero of mythic proportions, a man—and, I would argue, only a man—who makes his own rules and then lives by them, no matter how difficult that may be. With such a rubric in place, it is no wonder that 125 years were needed for authors to create a critical mass of women detectives. At the Round Table, in the Old West, and wherever else myths were made, women were either the cause of battles or the prize; the actors in those dramas were always men. And so, the private eye's vaunted code of honor—Sam Spade's loyalty or Spenser's indefinable sense of rightness—doesn't work for a female detective (unless she's completely derivative). The difference between men and women can be qualified in two phrases from Harvard psychologist Carol Gilligan— "ethic of rights" and "ethic of responsibility." Men, she concludes, have been socialized to the former, paying attention to what detectives in fiction like to call their code. It is abstract, judgmental, and rigid: something either conforms to the code or it doesn't. Women, Gilligan writes, have also been socialized; but what they have been taught to value is not the code but connection. Gilligan's "ethic of responsibility" defines women's concern for how their actions and decisions will affect the other people involved in the scenario. Their concern for connection is personal, flexible, and attentive to detail. It is no surprise, then, that women detectives who are believable, successful, and engaging cannot merely mimic the male models. Or, as Sydney Sloane insists in *Brotherly Love:* " 'I never said I have a responsibility to make the world a safer place, Ed, but I do have a responsibility to my client.' So there" (102).

The past six or seven transitional years have also been transformational. The early years of women as fictional detectives emphasized the improbability of women's filling the male heroic role; they were described as neither intellectual enough for the ratiocinative model nor physical enough for the physically active one. In those terms, authors resolved their problems by making the term "woman detective" an oxymoron. Now that authors have rejected the cultural restrictions on both terms, they have defined them anew. A few writers from the past half-dozen years have remained enmeshed within the formula (some have even accepted the derogatory readings of their characters);[5] many have modified or adapted received readings to shift the focus for their own uses. A few have intervened, under-cutting and realigning the genre, making it recognizable yet different.

What does it take to redefine the new woman p.i.? Leading the list of new women detectives is Linda Barnes's Carlotta Carlyle. Through five novels to date, Barnes has broken new ground in re-thinking both the genre and its protagonist. What Barnes gives readers is a distinctively new take on the woman p.i.; through both the form and the character, she challenges the standard in ways that are un-questionably feminist.

A six-foot-tall redhead, Carlyle would stand out in any crowd; further, Barnes molds her into a contemporary feminist. The message is deftly delivered through Carlotta's first-person observations half a dozen times in each novel without overpowering either the plot or the character. Early in the first novel, working the Irish bars, she observes:

> Someday unescorted women will walk into bars without getting the glad eyeball from every guy who can still lift his face from his beer. But that great day has not yet ar-rived. Oh, I'm not making a fuss—I'm not bitter, don't get me wrong. I just hate feeling like I've got a price tag hung on my ass. There's no way to stop it. No way to win or get even. Once I spent an entire summer wolf-whistling at construction workers, reaching new heights of hollow achievement when I made some poor jerk blush. (*Trouble* 27)

Barnes manages to deliver her complaint, acknowledge the limita-tions of protest, assess the injustice, and offer a payback-alternative without missing a beat. But, unlike Linda Grant, who reiterates the difficulty her detective Catherine Sayler has with her ex-husband's acknowledging her independence, Barnes chooses a different target for each jab. Older women's camouflage, sexism in the police force, women and sports injuries, women's song lyrics, sex versus celibacy, independence, and menstruation all provide Barnes and Carlyle op-portunities to make their point.

Equally important in carrying these novels' feminist message is the richness of women whose voices and presence reverberate throughout. From her union-organizing mother and grandmother, Carlotta gets Yiddishisms for every occasion; from her Aunt Bea, a house and a chatty parrot who is renamed for Emma Goldman. The performance artist Roz who lives upstairs gives Carlotta an unconventional slant on cases and a never-dull home life. Gloria, co-owner and dispatcher of Green and White Cab where Carlotta moonlights, is a great source of local information and junk food. Even Carlotta's volleyball team provides female advice and energy. But, Carlotta's greatest affection is captured by Paolina; connected through the Big Sister program with this seven-year-old Colombian immigrant, Carlotta tries to offer her support and encouragement. In this, she often comes up against the rare negative female voice in Barnes's novels as Marta, the girl's mother, reiterates traditional messages of female subordination. In this plethora of women's lives and ideas, Barnes has the makings of a communal female voice if she can avoid reductivism and stereotyping. Such heteroglossia (multiplicity of voices) undercuts the traditional voice of authority with which only the detective speaks.

Daughter of a cop and a union organizer, a former cop herself, Carlotta Carlyle seems to have absorbed both the regard for authority and a reasonable suspicion of it from her upbringing. In most of her cases, she cooperates fully with the police through her former boss, Lieutenant Mooney, who would like a romantic relationship. In three of the novels, the denouement consists of a joint effort by Carlyle, the Boston Police Department, and, in one case, the FBI. But, in *Snapshot*, she is also willing to arrange a deal with Paolina's father, a Colombian drug lord, to keep her license from being revoked. Her attitude is typically realistic—she carries a gun, arranges for backup, tempers her hunches with common sense—rather than idealistic. Little about her conforms with the traditional private eye out of Hammett and Chandler or even her Boston neighbor, Spenser.

Barnes limits the appearances of recurring male characters. After having been described in the first three novels as a brilliant musician and drug addict, Carlyle's ex-husband appears in *Steel Guitar* long enough to satisfy readers' curiosity, then leaves on a gig. Carlotta's sometime lover, Sam Gianelli, is a Boston mobster's son who did not follow in his father's business; he neither challenges Carlotta's independence nor provides advice, information, or backup in her professional life. Barnes allows only Mooney—Carlotta's former boss, one-time client, and regular P.D. contact—a significant presence in the novels. All three men are sexually interested in Carlotta and two are in a position to affect her professional standing. Still, only Mooney, relegated to cop, provides a setting for the realistic woman detective Barnes has created.

Arguably, Barnes has not jettisoned all that readers know and expect of detective fiction. Her novels are definitely part of a tradition almost 150 years old. But she has reconfigured the genre to make her concerns and her detective primary rather than just adaptations of familiar models. Similarly, in *Snapshot,* Carlotta Carlyle's Seder, derived from a more ancient and revered tradition, is transformed into a ritual that is exactly right for her. Keeping what is pleasurable, discarding what is stale, making room for change, Carlyle's celebration encapsulates the metaphor of Linda Barnes's novels and the possibilities inherent in these novels of new women detectives.

Like Linda Barnes, Karen Kijewski works to recast the mold for her hard-boiled detective, Kat Colorado. One of two unwanted children of an alcoholic single mother, Kat found her mother dead at the bottom of a flight of stairs, the victim of a drunken fall. At twelve she felt responsible for her three-year-old sister's death from pneumonia, but she never regrets being forced so young into adulthood: "People always thought that taking care of her was too much for a twelve-year-old kid, but that wasn't it at all. She saved me, taught me how to love and care the way our mother never did. I would have grown up hard and cold inside without her" (*Katwalk* 63). Maybe this is why she feels connected to other young women, especially when she helps a runaway teenager to leave prostitution. She even offers good-natured cautions to a streetwise troupe of teenaged hookers who show up with Lindy at her hospital bed. She also gives "revolutionary" advice to a group of pregnant women confined in a home for unmarried mothers. At this moment, in the Weyland Home, Kijewski has Kat voice Carolyn Heilbrun's feminist call. Rather than seeing this time of being hidden away from society as punishment, she urges them to consciousness-raising: "Write your own script . . . tell your own stories . . . talk to each other." Evading the Victorian regulations and those who enforce them, Kat assures the women, "Nobody can make you stop thinking your own way, or laughing and living your life" (*Katapult* 71). Kijewski plays out this message in her protagonist's life and thoughts.

Women are frequently the beneficiaries of Kat's hard-won wisdom. All of her cases focus on issues from women's perspectives—

incest, rape, fertility, divorce settlements, and birth mothers–while the majority offer female clients, including her best friend and her adopted grandmother. Kijewski has created a protagonist who seems driven to support and encourage other women. To a threatened client, Kat insists, "You are not ignorant and helpless. You are not a victim" (*Katapult* 131). She breaks through another woman's brainwashing and enslavement by repeatedly using the woman's true name rather than her captor's choice; together they disable the criminal and escape. Kijewski has used the familiar outlines of the hard-boiled mystery to reconsider the lives of women and children.

Joining Barnes and Kijewski in challenging the established boundaries of the genre is Linda Grant in her newest Catherine Sayler novel, *A Woman's Place,* an investigation of sexual harassment. Published almost simultaneously with Michael Crichton's *Disclosure*—a work that inverts harassment to claim a man victimized by a woman— *A Woman's Place* demonstrates with absolute clarity the gendered connections of power, violence, and sexual harassment. Sayler knows what neither her partner nor her lover can, for they are both male: "A man's body was his protection; a woman's is too often a liability" (83). And even though she has trained her body through Aikido to protect herself, she cannot escape the emotional vulnerability provoked by the implied threat of sexual power plays.[6]

Pushing the boundaries of the genre even further is the subset of lesbian detective fiction. The male heroic celebration of conventional novels, which has been shifted off-center by female private eyes, is even more threatened by a lesbian detective. Furthermore, the traditional narratives of crime and detection that are challenged by women-centered socialization patterns are dismantled by novels that see the patriarchy and heterosexual privilege as underlying more visible and identifiable "crimes." Published in numbers by small feminist presses—notably Niad and Seal–lesbian detective fiction is now also moving into mainstream publishing houses. The power of this fiction to disrupt what readers classify as detective fiction could have the same impact on the genre that Chandler and Hammett's hard-boiled mean streets had on Christie's and Conan Doyle's locked rooms and country house parties.[7]

As the lesbian feminist critic Bonnie Zimmerman notes, the detective novel has replaced science fiction as the lesbian adventure genre of choice. Such novels offer a built-in potential for critically examining the existing social system and challenging its norms and givens. Lesbian detective fiction concentrates on the prevailing sexism and homophobia of contemporary culture; typically crimes against women and girls, including murder, rape, sexual abuse, battering, incest, stalking, prostitution, pornography, and discrimination, are the focus of the investigation. Because the detective herself—as woman and lesbian—has often been the victim of sexist and homophobic treatment, she is the ideal sleuth, eventually revealing not only the criminal but also the socially established practices that make such crime hard to eradicate. Although readers can expect these plot elements in all the books published by feminist presses (Seal, Niad, Daughters, Spinsters/Aunt Lute), those from mainstream publishers like St. Martin's (Randye Lordon's *Brotherly Love* and Phyllis Knight's *Switching the Odds* and *Shattered Rhythms*) subordinate the lesbian feminist concerns under a more conventional crime narrative.

Even among feminist presses, lesbian private-eye novels differ in one marked respect from the amateur-detective or police-procedural novels. Many amateurs unravel the mystery of their own sexuality simultaneously with the mystery of crime—usually in the first one or two novels of a series—in "coming-out" stories. The very valuable connection between the detective's "criminal" sexuality and the acknowledged criminal's acts is lost in the majority of private-eye novels where the detective's sexual identity is open and acknowledged. By contrast, police detectives (for example, Katherine Forrest's Kate Delafield and Claire McNab's Carol Ashton) find that the system requires them to withhold public acknowledgment of their lesbianism; not until threatened with blackmail does Ashton face the formal "coming out." Again, the lesbian private-eye novels generally avoid this issue because the authors construct protagonists who are already "out," such as Lauren Wright Douglas's Caitlin Reese, Pat Welch's Helen Black, or Diana McRae's Eliza Pirex, who advertises herself as "All the Muscle You Need."

Sandra Scoppettone's three novels featuring p.i. Lauren Laurano are the only examples where mainstream publishing (Little, Brown in hardcover and Ballantine Books in paperback) and full-scale lesbian issues come together. In the first novel, *Everything You Have Is Mine*, Laurano investigates rape, maternal identity, and mother-daughter relationships to solve the crime just as she confronts her childhood, her mother, and her lover's brother's AIDS to resolve her own life.

In the second chapter, by relating the story of her own rape as a teenager, Lauren proves herself to a client whose sister has been date-raped; such credentials are not part of the average p.i.'s *bona fides* and signal the different connections through which the best lesbian detective fiction reimagines the genre. Set in New York's Greenwich Village, where the happily married Laurano is part of a well-established gay and lesbian network, the novels show her detecting friendship, the limits of self-and-other, love, and marriage as she investigates crime. Scoppettone uses the detective formula with its widespread popular appeal to open up the range of issues that circulate throughout American public discourse.

The role of feminist discourse—both academic and public–in these re-visions of the genre cannot be discounted. Over the past twenty-five years, feminist criticism has revealed the social construction of what had always been taken to be natural categories: male and female. Wrenching apart sex (biology) and gender (social role), feminists deconstructed the cultural imperatives of power. Detective fiction has always revolved around power; the ascendancy of the criminal over the victim gives way in the novel to the power of the detective over the criminal as the narrative of crime is overtaken by the narrative of detection. Feminism has imploded the way ordinary people look at the world; in detective fiction criticism, it has challenged everything from the "male" and "heroic" designation of the male heroic protagonist to the authoritative single voice of the detective to the anticipated closure of the final chapter. Feminist thought has provided novelists and readers not merely affirmative-action opportunities for new detectives (gay, female, lesbian, black, Asian, native American, etc.) but the challenges, disruptions, demands, and encouragement that assure the future of the genre.

Notes

1. Characters introduced before 1987 and continuing in novels published since include Liza Cody's Anna Lee, Sue Grafton's Kinsey Milhone, Janice Law's Anna Peters, Marcia Muller's Sharon McCone, Sara Paretsky's V. I. Warshawski, Susan Steiner's Alexandra Winter, and Eve Zaremba's Helen Keremos.

2. Two series have noncontemporary settings: Marian J. A. Jackson's novels are set in 1900 and Kerry Greenwood's in the "Roaring Twenties."

3. In chapter 10 I argue that the ready acceptance of the patriarchal police and legal system by the newest women detectives undermined a full feminist reexamination of the power structure. The most recent novelists have clearly adopted a liberal feminist position on this question, choosing to have their characters work within the system rather than challenge it.

4. At a recent mystery convention, a group of reader-reviewer-critics estimated the number of new women p.i.'s since 1987 at two hundred—almost three times the actual number. This exaggeration is similar to Dale Spender's findings in *Man Made Language* that women were judged to *dominate* male-female conversations long before their statistically verifiable participation reached even 50 percent. Both misperceptions begin from the premise that women's legitimate participation—in male-female conversations and in male-female p.i. novels—is well below half; consequently, long before women reach parity, they are perceived as dominating, overwhelming, or even controlling. Such perceptions are used to encourage and justify backlash; see Susan Faludi's *Backlash.*

5. Several examples stand out. Both of Catherine Dain's otherwise interesting novels have p.i. Freddie O'Neal trapped by the criminal and rescued by a man in the penultimate chapter, a favorite device of the early twentieth-century novelists who minimized the detective to glorify traditional femininity. Lillian O'Donnell's Gwen Ramadge and Kay Hooper's Lane Montana persist too long in their "I'm-just-an-amateur" routine despite novels that clearly show off their professional credentials. Valerie Frankel's Wanda Mallory, owner of the Do It Right Detective Agency in Times Square, plus the police, victims, suspects, and friends-of-the-detective are little more than caricatures in these hard-boiled cartoons. Michael Hendricks's two novels are as much about sex as detection. And, in Joseph Wambaugh's *Fugitive Nights*, p.i. Breda Burrows becomes overshadowed by the novel's two strange male cops.

6. At the same time as Grant and Kijewski, Sue Grafton continues her Kinsey Milhone series with *K is for Killer*. And, after a longer wait, Sara Paretsky's *Tunnel Vision* arrived to take away the bad taste left by Hollywood Pictures' sexist misrepresentation of her detective in *V. I. Warshawski*; see my essay, "Watching Warshawski."

7. For a fuller discussion of the role of lesbian detectives in transforming the genre, see my article, "*Habeas corpus:* Feminism and Detective Fiction."

Appendix: Women Private Eyes 1987–94

(Author's name is in parentheses.)

*Characters created before 1987 appearing in additional novels after that date.

Ashe, Kristin (Jennifer L. Jordan)

Baeier, Kate (Gillian Slovo)
Barrows, Breda (Joseph Wambaugh)
Black, Helen (Pat Welch)
Brannigan, Kate (Val McDermid)
Browne, Clio (Dolores Komo)
Bryant, Sydney (Patricia Wallace)
Buddenbrooks, Sister Cecile (Winona Sullivan)
Burke, Caley (Bridget McKenna)

Carlyle, Carlotta (Linda Barnes)
Colorado, Kat (Karen Kijewski)
Conrad, Claire (Melodie Johnson Howe)
Cross, Victoria (Penny Summer)

Danforth, Abagail Patience (Marian J. A. Jackson)
da Silva, Jane (K. K. Beck)
Delaney, Patricia (Sharon Gwyn Short)
Dillworth, Poppy (Dorothy Tell)
Donovan, Brigid (Karen Saum)

Doyle, Abagail (Anna Ashwood Collins)

Elliot, Maggie (Elizabeth Atwood Taylor)

Fisher, Phryne (Kerry Greenwood)
Flynn, Laura (Leslie Grant-Adamson)
Fury, Nell (Elizabeth Pincus)

Garrity, Callahan (Kathy Hogan Trocheck)
Guiu, Lonia (Maria-Antonia Oliver)

Hale, Tamara (Valerie Wilson Wesley)
Howard, Jeri (Janet Dawson)

Jasper, Jazz (Karin McQuillan)

*Keremos, Helen (Eve Zaremba)
Kinsella, Kate (Christine Green)
Knight, Michele (J. M. Redmann)

Lacey, Meg (Elisabeth Bowers)
Lake, Barrett (Shelley Singer)
Laurano, Lauren (Sandra Scoppettone)
*Lee, Anna (Liza Cody)

*McCone, Sharon (Marcia Muller)
MacDonald, Devon (Nancy Baker Jacobs)
McGrogan, Annie (Gillian B. Farrell)
Mallory, Wanda (Valerie Frankel)
Marlow, Daisy (D. Miller Morgan)
Martin, Dorie (Diane S. Dean)
Martin, Saz (Stella Duffy)
*Milhone, Kinsey (Sue Grafton)
Miller, Robin (Jaye Maiman)
Montana, Lane (Kay Hooper)

Nelson, Vicki (Tanya Huff)
Noonan, Rita (Michael Hendricks)

O'Connell, Cat (Pat Sweet)
O'Neal, Freddie (Catherine Dain)
O'Shaughnessy, Kiernan (Susan Dunlap)

Padgett, Lena (Lynn S. Hightower)
*Peters, Anna (Janice Law)
Pirex, Eliza (Diana McRae)
Principal, Laura (Michelle Spring)

Ramadge, Gwen (Lillian O'Donnell)
Randolph, Jess (Margaret Lucke)
Reece, Caitlin (Lauren Wright Douglas)
Reilly, Regan (Carol Higgins Clark)
Ritchie, Lil (Phyllis Knight)

Sayler, Catherine (Linda Grant)
Shugak, Kate (Dana Stabenow)
Siegel, Phoebe (Sandra West Prowell)
Sloane, Sydney (Randye Lordon)
St. James, Quin (T. J. MacGregor)
Stewart, Blaine (Sharon Zukowski)
Swift, Sabina (Dorothy Sucher)

Tanner, Alex (Anabel Donald)

Valentine, Claudia (Marele Day)
Ventana, Ronnie (Gloria White)

*Warshawski, V. I. (Sara Paretsky)
West, Delilah (Maxine O'Callaghan)
Wilder, Johanna (Agnes Bushell)
*Winter, Alexandra (Susan Steiner)
Wolfe, Hannah (Sarah Dunant)

Bibliography: Works Published prior to 1987

Detective Novels

This bibliography consists of all of the novels featuring professional women detectives that I was able to locate, using numerous sources. Dates of original publication are based on information provided in the copies I have used; where the information was lacking, I have supplied dates based on Allen J. Hubin's bibliography. Hubin is uncertain about the books listed under Carter Brown, believing that some may be unacknowledged reprints under new titles; this is more likely for the novels published in Australia.

Aiken, Albert W. *The Actress Detective; or, The Invisible Hand: The Romance of an Implacable Mission.* New York: Beadle and Adams, 1889.

―――. *The Female Barber Detective; or, Joe Phoenix in Silver City.* New York: Beadle and Adams, 1895.

―――. *La Marmoset, the Detective Queen; or, the Lost Heir of Morel.* New York: Beadle and Adams, 1882.

Beal, M. F. *Angel Dance.* New York: Daughters, 1977.

Bodkin, M. McDonnell. *The Capture of Paul Beck.* London: T. Fisher Unwin, 1909.

―――. *Dora Myrl, the Lady Detective.* London: Chatto and Windus, 1900.

Brown, Carter [Alan Geoffrey Yates]. *And the Undead Sing.* New York: Signet, 1974.

―――. *A Bullet for my Baby.* Sidney, Australia: Horwitz-Transport, 1955.

―――. *The Bump and Grind Murders.* New York: Signet, 1964.

―――. *Good Morning, Mavis.* Sidney, Australia: Horwitz-Transport, 1957.

————. *Honey, Here's Your Hearse*. Sidney, Australia: Horwitz-Transport, 1955.

————. *Lament for a Lousy Lover*. New York: Signet, 1960.

————. *The Loving and the Dead*. New York: Signet, 1959.

————. *Murder Is So Nostalgic!* New York: Signet, 1972.

————. *Murder Wears a Mantilla*. 1957. New York: Signet, 1962.

————. *None But the Lethal Heart*. New York: Signet, 1959.

————. *Seidlitz and the Super-Spy*. New York: Signet, 1967.

————. *Tomorrow Is Murder*. New York: Signet, 1960.

Buchanan, Patrick [Edwin Corley and Jack Murphy]. *A Murder of Crows*. New York: Stein and Day, 1970.

————. *A Parliament of Owls*. 1971. New York: Pyramid, 1974.

————. *A Requiem of Sharks*. New York: Dodd, Mead, 1973.

————. *A Sounder of Swine*. New York: Dodd, Mead, 1974.

Bullivant, Cecil L. *Millie Lynn, Shop Investigator*. 1920. London: Odhams, n.d.

Campbell, Hazel. *Olga Knaresbrook, Detective*. 1933. London: John Long Ltd., n.d.

Chanslor, Torrey. *Our First Murder*. New York: Frederick A. Stokes, 1940.

————. *Our Second Murder*. New York: Frederick A. Stokes, 1941.

Chetwynd, Bridget. *Death Has Ten Thousand Doors*. London: Hutchinson, 1951.

————. *Rubies, Emeralds and Diamonds*. London: Hutchinson, 1952.

Christie, Agatha. *By the Pricking of My Thumbs*. 1968. New York: Pocket Books, 1974.

————. *N or M?* 1941. New York: Dell, 1977.

————. *Partners in Crime*. 1929. New York: Dell, 1963.

————. *Postern of Fate*. 1973. New York: Bantam, 1974.

————. *The Secret Adversary*. 1922. New York: Bantam, 1970.

Cody, Liza. *Bad Company*. 1982. New York: Warner, 1984.

————. *Dupe*. 1981. New York: Warner, 1983.

————. *Headcase*. New York: Charles Scribner's Sons, 1986.

————. *Stalker*. New York: Charles Scribner's Sons, 1984.

————. *Under Contract*. New York: Scribner, 1987.

Conaway, Jim C. *Deadlier than the Male*. New York: Belmont Tower, 1977.

————. *They Do It with Mirrors*. New York: Belmont Tower, 1977.

Cross, Mark [Archibald Thomas Pechey]. *The Best-Laid Schemes*. London: Ward Lock, 1955.

————. *The Black Spider*. London: Ward Lock, 1953.

————. *Challenge to the Four*. London: Ward Lock, 1939.

————. *The Circle of Freedom*. London: Ward Lock, 1953.

————. *Desperate Steps*. London: Ward Lock, 1957.

———. *Find the Professor*. London: Ward Lock, 1940.

———. *Foul Deeds Will Arise*. London: Ward Lock, 1958.

———. *The Four at Bay*. London: Ward Lock, 1939.

———. *The Four Get Going*. London: Ward Lock, 1938.

———. *The Four Make Holiday*. London: Ward Lock, 1938.

———. *The Four Strike Home*. London: Ward Lock, 1937.

———. *The Green Circle*. London: Ward Lock, 1942.

———. *The Grip of the Four*. London: Ward Lock, 1934.

———. *The Hand of the Four*. London: Ward Lock, 1935.

———. *How Was It Done?* London: Ward Lock, 1941.

———. *In the Dead of Night*. London: Ward Lock, 1955.

———. *It Couldn't Be Murder*. London: Ward Lock, 1940.

———. *The Jaws of Darkness*. London: Ward Lock, 1952.

———. *The Mark of the Four*. London: Ward Lock, 1936.

———. *Missing from His Home*. London: Ward Lock, 1949.

———. *Murder As Arranged*. London: Ward Lock, 1943.

———. *Murder in Black*. London: Ward Lock, 1944.

———. *Murder in the Air*. London: Ward Lock, 1943.

———. *Murder in the Pool*. London: Ward Lock, 1941.

———. *Murder Will Speak*. London: Ward Lock, 1954.

———. *The Mystery of Gruden's Gap*. London: Ward Lock, 1942.

———. *The Mystery of Joan Marryat*. London: Ward Lock, 1945.

———. *The Mystery of the Corded Box*. London: Ward Lock, 1956.

———. *Not Long to Live*. London: Ward Lock, 1959.

———. *Once Too Often*. London: Ward Lock, 1960.

———. *Once Upon a Crime*. London: Ward Lock, 1961.

———. *On the Night of the 14th*. London: Ward Lock, 1950.

———. *Other Than Natural Causes*. London: Ward Lock, 1949.

———. *Over Thin Ice*. London: Ward Lock, 1958.

———. *Perilous Hazard*. London: Ward Lock, 1961.

———. *The Secret of the Grange*. London: Ward Lock, 1946.

———. *The Shadow of the Four*. London: Ward Lock, 1934.

———. *The Strange Affair at Greylands*. London: Ward Lock, 1948.

———. *The Strange Case of Pamela Wilson*. London: Ward Lock, 1954.

———. *Surprise for the Four*. London: Ward Lock, 1937.

———. *Third Time Unlucky*. London: Ward Lock, 1959.

———. *Wanted for Questioning*. London: Ward Lock, 1960.

———. *The Way of the Four*. London: Ward Lock, 1936.

———. *When Danger Threatens*. London: Ward Lock, 1959.

———. *When Thieves Fall Out*. London: Ward Lock, 1956.

———. *Who Killed Henry Wickenstrom?* London: Ward Lock, 1951.

Danvers, Milton. *A Desperate Dilemma; or, An Unheard of Crime*. London: Diprose and Bateman, 1892.

―――. *The Detective's Honeymoon; or, The Doctor of the "Pinjarrah."* London: Diprose and Bateman, 1894.

―――. *The Doctor's Crime; or, Simply Horrible*. London: Diprose and Bateman, 1891.

―――. *The Fatal Finger Mark, Rose Courtenay's First Case*. London: Diprose and Bateman, 1895.

―――. *The Grantham Mystery; or, Confidence and Crime*. London: Diprose and Bateman, 1893.

―――. *The "Lone Cross Manor" Mystery; or, Hugh Darrill's Confession*. London: Diprose and Bateman, 1896.

―――. *Mysterious Disappearance of a Bride; or, Who Was She?* London: Diprose and Bateman, 1895.

Fair, A. A. [Erle Stanley Gardner]. *All Grass Isn't Green*. 1970. New York: Pocket Books, 1971.

―――. *Bachelors Get Lonely*. 1961. New York: Pocket Books, 1971.

―――. *Bats Fly at Dusk*. 1942. New York: Dell, 1972.

―――. *Bedrooms Have Windows*. 1949. New York: Dell, n.d.

―――. *Beware the Curves*. 1956. New York: Pocket Books, 1960.

―――. *The Bigger They Come*. 1939. New York: Dell, 1963.

―――. *Cats Prowl at Night*. 1943. New York: Dell, n.d.

―――. *The Count of Nine*. 1958. New York: Pocket Books, 1962.

―――. *Crows Can't Count*. 1946. New York: Dell, 1972.

―――. *Cut Thin to Win*. 1965. New York: Pocket Books, 1966.

―――. *Double or Quits*. 1941. New York: Dell, 1966.

―――. *Fish or Cut Bait*. 1963. New York: Pocket Books, 1970.

―――. *Fools Die on Friday*. 1947. New York: Dell, 1961.

―――. *Give 'Em the Ax*. 1944. New York: Dell, 1962.

―――. *Gold Comes in Bricks*. 1940. New York: Dell, 1961.

―――. *Kept Women Can't Quit*. 1960. New York: Pocket Books, 1965.

―――. *Owls Don't Blink*. 1942. Philadelphia: Blakistan, 1947.

―――. *Pass the Gravy*. 1959. London: Transworld, 1961.

―――. *Shills Can't Cash Chips*. 1961. New York: Pocket Books, 1963.

―――. *Some Slips Don't Show*. 1957. New York: Pocket Books, 1964.

―――. *Some Women Won't Wait*. 1953. New York: Dell, 1960.

―――. *Spill the Jackpot!* 1941. New York: Dell, 1971.

―――. *Top of the Heap*. 1952. New York: Dell, 1972.

―――. *Traps Need Fresh Bait*. 1967. New York: The Detective Book Club, n.d.

―――. *Try Anything Once*. 1962. New York: Pocket Books, 1975.

―――. *Turn on the Heat*. 1940. New York: Dell, 1962.

————. *Up for Grabs.* 1964. New York: Pocket Books, 1964.

————. *Widows Wear Weeds.* 1966. New York: Dell, 1967.

————. *You Can Die Laughing.* 1957. New York: Pocket Books, 1975.

Fickling, G. G. [Gloria and Forrest E. Fickling]. *Blood and Honey.* 1961. New York: Pyramid, 1965.

————. *Bombshell.* New York: Pyramid, 1964.

————. *Dig a Dead Doll.* New York: Pyramid, 1960.

————. *Girl on the Loose.* 1958. New York: Pyramid, 1965.

————. *Girl on the Prowl.* 1959. New York: Pyramid, 1965.

————. *A Gun for Honey.* 1958. New York: Pyramid, 1965.

————. *Honey in the Flesh.* 1959. New York: Pyramid, 1965.

————. *Honey on Her Tail.* New York: Pyramid, 1971.

————. *Kiss for a Killer.* 1960. New York: Pyramid, 1965.

————. *Stiff as a Broad.* New York: Pyramid, 1971.

————. *This Girl for Hire.* New York: Pyramid, 1957.

Footner, Hulbert. *The Almost Perfect Murder: A Casebook of Madame Storey.* 1933. New York: Caxton House, 1939.

————. *The Casual Murder and Other Stories.* 1932. New York: J. B. Lippincott, n.d.

————. *Dangerous Cargo.* New York: Harper, 1934.

————. *The Doctor Who Held Hands.* New York: Doubleday, 1929.

————. *Easy to Kill.* New York: Harper, 1931.

————. *Madame Storey.* New York: George H. Doran, 1926.

————. *The Under Dogs.* New York: George H. Doran, 1925.

————. *The Velvet Hand.* New York: Doubleday, Doran, 1928.

————. *The Viper.* London: Collins, 1930.

Forrester, Jun., Andrew. *The Female Detective.* London: Ward and Lock, 1864.

————. "The Unknown Weapon." In *Three Victorian Detective Novels,* edited by E. F. Bleiler, 1–6. New York: Dover, 1978.

Gallagher, Gale [Will Oursler and Margaret Scott]. *Chord in Crimson.* 1949. New York: Collier, 1962.

————. *I Found Him Dead.* New York: Coward-McCann, 1947.

Galloway, David. *Lamaar Ransom, Private Eye.* London: John Calder, 1979.

Grafton, Sue. *"A" is for Alibi.* 1982. New York: Signet, 1984.

————. *"B" is for Burglar.* New York: Holt, Rinehart, and Winston, 1985.

————. *"C" is for Corpse.* New York: Henry Holt, 1986.

————. *"D" is for Deadbeat.* New York: Henry Holt, 1987.

Green, Anna Katherine. *The Golden Slipper and Other Problems for Violet Strange.* New York: G. P. Putnam's Sons, 1915.

Groom, Mrs. Sidney. *Detective Sylvia Shale.* 1923. London: Hurst and Blackett, n.d.

Hayward, W. Stephens. *The Experiences of a Lady Detective.* 1864. London: Charles Henry Clarke, n.d.

Huston, Fran [Ron S. Miller]. *The Rich Get It All.* New York: Doubleday, 1973.

James, P. D. *An Unsuitable Job for a Woman.* New York: Popular Library, 1972.

―――. *The Skull Beneath the Skin.* 1982. New York: Warner Books, 1983.

Kane, Henry. *Kisses of Death.* New York: Belmont, 1962.

―――. *Private Eyeful.* 1959. New York: Pyramid Books, 1962.

Kaplan, Arthur. *A Killing for Charity.* 1976. New York: Berkley, 1977.

Kaufman, Reginald W. *Miss Frances Baird, Detective: A Passage from Her Memoirs.* Boston: L. C. Page, 1906.

―――. *My Heart and Stephanie: A Novel.* Boston: L. C. Page, 1910.

Law, Janice. *The Big Payoff.* Boston: Houghton Mifflin, 1976.

―――. *Death under Par.* Boston: Houghton Mifflin, 1981.

―――. *Gemini Trip.* Boston: Houghton Mifflin, 1977.

―――. *The Shadow of the Palms.* Boston: Houghton Mifflin, 1980.

―――. *Under Orion.* Boston: Houghton Mifflin, 1978.

Lawrence, James D. *The Dream Girl Caper.* New York: Pyramid, 1975.

―――. *The Emerald Oil Caper.* New York: Pyramid, 1975.

―――. *The Gilded Snatch Caper.* New York: Pyramid, 1975.

―――. *The Godmother Caper.* New York: Pyramid, 1975.

Lee, Austin. *Call In Miss Hogg.* London: Jonathan Cape, 1956.

―――. *Miss Hogg and the Bronte Murders.* London: Jonathan Cape, 1956.

―――. *Miss Hogg and the Covent Garden Murders.* London: Jonathan Cape, 1960.

―――. *Miss Hogg and the Dead Dean.* London: Jonathan Cape, 1958.

―――. *Miss Hogg and the Missing Sisters.* London: Jonathan Cape, 1961.

―――. *Miss Hogg and the Squash Club Murders.* London: Jonathan Cape, 1957.

―――. *Miss Hogg Flies High.* London: Jonathan Cape, 1958.

―――. *Miss Hogg's Last Case.* London: Jonathan Cape, 1963.

―――. *Sheep's Clothing.* London: Jonathan Cape, 1955.

Lee, Jeannette. *Dead Right.* New York: Charles Scribner's Sons, 1925.

―――. *The Green Jacket.* New York: Charles Scribner's Sons, 1917.

―――. *The Mysterious Office.* New York: Charles Scribner's Sons, 1922.

Leighton, Marie Connor. *Joan Mar, Detective.* London: Ward Lock, 1910.

―――. *Lucille Dare, Detective.* London: Ward Lock, 1919.

Linzee, David. *Belgravia.* 1979. New York: Dell, 1981.

―――. *Discretion.* New York: Seaview, 1977.

McGraw, Lee. *Hatchett.* New York: Ballantine, 1976.

McIntosh, J. T. [James M. MacGregor]. *A Coat of Blackmail.* 1970. New York: Doubleday, 1971.

————. *Take a Pair of Private Eyes*. London: Frederick Muller, 1968.

Miller, Victor B. *Fernanda*. New York: Pocket Books, 1976.

Montrose, Graham [Charles Roy Mackinnon]. *Angel Abroad*. London: Robert Hale, 1969.

————. *Angel and the Nero*. London: Robert Hale, 1971.

————. *Angel and the Red Admiral*. London: Robert Hale, 1972.

————. *Angel at Arms*. London: Robert Hale, 1971.

————. *Angel in Paradise*. London: Robert Hale, 1970.

————. *Angel of Death*. London: Robert Hale, 1968.

————. *Angel of No Mercy*. London: Robert Hale, 1968.

————. *Angel of Vengeance*. London: Robert Hale, 1970.

————. *Ask Angel*. London: Robert Hale, 1970.

————. *Fanfare for Angel*. London: Robert Hale, 1971.

————. *A Matter of Motive*. London: Robert Hale, 1969.

————. *Send for Angel*. London: Robert Hale, 1970.

————. *Where Angels Tread*. London: Robert Hale, 1969.

Muller, Marcia. *Ask the Cards a Question*. New York: St. Martin's, 1982.

————. *The Cheshire Cat's Eye*. New York: St. Martin's, 1983.

————. *Edwin of the Iron Shoes*. New York: Penguin, 1977.

————. *Games to Keep the Dark Away*. New York: St. Martin's, 1984.

————. *Leave a Message for Willie*. New York: St Martin's, 1984.

————. *There's Nothing to be Afraid of*. New York: St. Martin's, 1985.

Muller, Marcia, and Bill Pronzoni. *Double*. New York: St. Martin's, 1984.

Old Sleuth [Harlan P. Halsey]. *Cad Metti, The Female Detective Strategist; or Dudie Dunne Again in the Field*. New York: J. S. Ogilvie, 1895.

————. *The Lady Detective*. 1880. New York: George Munro, 1892.

————. *Mademoiselle Lucie, the French Lady Detective*. New York: George Munro's Sons, 1904.

Oppenheim, E. Phillips. *Advice Limited*. London: Hodder, 1935.

————. *Ask Miss Mott*. 1936. Boston: Little, Brown, 1937.

Paretsky, Sara. *Bitter Medicine*. New York: Morrow, 1987.

————. *Deadlock*. 1984. New York: Ballantine, 1985.

————. *Indemnity Only*. 1982. New York: Ballantine, 1983.

————. *Killing Orders*. New York: William Morrow, 1985.

Pirkis, C. L. *The Experiences of Loveday Brooke, Lady Detective*. London: Hutchinson, 1894.

Popkin, Zelda. *Dead Man's Gift*. New York: J. B. Lippincott, 1941.

————. *Death Wears a White Gardenia*. New York: J. B. Lippincott, 1938.

————. *Murder in the Mist*. 1940. New York: J. B. Lippincott, 1941.

————. *No Crime for a Lady*. New York: J. B. Lippincott, 1942.

————. *Time Off for Murder*. New York: J. B. Lippincott, 1940.

Sims, George R. *Dorcas Dene, Detective.* Second Series. London: F. V. White, 1898.

————. *Dorcas Dene, Detective: Her Adventures.* London: F. V. White, 1897.

Solomon, Brad. *The Open Shadow.* 1979. New York: Avon, 1980.

Spain, Nancy. *Cinderella Goes to the Morgue.* London: Hutchinson, 1950.

————. *Death Goes on Skis.* 1949. London: Hutchinson, 1950.

————. *Not Wanted on Voyage.* 1951. London: Penguin Books, 1956.

————. *Out, Damned Tot.* London: Hutchinson, 1952.

————. *Poison for Teacher.* London: Hutchinson, 1949.

————. *R in the Month.* London: Hutchinson, 1950.

Steiner, Susan. *Murder on Her Mind.* New York: Fawcett, 1985.

Stout, Rex. *The Hand in the Glove.* 1937. New York: Pyramid, 1976.

————. "Too Many Detectives." 1956. In *Three for the Chair*, 100–54. New York: Bantam, 1981.

Strahan, Kay Cleaver. *Death Traps.* New York: Doubleday, Doran, 1930.

————. *The Desert Lake Mystery.* 1936. London: Methuen, 1937.

————. *The Desert Moon Mystery.* 1928. New York: Caxton House, 1939.

————. *Footprints.* New York: Doubleday, Doran, 1929.

————. *The Hobgoblin Murder.* Indianapolis: Bobbs-Merrill, 1934.

————. *The Meriweather Mystery.* New York: Doubleday, Doran, 1932.

————. *October House.* New York: Grosset and Dunlap, 1931.

Stringer, Arthur. *The Diamond Thieves.* 1914. Indianapolis: Bobbs-Merrill, 1923.

————. *The House of Intrigue.* New York: A. L. Burt, 1918.

Swan, Phyllis. *The Death Inheritance.* New York: Leisure Books, 1980.

————. *Find Sherri!* New York: Leisure Books, 1979.

————. *Trigger Lady.* New York: Leisure Books, 1979.

Tone, Teona. *Full Cry.* New York: Fawcett, 1985.

————. *Lady on the Line.* New York: Fawcett, 1985.

Valentine [Archibald Thomas Pechey]. *The Adjustors.* London: Anglo-Eastern, 1930.

————. *A Flight to a Finish.* London: Ward Lock, 1929.

————. *Strange Experiment.* London: Ward Lock, 1937.

————. *The Unseen Hand.* London: Jarrolds, 1924.

Wager, Walter. *Blue Leader.* 1979. New York: Berkley, 1981.

————. *Blue Moon.* 1980. New York: Berkley, 1981.

————. *Blue Murder.* 1981. New York: Berkley, 1982.

Walden, Amelia. *Where Was Everyone When Sabrina Screamed?* New York: Scholastic Book Services, 1974.

Weir, Hugh. *Miss Madeline Mack, Detective.* Boston: Page, 1914.

Wells, Anna Mary. *Murderer's Choice.* 1943. New York: Perennial Library, 1981.

————. *A Talent for Murder.* 1942. New York: Perennial Library, 1981.

Wentworth, Patricia. [Nora Amy Dillon Turnbull]. *The Alington Inheritance.* 1958. New York: Pyramid Books, 1966.

————. *The Benevent Treasure.* New York: J. B. Lippincott, 1954.

————. *The Brading Collection.* 1950. London: Coronet, 1975.

————. *The Case Is Closed.* 1937. New York: Warner, 1986.

————. *The Case of William Smith.* New York: J. B. Lippincott, 1948.

————. *The Catherine Wheel.* 1949. London: Hodder and Stoughton, 1951.

————. *The Chinese Shawl.* 1943. New York: Pyramid, 1973.

————. *The Clock Strikes Twelve.* 1944. London: Coronet, 1979.

————. *Danger Point.* 1942. London: Coronet, 1974.

————. *Death at Deep End.* 1951. New York: Pyramid, 1973.

————. *Eternity Ring.* 1948. London: Hodder and Stoughton, 1958.

————. *The Fingerprint.* 1956. London: Coronet, 1974.

————. *The Girl in the Cellar.* 1961. London: Coronet, 1980.

————. *Grey Mask.* 1928. London: Berkley, 1972.

————. *The Ivory Dagger.* 1950. New York: Bantam, 1980.

————. *The Key.* 1944. London: Coronet, 1946.

————. *Ladies' Bane.* 1952. London: Hodder and Stoughton, 1954.

————. *Latter End.* 1947. London: Coronet, 1979.

————. *The Listening Eye.* 1955. London: Hodder and Stoughton, 1960.

————. *Lonesome Road.* New York: J. B. Lippincott, 1939.

————. *Miss Silver Comes to Stay.* 1949. London: Coronet, 1974.

————. *Miss Silver Intervenes.* 1944. London: Coronet, 1974.

————. *Out of the Past.* 1953. New York: Berkley, 1971.

————. *Pilgrim's Rest.* New York: J. B. Lippincott, 1946.

————. *Poison in the Pen.* 1955. New York: Pyramid, 1973.

————. *She Came Back.* 1945. New York: Pyramid, 1973.

————. *The Silent Pool.* New York: J. B. Lippincott, 1954.

————. *The Summerhouse.* 1955. New York: Pyramid, 1972.

————. *Through the Wall.* 1950. New York: Pyramid, 1973.

————. *Vanishing Point.* 1953. New York: Berkley Medallion, 1971.

————. *The Watersplash.* New York: J. B. Lippincott, 1951.

————. *Wicked Uncle.* New York: J. B. Lippincott, 1947.

Wheeler, Edward L. *New York Nell, the Boy-Girl Detective.* New York: Beadle and Adams, 1886.

Yardley, James A. *A Kiss a Day Keeps the Corpses Away.* New York: Signet, 1971.

————. *Kiss the Boys and Make Them Die.* New York: Signet, 1970.

Zaremba, Eve. *A Reason to Kill.* Markham, Ontario, Canada: Paper Jacks, 1978.

Secondary Sources

Albert, Walter. *Detective and Mystery Fiction: An International Bibliography of Secondary Sources.* Madison, Ind.: Brownstone Books, 1985.

Allen, Dick, and David Chacko, eds. *Detective Fiction, Crime and Compromise.* New York: Harcourt Brace Jovanovich, 1974.

Altick, Richard. *The English Common Reader: A Social History of the Mass Reading Public, 1800–1900.* Chicago: University of Chicago Press, 1957.

Anderson, Karen. *Wartime Women: Sex Roles, Family Relations, and the Status of Women during World War II.* Westport, Conn.: Greenwood Press, 1981.

Atkinson, Paul. "Fitness, Feminism and Schooling." In *The Nineteenth Century Woman, Her Cultural and Physical World,* edited by Lorna Duffin and Sara Delamont, 92–133. New York: Barnes and Noble, 1978.

Aron, Cindy S. " 'To Barter Their Souls for Gold': Female Clerks in Federal Government Offices, 1862–1890." *Journal of American History* 67 (March 1981): 835–53.

Auden, W. H. "The Guilty Vicarage." In *Detective Fiction: A Collection of Critical Essays,* edited by Robin W. Winks, 15–24. Englewood Cliffs, N.J.: Prentice-Hall, 1980.

Bakerman, Jane S. "Cordelia Gray: Apprentice and Archetype." *Clues* 5.1 (Spring, Summer 1984): 101–23.

Bakhtin, M. M. *The Dialogic Imagination: Four Essays.* Translated by Caryl Emerson and Michael Holquist. Edited by Michael Holquist. Austin: University of Texas Press, 1982.

Ball, John, ed. *The Mystery Story.* San Diego: University Extension, University of California, San Diego–Publisher's Inc., 1976.

Banks, J. A., and Olive Banks. *Feminism and Family Planning in Victorian England.* Liverpool: Liverpool University Press, 1964.

Barbu, Zev. "Popular Culture: A Sociological Approach." In *Approaches to Popular Culture,* edited by C. W. E. Bigsby, 39–68. Bowling Green, Ohio: Bowling Green University Popular Press, 1976.

Barker-Benfield, G. L. *The Horrors of the Half-Known Life: Male Attitudes Toward Women and Sexuality in Nineteenth-Century America.* New York: Harper and Row, 1976.

Barrett, Michele. "Ideology and the Cultural Production of Gender." In *Feminist Criticism and Social Change,* edited by Judith Newton and Deborah Rosenfelt, 65–85. New York: Methuen, 1985.

Barzun, Jacques, and Wendell Hertig Taylor. *A Catalogue of Crime.* New York: Harper and Row, 1971.

Batsleer, Janet, Tony Davies, Rebecca O'Rourke, and Chris Weedon. *Rewriting English: Cultural Politics of Gender and Class.* London: Methuen, 1985.

Bearchell, Chris. "Making It in the Murder Market." *The Body Politic,* August 1978.

Belsey, Catherine. "Constructing the Subject: Deconstructing the Text." In *Feminist Criticism and Social Change,* edited by Judith Newton and Deborah Rosenfelt, 45–64. New York: Methuen, 1985.

Bergold, Laurel R. "The Changing Legal Status of American Women." *Current History* (May 1976): 206–10.

Bigsby, C. W. E. "The Politics of Popular Culture." In *Approaches to Popular Culture,* edited by C. W. E. Bigsby, 2–26. Bowling Green, Ohio: Bowling Green University Popular Press, 1976.

Bird, Carolyn. *Born Female.* New York: David McKay, 1968.

Blau, Francine D. "The Data on Women Workers, Past, Present and Future." In *Women Working,* edited by Anne H. Stromberg and Shirley Harkess, 29–62. Palo Alto, Cal.: Mayfield, 1978.

Bleiler, E. F., ed. Introduction. *Three Victorian Detective Novels.* New York: Dover, 1978.

————. "Female Detectives, Ghost Books and the Relative Importance of It All." *The Armchair Detective* 8.3 (May 1975): 202.

Bouchier, David. *The Feminist Challenge.* New York: Schocken, 1984.

Braybon, Gail. *Women Workers in the First World War: The British Experience.* London: Croom Held, 1981.

Brittain, Vera. *Lady into Woman: A History of Women from Victoria to Elizabeth II.* New York: Macmillan, 1953.

————. *The Women at Oxford.* New York: Macmillan, 1960.

Brownstein, Rachel M. *Becoming a Heroine: Reading about Women in Novels.* New York: Penguin, 1984.

Calder, Angus. *The People's War Britain, 1939–1945.* New York: Pantheon, 1969.

Carter, Steven R. "On Teaching Detective Fiction." *The Armchair Detective* 17 (1984): 404.

Cawelti, John G. *Adventure, Mystery, and Romance: Formula Stories as Art and Popular Culture.* Chicago: University of Chicago Press, 1976.

Chafe, William H. *The American Woman: Her Changing Social, Economic, and Political Roles 1920–1970.* New York: Oxford University Press, 1972.

————. *Women and Equality: Changing Paterns in American Culture.* New York: Oxford University Press, 1977.

Champigny, Robert. *What Will Have Happened: A Philosophical and Technical Essay on Mystery Stories.* Bloomington: Indiana University Press, 1977.

Chandler, Raymond. "The Simple Art of Murder, an essay." In *The Simple Art of Murder*, 519–33. New York: Houghton Mifflin, 1950.

Collins, Wilkie. *The Woman in White*. 1860. New York: Dutton, 1972.

Cornillon, John. "A Case for Violet Strange." In *Images of Women in Fiction: Feminist Perspectives*, edited by Susan Koppelman Cornillon, 206–16. Bowling Green, Ohio: Bowling Green University Popular Press, 1972.

Cott, Nancy, and Elizabeth H. Pleck. *A Heritage of Her Own*. New York: Touchstone, 1979.

Coward, Rosalind. "Are Women's Novels Feminist Novels?" In *The New Feminist Criticism*, edited by Elaine Showalter, 225–39. New York: Pantheon, 1985.

Cox, J. Randolph. "The Detective-Hero in the American Dime Novel." *Dime Novel Roundup* 50 (1981): 2–13.

Craig, Patricia, and Mary Cadogan. *The Lady Investigates: Women Detectives and Spies in Fiction*. New York: St. Martin's, 1981.

Critchley, T. A. *A History of Police in England and Wales, 1900–1966*. London: Constable, 1967.

Cross, Amanda. [Carolyn G. Heilbrun]. *Death in a Tenured Position*. 1981. New York: Ballantine, 1982.

————. *No Word from Winifred*. New York: Dutton, 1986.

Crow, Duncan. *The Victorian Woman*. London: George Allen and Unwin, 1971.

Cunningham, Gail. *The New Woman and the Victorian Novel*. New York: Barnes and Noble, 1978.

Davidoff, Leonore. *The Best Circles: Society, Etiquette and the Season*. New York: Rowman, 1973.

De Beauvoir, Simone. *The Second Sex*. Translated by H. M. Parshley. New York: Bantam, 1961.

Degler, Carl. *At Odds: Women and the Family in America from the Revolution to the Present*. New York: Oxford University Press, 1980.

Delamont, Sara. "The Contradictions in Ladies' Education." In *The Nineteenth-Century Woman, Her Cultural and Physical World*, edited by Lorna Duffin and Sara Delamont, 134–63. New York: Barnes and Noble, 1978.

DeMarr, Mary Jean. "Kay Cleaver Strahan: A Forgotten Detective Novelist." *Clues* 2.1 (Spring/Summer 1981): 53–61.

————. "The Mysteries of Zelda Popkin." *Clues* 3.1 (Spring/Summer, 1982): 1–8.

Dilnot, George. *The Story of Scotland Yard*. Boston: Houghton Mifflin, 1927.

Douglas, Ann. *The Feminization of American Culture*. New York: Avon, 1977.

Dove, George. "The Criticism of Detective Fiction." In *Detective Fiction: A Collection of Critical Essays*, edited by Robin W. Winks, 203–8. Englewood Cliffs, N.J.: Prentice-Hall, 1980.

————. *The Police Procedural.* Bowling Green, Ohio: Bowling Green University Popular Press, 1982.

DuBois, Ellen. "The Radicalism of the Woman Suffrage Movement: Notes Toward the Reconstruction of Nineteenth-Century Feminism." *Feminist Studies* 3 (1975): 63–71.

DuBois, Ellen Carol, Gail Paradise Kelly, Elizabeth Lapovsky Kennedy, Carolyn W. Korsmeyer, and Lillian Robinson. *Feminist Scholarship: Kindling in the Groves of Academe.* Urbana: University of Illinois Press, 1985.

Duffin, Lorna. "The Conspicuous Consumptive: Woman as Invalid." In *The Nineteenth-Century Woman, Her Cultural and Physical World,* edited by Lorna Duffin and Sara Delamont, 26–56. New York: Barnes and Noble, 1978.

Durham, Phillip. "Dime Novels." *The Western Humanities Review* 9.1 (Winter 1954–5): 33–43.

Dyhouse, Carol. *Girls Growing Up in Late Victorian and Edwardian England.* London: Routledge and Kegan Paul, 1981.

Edenbaum, Robert. "The Politics of the Private Eye: The Novels of Dashiell Hammett." In *Tough Guy Writers of the Thirties,* edited by David Madden, 80–104. Carbondale: Southern Illinois University Press, 1968.

Ehrenreich, Barbara. *The Hearts of Men; American Dreams and the Flight from Commitment.* Garden City, N.J.: Anchor Press-Doubleday, 1983.

Ehrenreich, Barbara, and Deirdre English. *For Her Own Good: 150 Years of the Experts' Advice to Women.* New York: Anchor Press-Doubleday, 1978.

Escarpit, Robert. *The Book Revolution.* London: George G. Harrap, 1966.

Farahger, John Mack. *Women and Men on the Overland Trail.* New Haven: Yale University Press, 1979.

Fetterley, Judith. *The Resisting Reader: A Feminist Approach to American Fiction.* Bloomington: Indiana University Press, 1978.

Flexner, Eleanor. *Century of Struggle.* 1959. New York: Atheneum, 1974.

Freeman, Lucy, ed. *The Murder Mystique: Crime Writers on their Art.* New York: Frederick Ungar, 1982.

Fritz, Kathlyn Ann, and Natalie Kaufman Hevener. "An Unsuitable Job for a Woman: Female Protagonists in the Detective Novel." *International Journal of Women's Studies* 2.2 (March/April 1979): 105–28.

Frye, Joanne S. "Consensus or Community: Women Writers and the Locus of Narrative Authority." Unpublished paper presented at Midwest MLA meeting, 1986.

Gans, Herbert J. *Popular Culture and High Culture: An Analysis and Evolution of Taste.* New York: Basic Books, 1974.

Geherin, David. *Sons of Sam Spade: The Private-Eye Novels in the 70s.* New York: Frederick Ungar, 1980.

Gilbert, Elliot L., ed. *The World of Mystery Fiction.* Del Mar, Cal: Publishers' Inc., 1978.

Gilbert, Sandra M., and Susan Gubar. *The Madwoman in the Attic: The Woman Writer and the Nineteenth-Century Literary Imagination.* New Haven: Yale University Press, 1979.

Gilligan, Carol. *In a Different Voice.* Cambridge: Harvard University Press, 1982.

Gilman, Charlotte Perkins. *Women and Economics.* 1898. Edited by Carl Degler. New York: Harper and Row, 1966.

Glover, David. "The Frontiers of Genre." *Journal of American Studies* 15 (August 1981): 249–52.

Glover, Dorothy, and Graham Greene. *Victorian Detective Fiction.* London: The Bodley Head, 1966.

Graham, Patricia Albjerg. "Expansion and Exclusion: A History of Women in American Higher Education." *Signs* 3 (Summer 1978): 759–73.

Greene, Gayle, and Coppelia Kahn. *Making a Difference: Feminist Literary Criticism.* London: Methuen, 1985.

Greenwald, Maurine Weiner. *Women, War and Work: The Impact of World War I on Women Workers in the United States.* Westport, Conn: Greenwood Press, 1980.

Grella, George. "The Hard-Boiled Detective Novel." In *Detective Fiction: A Collection of Critical Essays,* edited by Robin W. Winks, 103–20. Englewood Cliffs, N.J.: Prentice Hall, 1980.

Grossvogel, David I. *Mystery and Its Fictions: From Oedipus to Agatha Christie.* Baltimore: The Johns Hopkins University Press, 1979.

Hackett, Alice Payne. *Seventy Years of Best Sellers 1895–1965.* New York: Bowker, 1967.

————. *Sixty Years of Best Sellers 1895–1955.* New York: Bowker, 1956.

Hackett, Alice Payne, and James Henry Burke. *Eighty Years of Best Sellers 1895–1975.* New York: Bowker, 1977.

————. *Fifty Years of Best Sellers 1895–1945.* New York: Bowker, 1945.

Hammerton, A. James. "Feminism and Female Emigration, 1861–1866." In *A Widening Sphere, Changing Roles of Victorian Women,* edited by Martha Vicinus, 52–71. Bloomington: Indiana University Press, 1977.

Harkness, Bruce. "P. D. James." In *Art in Crime Writing: Essays on Detective Fiction,* edited by Bernard Benstock, 123–34. New York: St. Martin's, 1983.

Harrison, Brian H. *Separate Spheres: The Opposition to Women's Suffrage in Britain.* New York: Holmes and Meier, 1978.

Hart, James D. *The Popular Book: A History of America's Literary Taste.* New York: Oxford University Press, 1950.

Hartman, Susan M. *The Home-Front and Beyond: American Women in the 1940s.* Boston: Twayne, 1982.

Haskell, Molly. *From Reverence to Rape: The Treatment of Women in the Movies.* New York: Penguin, 1974.

Haycraft, Howard. *Murder for Pleasure: The Life and Times of the Detective Story.* New York: Appleton-Century, 1941.

————. "The Whodunit in World War II and after." In *The Art of the Mystery Story,* edited by Howard Haycraft, 536–42. New York: Simon and Schuster, 1946.

Hayne, Barrie. "Anna Katharine Green." In *Ten Women of Mystery,* edited by Earl F. Bargainnier, 152–78. Bowling Green, Ohio: Bowling Green University Popular Press, 1981.

Heilbrun, Carolyn. "Female Sleuths and Others." *Hecate* 2 (July 1976): 74–79.

————. "Why I Don't Read Science Fiction." *Women's Studies International Forum* 7.2 (1984): 117–19.

Heilbrun, Carolyn, and Catharine Stimpson. "Theories of Feminist Criticism: A Dialogue." In *Feminist Literary Criticism: Explorations in Theory,* edited by Josephine Donovan, 61–73. Lexington: University Press of Kentucky, 1975.

Hersh, Blanche Glassman. *The Slavery of Sex: Feminist-Abolitionists in America.* Urbana: University of Illinois Press, 1978.

Hoffman, Nancy Y. "Mistresses of Malfeasance." In *Dimensions of Detective Fiction,* edited by Larry N. Landrum, Pat Browne, and Ray B. Browne, 97–101. Bowling Green, Ohio: Bowling Green University Popular Press, 1976.

Holcombe, Lee. "Victorian Wives and Property: Reform of the Married Woman's Property Law 1857–1882." In *A Widening Sphere, Changing Roles of Victorian Women,* edited by Martha Vicinus, 3–28. Bloomington: Indiana University Press, 1977.

Honey, Maureen. "The Working-Class Woman and Recruitment Propaganda during World War II: Class Differences in the Portrayal of War Work." *Signs* 8 (Summer 1983): 672–87.

Hoppenstand, Gary, ed. *The Dime Novel Detective.* Bowling Green, Ohio: Bowling Green University Popular Press, 1982.

Horner, Matina S. "Toward an Understanding of Achievement-Related Conflicts in Women." *Journal of Social Issues* 28.2 (1972): 157–75.

Howe, Sir Ronald. *The Story of Scotland Yard.* London: Arthur Baker Limited, 1965.

Hubin, Allen J. *Crime Fiction, 1749–1980: A Comprehensive Bibliography.* New York: Garland, 1984.

Huff, Cynthia A. "Chronicles of Confinement: Reactions to Childbirth in British Women's Diaries." *Women's Studies International Forum* 10.1 (1987): 63–68.

Illich, Ivan. *Gender.* New York: Pantheon, 1982.

Jameson, F. R. "On Raymond Chandler." In *The Poetics of Murder: Detective Fiction and Literary Theory,* edited by Glenn W. Most and William W. Stowe, 122–48. New York: Harcourt Brace Jovanovich, 1983.

Johannsen, Albert. *The House of Beadle and Adams and Its Dime and Nickle Novels: The Story of a Vanished Literature.* Norman: University of Oklahoma Press, 1950.

Jones, Mary Jane. "The Spinster Detective." *Journal of Communications* 25.2 (Spring 1975): 109–26.

Joyner, Nancy J. "P. D. James." In *Ten Women of Mystery,* edited by Earl F. Bargainnier, 109–26. Bowling Green, Ohio: Bowling Green University Popular Press, 1981.

Kennedy, Susan Estabrook. *All We Did Was to Weep at Home: A History of White Working-Class Women in America.* Bloomington: Indiana University Press, 1979.

Kessler-Harris, Alice. *Out to Work: A History of Wage-Earning Women in the United States.* New York: Oxford University Press, 1982.

Klein, Kathleen Gregory, and Joseph Keller. "Deductive Detective Fiction: The Self-Destructive Genre." *Genre* 19.2 (Summer 1986): 155–72.

Knepper, Marty S. "Agatha Christie, Feminist." *The Armchair Detective* 16.4 (Winter 1983): 389–406.

———. "Why Are So Many Feminists So Hopelessly Addicted to Detective Fiction?" Unpublished paper presented at Midwest Popular Culture Association meeting, 1982.

Knight, Stephen. *Form and Ideology in Crime Fiction.* Bloomington: Indiana University Press, 1980.

Kolodny, Annette. "Dancing through the Minefield: Some Observations on the Theory, Practice, and Politics of Feminist Literary Criticism." In *The New Feminist Criticism,* edited by Elaine Showalter, 144–67. New York: Pantheon, 1985.

Lawrence, Barbara. "Female Detectives: The Feminist–Anti-Feminist Debate." *Clues* 3.1 (Spring, Summer 1982): 38–48.

Lerner, Gerda. "The Lady and the Mill Girl: Changes in the Status of Women in the Age of Jackson, 1800–1840." In *A Heritage of Her Own,* edited by Nancy Cott and Elizabeth H. Pleck, 182–96. New York: Touchstone, 1979.

Macdonald, Dwight. *Against the American Grain*. New York: Random House, 1962.

McGuinn, Nicholas. "George Eliot and Mary Wollstonecraft." In *The Nineteenth-Century Woman, Her Cultural and Physical World*, edited by Lorna Duffin and Sara Delamont, 188–205. New York: Barnes and Noble, 1978.

Macherey, Pierre. *A Theory of Literary Production*. London: Routledge and Kegan Paul, 1978.

McIntosh, Peter C. *Physical Education in England since 1800*. Revised Edition. London: G. Bell and Sons, 1968.

McWilliams-Tullberg, Rita. *Women at Cambridge*. London: Victor Gollancz, 1975.

Mandel, Ernest. *Delightful Murder: A Social History of the Crime Story*. London: Pluto Press, 1984.

Mann, Jessica. *Deadlier than the Male*. New York: Macmillan, 1981.

Marcus, Steven. "Dashiell Hammett." In *The Poetics of Murder: Detective Fiction and Literary Theory*, edited by Glenn W. Most and William W. Stowe, 197–209. New York: Harcourt Brace Jovanovich, 1983.

Margolies, Edward. *Which Way Did He Go? The Private Eye in Dashiell Hammett, Raymond Chandler, Chester Himes and Ross Macdonald*. New York: Holmes and Meier, 1982.

Marwick, Arthur. *Britain in the Century of Total War*. Boston: Little, Brown and Company, 1968.

Mason, Bobbie Ann. *The Girl Sleuth: A Feminist Guide*. Old Westbury, N.Y.: Feminist Press, 1975.

Maugham, W. Somerset. "The Decline and Fall of the Detective Story." *The Vagrant Mood*, 101–32. New York: Doubleday, 1952.

Mead, Margaret. *Male and Female: A Study of the Sexes in a Changing World*. New York: Mentor, 1946.

Millett, Kate. *Sexual Politics*. Garden City, N.Y.: Doubleday, 1969.

Miner, Valerie. *Murder in the English Department*. London: Women's Press, 1982.

Modleski, Tania. *Loving With A Vengeance: Mass-Produced Fantasies For Women*. Hamden, Conn.: Archon Books, 1982.

Moers, Ellen. *Literary Women: The Great Writers*. Garden City, N.Y.: Anchor Books, 1977.

Monteith, Moira, ed. *Women's Writing: A Challenge to Theory*. Brighton, England: Harvester, 1986.

Muller, Marcia. "Creating a Female Sleuth." *The Writer* (October 1978): 20–22, 45.

Murch, A. E. *The Development of the Detective Novel*. 1958. New York: Greenwood Press, 1968.

Naremore, James. "Dashiell Hammett and the Poetics of Hard-Boiled Detection." In *Art in Crime Writing: Essays on Detective Fiction,* edited by Bernard Benstock, 49–72. New York: St. Martin's, 1983.

Newton, Judith, and Deborah Rosenfelt, eds. *Feminist Criticism and Social Change.* New York: Methuen, 1985.

Nicolson, Marjorie Hope. "The Professor and the Detective." In *The Art of the Mystery Story,* edited by Howard Haycraft, 110–27. New York: Simon and Schuster, 1946.

Nietzel, Michael T., and Robert Baker. "Eye to Eye: A Survey of the P. I. Writers of America." *The Armchair Detective* 16.3 (Summer 1983): 228–34.

Oakley, Ann. *Subject Women.* London: Fontana, 1982.

————. *Woman's Work: The Housewife, Past and Present.* New York: Pantheon, 1974.

O'Faolain, Julia, and Lauro Martines, eds. *Not in God's Image: Women in History from the Greeks to the Victorians.* New York: Harper and Row, 1974.

O'Neill, William. *Everyone Was Brave.* Chicago: Quadrangle, 1969.

Palmer, Jerry. *Thrillers: Genesis and Structure of a Popular Genre.* New York: St. Martin's, 1979.

Panek, LeRoy. *Watteau's Shepherds: The Detective Novel in Britain 1914–1940.* Bowling Green, Ohio: Bowling Green University Popular Press, 1979.

Parker, Gail. *The Oven Birds.* New York: Anchor Books, 1972.

Paul, Barbara. *The Renewable Virgin.* 1984. New York: Bantam Books, 1986.

Porter, Dennis. *The Pursuit of Crime: Art and Ideology in Detective Fiction.* New Haven: Yale University Press, 1981.

Pratt, Annis. *Archetypal Patterns in Women's Fiction.* Bloomington: Indiana University Press, 1981.

Queen, Ellery. *Queen's Quorum.* New York: Biblio and Tannen, 1969.

————, ed. *The Female of the Species: The Great Women Detectives and Criminals.* New York: Little, Brown and Company, 1944.

Radway, Janice A. *Reading the Romance: Women, Patriarchy, and Popular Literature.* Chapel Hill: University of North Carolina Press, 1984.

Real, Michael R. *Mass-Mediated Culture.* Englewood Cliffs, N.J.: Prentice-Hall, 1977.

Reddy, Maureen T. "She Done It." *The Women's Review of Books* 4.3 (December 1986): 7–8.

Reilly, John M. "Classic and Hard-Boiled Detective Fiction." *The Armchair Detective* 9.4 (1975/6): 289–91, 334.

————, ed. *Twentieth-Century Crime and Mystery Writers.* New York: St. Martin's, 1980.

Robbins, Frank E. "The Firm of Cool and Lam." In *The Mystery Writer's Art,* edited by Francis M. Nevins, Jr., 136–48. Bowling Green, Ohio: Bowling Green University Popular Press, 1970.

Robinson, Lillian S. "Dwelling in Decencies: Radical Criticism and the Feminist Perspective." In *Feminist Criticism: Essays on Theory, Poetry and Prose,* edited by Cheryl L. Brown and Karen Olsen, 21–36. Metuchen, N.J.: Scarecrow Press, 1978.

Roosevelt, Mrs. Franklin D. [*sic*] *It's up to the Women.* New York: Frederick A. Stokes, 1944.

Rossi, Alice S., ed. *Essays on Sex Equality by John Stuart Mill and Harriett Taylor Mill.* Chicago: University of Chicago Press, 1970.

Rothman, Sheila N. *Woman's Proper Place: A History of Changing Ideals and Practices, 1870 to the Present.* New York: Basic Books, 1978.

Rowbotham, Sheila. *Hidden from History: Rediscovering Women in History from the Seventeenth Century to the Present.* New York: Pantheon, 1973.

Rubin, Gayle. "The Traffic in Women: Notes on the 'Political Economy' of Sex." In *Toward an Anthropology of Women,* edited by Rayna R. Reiter, 157–210. New York: Monthly Review Press, 1975.

Ruehlmann, William. *Saint with a Gun: The Unlawful American Private Eye.* New York: New York University Press, 1974.

Rupp, Leila J. "Women's Place Is in the War: Propaganda and Public Opinion in the United States and Germany, 1939–1945." In *Women of America: A History,* edited by Carol Berkin and Mary Beth Norton, 342–59. Boston: Houghton Mifflin, 1979.

Russ, Joanna. *The Female Man.* New York: Bantam, 1975.

———. "What Can a Heroine Do? or Why Women Can't Write." In *Images of Women in Fiction: Feminist Perspectives,* edited by Susan Koppelman Cornillon, 3–20. Bowling Green, Ohio: Bowling Green University Popular Press, 1972.

Russell, Sharon A. "From Mystery to Fantasy: Chelsea Quinn Yarbro and the Mystery Genre." Unpublished paper.

Sampson, Robert. "A Practical Psychologist, Specializing in the Feminine." *The Armchair Detective* 16 (Winter 1983): 363–74.

Sayers, Dorothy L. "Aristotle on Detective Fiction." *Unpopular Opinions.* London: Victor Gollancz: 1946.

———. "Introduction." In *The Art of the Mystery Story,* edited by Howard Haycraft, 71–109. New York: Simon and Schuster, 1946.

Scharf, Lois. *To Work and To Wed: Female Employment, Feminism, and the Great Depression.* Westport, Conn.: Greenwood Press, 1980.

Scott, Donald M. "The Popular Lecture and the Creation of a Public in Mid-Nineteenth Century America." *Journal of American History* 66 (March 1980): 791–809.

Seidman, Michael, and Otto Penzler. "*The Armchair Detective* Readers' Survey." *The Armchair Detective* 17.3 (Spring 1984): 128–30.

Showalter, Elaine. "Feminist Criticism in the Wilderness." In *The New Feminist Criticism*, edited by Elaine Showalter, 243–70. New York: Pantheon, 1985.

———. *A Literature of Their Own: British Women Novelists from Bronte to Lessing*. Princeton: Princeton University Press, 1977.

———. "Toward a Feminist Poetics." In *The New Feminist Criticism*, edited by Elaine Showalter, 125–43. New York: Pantheon, 1985.

Siebenheller, Norma. *P. D. James*. New York: Frederick Ungar, 1981.

"A Sleuth's Hall of Fame." *Newsweek* (22 April 1985): 64.

Slung, Michele, ed. *Crime on Her Mind: Fifteen Stories of Female Sleuths from the Victorian Era to the Forties*. New York: Pantheon, 1975.

Smith, Daniel Scott. "Family Limitation, Sexual Control and Domestic Feminism in Victorian America." In *A Heritage of Her Own*, edited by Nancy Cott and Elizabeth H. Pleck, 222–45. New York: Touchstone, 1979.

Smith, F. Barry. "Sexuality in Britain, 1800–1900: Some Suggested Revisions." In *A Widening Sphere, Changing Roles of Victorian Women*, edited by Martha Vicinus, 182–98. Bloomington: Indiana University Press, 1977.

Smith, Page. *Daughters of the Promised Land: Women in American History*. Boston: Little, Brown and Company, 1970.

Smith, Roger N. *Paperback Parnassus*. Boulder, Colo: Westview Press, 1976.

Spender, Dale. *Women of Ideas (and What Men Have Done to Them)*. London: Arc Paperbacks, 1983.

Steinbrunner, Chris, and Otto Penzler, eds. *Encyclopedia of Mystery and Detection*. New York: McGraw Hill, 1976.

Stenton, Doris Mary. *The English Woman in History*. 1957. Reprint. New York: Schocken, 1977.

Stephens, Reed. *The Man Who Killed His Brother*. New York: Ballantine, 1980.

———. *The Man Who Risked His Partner*. New York: Ballantine, 1984.

Stout, Rex. "Watson Was a Woman." In *The Art of the Mystery Story*, edited by Howard Haycraft, 311–18. New York: Simon and Schuster, 1946.

Strachey, Ray. *The Cause: A History of the Women's Movement in Great Britain*. 1928. New York: Kennikat, 1969.

Symons, Julian. *Mortal Consequences: A History from the Detective Story to the Crime Novel*. New York: Schocken, 1973.

Thorwald, Jurgen. *The Century of the Detective*. New York: Harcourt Brace World, 1964.

Todorov, Tzvetan. *The Poetics of Prose*. Translated by Richard Howard. Ithaca, N.Y.: Cornell University Press, 1977.

Van Dover, J. Kenneth. _Murder In the Millions: Erle Stanley Gardner, Mickey Spillane, Ian Fleming._ New York: Frederick Ungar, 1984.

Vicinus, Martha, ed. _Suffer and Be Still: Women in the Victorian Age._ Bloomington: Indiana University Press, 1972.

Walkowitz, Judith. _Prostitution and Victorian Society: Women, Class and the State._ New York: Cambridge University Press, 1980.

Ware, Susan. _Beyond Suffrage: Women in the New Deal._ Cambridge: Harvard University Press, 1981.

————. _Holding Their Own: American Women in the 1930s._ Boston: Twayne, 1982.

Watson, Colin. _Snobbery with Violence: Crime Stories and Their Audience._ London: Eyre and Spottiswoode, 1971.

Weibel, Kay. "Mickey Spillane as a Fifties Phenomenon." In _Dimensions of Detective Fiction,_ edited by Larry N. Landrum, Pat Browne, and Ray B. Browne, 114–23. Bowling Green, Ohio: Bowling Green University Popular Press, 1976.

————. _Mirror Mirror: Images of Women Reflected in Popular Culture._ Garden City, N. Y.: Anchor Books, 1977.

Welter, Barbara. "The Cult of True Womanhood: 1820–1860." _American Quarterly_ 18 (Summer 1966): 151–74.

Wensley, F. P. _Forty Years of Scotland Yard._ 1930. Westport, Conn.: Greenwood Press, 1968.

Williams, Raymond. _The Long Revolution._ Westport, Conn.: Greenwood Press, 1961.

Wilson, Barbara. _Murder in the Collective._ Seattle: Seal, 1984.

————. _Sisters of the Road._ Seattle: Seal, 1986.

Wilson, Elizabeth. _Only Halfway to Paradise: Women in Post-War Britain, 1945–1968._ London: Tavistock, 1980.

Winks, Robin W. "American Detective Fiction." _American Studies International_ 19, no. 1 (Autumn 1980): 3–16.

————. _Modus Operandi: An Excursion into Detective Fiction._ Boston: David R. Godine, 1982.

Wolfe, Peter. _Beams Falling: The Art of Dashiell Hammett._ Bowling Green, Ohio: Bowling Green University Popular Press, 1980.

Woolf, Virginia. _A Room of One's Own._ 1929. New York: Harcourt, Brace and World, 1957.

————. _Three Guineas._ New York: Harcourt, Brace and World, 1938.

Wright, Will. _Sixguns and Society: A Structural Study of the Western._ Berkeley: University of California Press, 1975.

Wynne, Nancy Blue. "Patricia Wentworth Revisited." _The Armchair Detective_ 14.1 (Winter 1981): 90–92.

Yeager, Linda S. " 'Because a Fire Was in My Head': Eudora Welty and the Dialogic Imagination." _PMLA_ 99.5: 955–73.

Bibliography: Works Published 1987–94

Detective Novels

*Series created before 1987 and continuing beyond that date.

Barnes, Linda. *Coyote*. New York: Delacorte, 1990.
————. *Snake Tattoo*. New York: St. Martin's, 1989.
————. *Snapshot*. New York: Delacorte, 1993.
————. *Steel Guitar*. New York: Delacorte, 1991.
————. *Trouble of Fools*. New York: St. Martin's, 1987.
Beck, K. K. *Amateur Night*. New York: Mysterious Press, 1993.
————. *A Hopeless Case*. New York: Warner, 1992.
Bowers, Elisabeth. *Ladies Night*. Seattle: Seal, 1988.
————. *No Forwarding Address*. Seattle: Seal, 1991.
Bushell, Agnes. *Death by Crystal*. Portland, Maine: Astarte Shell Press, 1993.
————. *Shadow Dance*. Freedom, Calif.: Crossing Press, 1989.
Clark, Carol Higgins. *Decked*. New York: Warner, 1992.
————. *Snagged*. New York: Warner, 1993.
*Cody, Liza. *Backhand*. New York: Doubleday, 1992.
Collins, Anna Ashwood. *Deadly Resolutions*. New York: Walker, 1989.
————. *Red Roses for a Dead Trucker*. New York: Walker, 1990.
Dain, Catherine. *Lament for a Dead Cowboy*. New York: Berkley, 1994.
————. *Lay It On the Line*. New York: Jove, 1992.
————. *Sing A Song of Death*. New York: Jove, 1993.
Dawson, Janet. *Don't Turn Your Back on the Ocean*. New York: Fawcett, 1994.
————. *Kindred Crimes*. New York: St. Martin's, 1990.

———. *Take a Number.* New York: Fawcett, 1993.

———. *Till the Old Men Die.* New York: Fawcett, 1993.

Day, Marele. *The Case of the Chinese Boxes.* New South Wales: Allen and Unwin, 1990.

———. *Last Tango of Dolores Delgado.* New South Wales: Allen and Unwin, 1992.

Dean, Diane S. *Unauthorized Access.* New York: Avalon, 1992.

Donald, Anabel. *In at the Deep End.* London: Virago, 1994.

———. *An Uncommon Murder.* London: Macmillan, 1992.

Douglas, Lauren Wright. *The Always Anonymous Beast.* Tallahassee, Fla.: Niad, 1987.

———. *The Daughters of Artemis.* Tallahassee, Fla.: Niad, 1991.

———. *Goblin Market.* Tallahassee, Fla.: Niad, 1993.

———. *Ninth Life.* Tallahassee, Fla.: Niad, 1990.

———. *A Rage of Madness.* Tallahassee, Fla.: Niad, 1994.

———. *A Tiger's Heart.* Tallahassee, Fla.: Niad, 1992.

Duffy, Stella. *Calendar Girl.* New York and London: Serpent's Tail, 1994.

Dunlap, Susan. *High Fall.* New York: Delacorte, 1994.

———. *Pious Deception.* New York: Villard, 1989.

———. *Rogue Wave.* New York: Villard, 1991.

Dunant, Sarah. *Birth Marks.* New York: Doubleday, 1992.

———. *Fatlands.* London: Hamish Hamilton, 1993.

Farrell, Gillian B. *Alabi for an Actress.* New York: Pocket Books, 1992.

———. *Murder and a Muse.* New York: Pocket Books, 1994.

Frankel, Valerie. *A Deadline for Murder.* New York: Pocket Books, 1991.

———. *Murder on Wheels.* New York: Pocket Books, 1992.

*Grafton, Sue. *"E" is for Evidence.* New York: Henry Holt, 1988.

———. *"F" is for Fugitive.* New York: G. K. Hall, 1989.

———. *"G" is for Gumshoe.* New York: Henry Holt, 1990.

———. *"H" is for Homicide.* New York: Henry Holt, 1991.

———. *"I" is for Innocent.* New York: Henry Holt, 1992.

———. *"J" is for Judgment.* New York: Henry Holt, 1993.

———. *"K" is for Killer.* New York: Henry Holt, 1993.

Grant, Linda. *Blind Trust.* New York: Scribner's, 1990.

———. *Love nor Money.* New York: Macmillan, 1991.

———. *Random Access Murder.* New York: Avon, 1988.

———. *A Woman's Place.* New York: Scribner's, 1994.

Grant-Adamson, Leslie. *Too Many Questions.* New York: St. Martin's, 1991.

Green, Christine. *Deadly Admirer.* New York: Walker, c. 1992.

———. *Deadly Errand.* New York: Walker, 1991.

Greenwood, Kerry. *Death by Misadventure.* New York: Fawcett, 1991.

———. *Flying Too High.* New York: Fawcett, 1990.

————. *Murder on the Ballarat Train.* New York: Fawcett, 1993.

Hendricks, Michael. *Friends in High Places.* New York: Scribner's, 1991.

————. *Money to Burn.* New York: Dutton, 1989.

Hightower, Lynn S. *Satan's Lambs.* New York: Walker, 1993.

Hooper, Kay. *Crime of Passion.* New York: Avon, 1991.

————. *House of Cards.* New York: Avon, 1991.

Huff, Tanya. *Blood Lines.* DAW, 1993.

————. *Blood Price.* DAW, 1991.

————. *Blood Trail.* DAW, 1992.

Howe, Melodie Johnson. *The Mother Shadow.* New York: Penguin, 1989.

Jackson, Marian J. A. *The Arabian Pearl.* New York: Walker, 1993.

————. *Diamond Head.* New York: Walker, 1992.

————. *Sunken Treasure.* New York: Walker, 1994.

Jacobs, Nancy Baker. *The Silver Scalpel.* New York: Putnam, 1993.

————. *A Slash of Scarlet.* New York: Putnam, 1992.

————. *The Turquoise Tattoo.* New York: Putnam, 1991.

Jordan, Jennifer L. *Existing Solutions.* Denver, Colo.: Our Power Press, 1993.

————. *A Safe Place to Sleep.* Denver, Colo.: Our Power Press, 1992.

Kijewski, Karen. *Copy Kat.* New York: Doubleday, 1992.

————. *Katapult.* New York: St. Martin's, 1990.

————. *Kat's Cradle.* New York: Doubleday, 1992.

————. *Katwalk.* New York: St. Martin's, 1989.

————. *Wild Kat.* New York: Doubleday, 1994.

Knight, Phyllis. *Shattered Rhythms.* New York: St. Martin's, 1994.

————. *Switching the Odds.* New York: St. Martin's, 1992.

Komo, Dolores. *Clio Browne, Private Investigator.* Freedom, Calif.: Crossing Press, 1988.

*Law, Janice. *A Safe Place to Die.* New York: St. Martin's, 1993.

————. *Time Lapse.* New York: Walker, 1992.

Lordon, Randye. *Brotherly Love.* New York: St. Martin's, 1993.

————. *Sisters Keeper.* New York: St. Martin's, 1994.

Lucke, Margaret. *Bridge to Nowhere.* New York: St. Martin's, 1993.

————. *A Relative Stranger.* New York: St. Martin's, 1991.

McDermid, Val. *Crackdown.* New York: HarperCollins, 1994.

————. *Deadbeat.* London: Gollancz, 1992.

————. *Kick Back.* London: Gollancz, 1993.

MacGregor, T. J. *Blue Pearl.* New York: Hyperion, 1994.

————. *Dark Fields.* New York: Ballantine, 1987.

————. *Death Flats.* New York: Ballantine, 1991.

————. *Death Sweet.* New York: Ballantine, 1988.

————. *Kill Flash.* New York: Ballantine, 1987.

————. *Kin Dread.* New York: Ballantine, 1990.

————. *On Ice.* New York: Ballantine, 1989.

————. *Spree.* New York: Ballantine, 1992.

————. *Storm Surge.* New York: Hyperion, 1993.

McKenna, Bridget. *Murder Beach.* New York: Diamond, 1993.

McQuillan, Karin. *The Cheetah Chase.* New York: Ballantine, 1994.

————. *Elephants' Graveyard.* New York: Ballantine, 1993.

McRae, Diana. *All the Muscle You Need.* San Francisco: Spinsters/Aunt Lute, 1988.

Maiman, Jaye. *Crazy for Loving.* Tallahassee, Fla.: Niad, 1992.

————. *Under My Skin.* Tallahassee, Fla.: Niad, 1993.

Morgan, D. Miller. *A Lovely Night to Kill.* New York: Dodd, Mead, 1994.

————. *Money Leads to Murder.* New York: Dodd, Mead, forthcoming.

*Muller, Marcia. *Eye of the Storm.* New York: St. Martin's, 1988.

————. *The Shape of Dread.* New York: Mysterious Press, 1989.

————. *There's Something in a Sunday.* New York: Mysterious Press, 1989.

————. *Trophies and Dead Things.* New York: Mysterious Press, 1990.

————. *Where Echoes Live.* New York: Mysterious Press, 1991.

————. *Wolf in the Shadows.* New York: Mysterious Press, 1993.

O'Callaghan, Maxine. *Hit and Run.* New York: St. Martin's, 1989.

————. *Set-Up.* New York: St. Martin's, 1991.

————. *Trade-Off.* New York: St. Martin's, 1994.

O'Donnell, Lillian. *Used to Kill.* New York: Putnam, 1993.

————. *A Wreath for the Bride.* New York: Putnam, 1990.

Oliver, Maria-Antonia. *Antipodes.* Seattle: Seal, 1989.

————. *Study in Lilac.* Seattle: Seal, 1987.

*Paretsky, Sara. *Blood Shot.* New York: Delacorte, 1988.

————. *Burn Marks.* New York: Delacorte, 1990.

————. *Guardian Angel.* New York: Delacorte, 1992.

————. *Tunnel Vision.* New York: Delacorte, 1994.

Pincus, Elizabeth. *The Solitary Twist.* Minneapolis: Spinsters, 1993.

————. *The Two-Bit Tango.* Minneapolis: Spinsters, 1992.

Prowell, Sandra West. *By Evil Means.* New York: Walker, 1993.

————. *The Killing of Monday Brown.* New York: Walker, 1994.

Redmann, J. M. *Death by the Riverside.* Norwich, Vt.: New Victoria, 1990.

Saum, Karen. *Murder Is Germane.* Tallahassee, Fla.: Niad, 1991.

————. *Murder Is Relative.* Tallahassee, Fla.: Niad, 1990.

Scoppettone, Sandra. *Everything You Have Is Mine.* Boston: Little Brown, 1991.

————. *I'll Be Leaving You Always.* Boston: Little Brown, 1993.

————. *My Sweet Untraceable You.* Boston: Little Brown, 1994.

Short, Sharon Gwyn. *Angel's Bidding.* New York: Fawcett, 1994.

Singer, Shelley. *Following Jane.* New York: NAL-Dutton, 1993.

————. *Interview with Mattie.* New York: Signet, 1995.

————. *Picture of David.* New York: NAL-Dutton, 1993.

————. *Searching for Sara.* New York: Signet, 1994.

Slovo, Gillian. *Catnip.* London: Michael Joseph, 1994.

————. *Death Comes Staccato.* London: Women's Press, 1987.

Spring, Michelle. *Every Breath You Take.* New York: Pocket Books, 1994.

Stabenow, Dana. *A Cold-Blooded Business.* New York: Berkley, 1994.

————. *A Cold Day for Murder.* New York: Berkley, 1992.

————. *Dead in the Water.* New York: Berkley, 1993.

————. *A Fatal Thaw.* New York: Berkley, 1993.

*Steiner, Susan. *Library: No Murder Aloud.* New York: Fawcett, 1993.

Sucher, Dorothy. *Dead Men Don't Give Seminars.* New York: St. Martin's, 1988.

————. *Dead Men Don't Marry.* New York: St. Martin's, 1989.

Sullivan, Winona. *A Sudden Death at the Norfolk Cafe.* New York: St. Martin's, 1993.

Summer, Penny. *Cross Words.* Tallahassee, Fla.: Niad, 1994.

————. *End of April.* Tallahassee, Fla.: Niad, 1992.

Sweet, Pat. *Troubled Waters.* London: Virago, 1994.

Taylor, Elizabeth Atwood. *Murder at Vassar.* New York: Ivy Books, 1988.

————. *The Northwest Murders.* New York: St. Martin's, 1992.

Tell, Dorothy. *The Hallelujah Murders.* Tallahassee, Fla.: Niad, 1991.

————. *Murder at Red Rook Ranch.* Tallahassee, Fla.: Niad, 1990.

————. *Wilderness Trek.* Tallahassee, Fla.: Niad, 1990.

Trocheck, Kathy Hogan. *Every Crooked Nanny.* New York: HarperCollins, 1992.

————. *To Live and Die in Dixie.* New York: HarperCollins, 1993.

Wallace, Patricia. *Deadly Devotion.* New York: Zebra, 1994.

Wambaugh, Joseph. *Fugitive Nights.* New York: Morrow, 1992.

Welch, Pat. *Murder By the Book.* Tallahassee, Fla.: Niad, 1990.

————. *A Proper Burial.* Tallahassee, Fla.: Niad, 1993.

————. *Still Waters.* Tallahassee, Fla.: Niad, 1991.

Wesley, Valerie Wilson. *When Death Comes Stealing.* New York: Putnam, 1994.

White, Gloria. *Charged with Guilt.* Forthcoming.

————. *Money to Burn.* Dell, 1993.

————. *Murder on the Run.* New York: Dell, 1991.

*Zaremba, Eve. *Beyond Hope.* Toronto: Amanita, 1987.

————. *The Butterfly Effect.* Toronto: Second Story Press, 1994.

————. *Work for a Million.* Toronto: Amanita, 1987.

Zukowski, Sharon. *Dancing in the Dark.* New York: St. Martin's, 1992.

————. *The Hour of the Knife.* New York: St. Martin's, 1991.

Secondary Sources

Cranny-Francis. *Feminist Fiction: Feminist Uses of Generic Fiction.* New York: St. Martin's, 1990.

DellaCava, Frances A., and Madeline H. Engel. *Female Detectives in American Novels.* New York: Garland, 1993.

Faludi, Susan. *Backlash: The Undeclared War against American Women.* New York: Crown, 1991.

Heilbrun, Carolyn G. *Writing a Woman's Life.* New York: Norton, 1988.

Klein, Kathleen Gregory. "*Habeas Corpus:* Feminism and Detective Fiction." In *Gender and Genre Bending: Essays on the Woman Detective,* edited by Glenwood Irons. Toronto: University of Toronto Press, forthcoming.

————. "Watching Warshawski." In *It's A Print,* edited by Elizabeth A. Trembley and William Reynolds. Bowling Green, Ohio: Popular Press, 1994.

————, ed. *Great Women Mystery Writers: Classic to Contemporary.* Westport, Conn.: Greenwood, 1994.

Nichols, Victoria, and Susan Thompson. *Silk Stalkings: When Women Write of Murder.* Berkeley, Calif.: Black Lizard Books, 1988.

Reddy, Maureen. "The Feminist Counter-Tradition in Crime: Cross, Grafton, Paretsky, and Wilson." In *The Cunning Craft: Original Essays on Detective Fiction and Contemporary Literary Theory,* edited by Ronald G. Walker and June M. Frazer, 174-87. An Essays in Literature Book. Macomb, Ill.: Yeast Printing, 1990.

————. *Sisters in Crime.* New York: Continuum, 1988.

Spender, Dale. *Man Made Language.* London: Routledge and Kegan Paul, 1980.

Swanson, Jean, and Dean James. *By a Woman's Hand: A Guide to Mystery Fiction by Women.* New York: Berkley, 1994.

Zimmerman, Bonnie. *The Safe Sea of Women: Lesbian Fiction, 1969- 1989.* Boston: Beacon, 1990.

Index of Women Detectives

(Author's name is in parentheses.)

Subject Index

Note on the Author

KATHLEEN GREGORY KLEIN, the author of numerous articles and reviews on detective fiction and feminist criticism, is the editor of *Great Women Mystery Writers: Classic to Contemporary* (1994) and *Women Times Three: Writers, Detectives, Readers* (1995). She is a member of the advisory boards of *The Oxford Companion to Crime and Mystery Writing, Twentieth-Century Crime and Mystery Writers,* and *Clues: A Journal of Detection.*